THE LAST ADVENTURE OF LIFE

Inspiring approaches to living and dying

Maria Dancing Heart Hoaglund

Bridge to Dreams Publishing

The Last Adventure of Life: Inspiring approaches to living and dying

First published by Bridge to Dreams Publishing 2005
Second edition published by Findhorn Press 2008
Third edition published by Finch Publishing 2009

This edition published in 2014 by Bridge to Dreams Publishing, 105 Sugarloaf St., Sedona, AZ 86351

ISBN: 978-0-9752932-2-5
Library of Congress Control Number: 2014904086

Edited by Jean Semrau
Cover design by Joanna Hunt
Cover photography by Larry J. Rosenberg
Layout by Pam Bochel
Printed and bound by Create Space

This book was published in a grassroots fashion. The author maintained full control of the content in order to protect the integrity and layout of the material. None of the information herein is intended to replace any medical or spiritual care or relationships with health care or spiritual care professionals. Rather, the aim is to enhance and complement those relationships and communication, allowing everyone to explore more deeply and fully.

Email: info@ChangewithCourage.com

www.changewithcourage.com

If we are devoted to the cause of humanity,
we will soon be crushed and brokenhearted.
But if our motive is to love God,
no ingratitude can hinder us
from serving our fellow human beings.

~ Eleanor Roosevelt

To my mother, Betty
who has blessed me on Earth
and from the other side
in countless ways;

To my father, Alan
who taught me the love of books
and who recently made his own journey
across to the other side;

And to my daughter, Heather
and all the children of the world,
who are a continuing inspiration
and light for us all.

Souls live forever, so dying isn't possible.

~Heather Hoaglund-Biron

There are no real endings in this world, Bobby. Just discoveries.

I've been making discoveries all my life,

and this last one is going to be the biggest!

~A dying man speaking to his grandson

in *To Dance with the White Dog,* by Terry Kay

About the Artists

Reiko Mittet, calligrapher of the characters used throughout the book, was born in Japan. She is a sumi-e artist, and a Japanese language teacher. As a Buddhist, she has been studying various aspects of spiritualism.

Larry Rosenberg the photographer of the Cathedral Rock photo on the front cover, combines spirituality and creativity in his work. He is based in Sedona, AZ and can be reached at: www.facebook.com/LarryJRosenberg

Contents

Foreword to the Second Edition

FOR THOUSANDS of years of human history every phase and passage of life was lived out within the small nest of family, tribe, community. From the first cry of the newborn to the last breath of life, we lived among those for whom the passages of life were ever present and all of our experiences were lived out within the close, supportive circle of family and tradition.

The wisdom lines – the ancient knowledge of what was needed and necessary in the midst of each of passage – flowed unbroken from mother to daughter, from father to son, as each shared in the collective journey as predictably as the season changed...and changed again.

It has not been long now that humans have been living away from the nest, away from the tribes and farms and villages in which they often spent the whole of their lives. It has been a very short time indeed to learn new ways of living to help us move into and through life's most important and numinious moments, for our loved ones and for ourselves.

Is it any wonder that we are now so deeply in need of the wisdom that has been absent in our modern way of life? I believe that our greatest need for healing is that around the passage of death and dying. That endless eternal flow of life onward, from physical to non-physical, frightens us and wounds us as we encounter the experience without benefit of tradition, and without guidance or guides to help us navigate the journey that lies ahead.

Death. There is no greater mystery in human life. Regardless of your belief in the afterlife – call it heaven, nirvana, paradise, purgatory or hell – or your lack of belief in an afterlife, dying is a time of tremendous change and uncertainty. There is often great emotional suffering and grief as our loved ones, or perhaps we ourselves, are called upon to release all that we hold most dear in this life, to venture forward into the unknown.

The wisdom and customs of earlier times provided a container for this passage. Because this container has been mostly lost to our modern life, it is a blessing that we have a wise teacher, Maria Dancing Heart, to reacquaint us with some of the most important ways of healing for ourselves and our loved ones.

Dancing Heart brings together healing words and practices, from her own rich experience in hospice care along with the wisdom of many others, to help each of us

1

recall old ways of caring – and perhaps find some new ones – that can help us be fully present and alive as life changes form once again. She gives us the gift of knowledge that will soothe and comfort during this most difficult of times. I personally believe that the soul takes pretty good care of itself... and that it is the human mind and heart that are so in need of our care and healing attention. Dancing Heart's work brings the medicine of tender compassion to the human heart suffering the pain and loss of separation. Let her be your guide. Gain strength and comfort in her loving hands.

Lee Lawson

Lee Lawson is an artist and the author of *Love Letters from the Infinite: For Anyone Who Has Lost a Loved One* (Thorsons/HarperCollins, 2000); published in the US as *Visitations from the Afterlife: True Stories of Love and Healing* (HarperCollins, 2000). Website www.LeeLawson.com

Introduction

Dying as a Cause for Joy

There were once three "laughing monks" who lived in India. They would go from town to town, making people laugh. After entering a town, they would find the marketplace, then simply start laughing. After they got the whole marketplace laughing, they would move on to the next town and start the whole process over again.

One day, one of the monks became extremely ill. He told the other monks that after he died, he wanted to be buried just as he was, with the clothes on his back – no muss, no fuss. The monks honored his request. After his death, his body was placed on a barge to be taken down the river. The townspeople had lined the riverbank to mourn his loss. Shortly after his body was lit to be cremated, there was suddenly a large, beautiful display of fireworks! The monk had hidden the fireworks in his robe so that they would ignite and make the people laugh – which they did. His wish was granted; and the people of the town were able to realize an important aspect of death: it is graduation time, a time for the person to be honored and celebrated.

~ Received by e-mail; source unknown

WE ARE living in one of the most exciting and challenging times in the history of humankind. The human race is moving through a change in consciousness, and part of this change is facing how we think about our life and death. Have you noticed how many books on spirituality have made the bestseller lists in recent years? Likewise, have you noticed that we gradually are becoming more open to reading, studying, and even talking about the subject of our own dying and death? We are living in a time when we are being given the possibility to shift our fearful thinking around death – to see death as a celebration and something to laugh and be joyful about, just as the monk was helping others to do in this story from India.

3

Elisabeth Kübler-Ross was a pioneer in the area of dying, beginning with her classic book, *On Death and Dying.* Since then, Raymond Moody, Stephen Levine, Dr. Melvin Morse, and many others – including Betty Eadie, who actually experienced the process of dying through a near death experience – have begun to help us face not only the reality but also the hopeful and beautiful nature of death. The reality is that death is not to be feared. Anyone who calls him/herself a "believer" in most faith traditions believes that we have some kind of life after this one on earth. As a Christian, for example, I believe in eternal life; and when I leave this earth through death, I have faith that I will enjoy a kind of resurrection through the love and grace of God, Jesus Christ, and the power of the Holy Spirit. It was Mother Teresa who wrote: "Death... is only the easiest and quickest means to go back to God.... We come from God and we have to go back to [God]!"

How I Came to Write This Book

I served as a parish minister for ten years in the United Church of Christ before coming to hospice work. I am grateful for the experience in that ministry. However, toward the end of my time in church work, I began to feel stifled; the "free spirit" part of me was feeling boxed in. I found myself asking God how I could bring the joy back into my ministry. Shortly before completely letting go of parish work, the word "hospice" came to me while I was meditating one day. About six months later, after an intensive job search and significant soul work, I landed a part-time position as a bereavement counselor with a local hospice. One thing led to another, and soon I was doing spiritual counseling, as well. I found that I took to this work like a fish to water.

My parents were Lutheran missionaries to Japan, and I was given the gift of being born and raised in that country. Since my parents were adventuresome and willing to live "out of the box" to a certain extent, I enjoyed a thoroughly bi-cultural upbringing – attending Japanese public schools through eighth grade, for instance. It never made any sense to me that my loving, polite, gentle Japanese friends were going to "go to hell," just because they did not believe in Jesus Christ. Today I have a whole new appreciation of what I sensed intuitively as a child. We are each one a child of God! We each travel wonderfully varied paths to reach the same destination – to become loving, compassionate, joyous individuals who walk closely with God/Goddess, the divinity that resides in all living things.

So I learned, even while very young, about the diverse ways in which human beings interact. My hospice work continues to expand my thinking, bringing me into contact with a rich variety of people who continue to teach me much about the various ways in which we can live and die. I deeply appreciate this aspect of my work with hospice.

Now, after almost ten years in hospice as a spiritual counselor or "chaplain," the great challenge is to describe how much hospice work has taught me and expanded the way I think and feel about God. For example, I see much more clearly now that every single human being is a "child of God." It is simply a matter of awareness; some people are more in touch with their divine inheritance than others. Some people receive more love and nurturing as children, so it appears easier for them to see and feel the divine in themselves and pass it on to others. Still others have had a powerful, direct experience of God in their lives. Then there are those who have developed their spiritual lives along other paths and have added solace and strength to their spiritual growth and development.

I am learning that the spiritual journey is about opening up to love and to our inner guidance. Some religions and denominations seem to be better able to help people to awaken to their spiritual nature. However, in the end, it is not our religion, but the full understanding and acceptance of our true essence that will save or heal us. It is through the way we live our lives every day – through our love and service, our joy and understanding – that we will heal ourselves and our world.

One of the reasons I began putting this book together is because the more hospice work I do, the more I realize the interconnectedness of all. The value of all things and everyone, not to mention everything that happens to us, is special and very necessary. I have seen how All Is One, and there is no cause for us to judge another. Another reason for the book is that, after gathering a great deal of interesting and useful inspirational material, I felt it was time to share it with others. It has brought me great satisfaction to bring together these resources, to share a sampling of various teachings and support for reflecting on life and preparing for death.

Because our culture is materially focused, many people wait until the last minutes of life to talk about death. I have come to see that talking, reading, and thinking about one's death – even visualizing it – can be one of the most rewarding experiences of a lifetime. Facing death is definitely something we do not want to wait until the last minute to deal with, when our body strength may be dwindling, our concentration weakening, and our emotions distracted by death's encroachment. In fact, I am convinced that facing the reality of death can be a catalyst to help us let go of our fears and live more fully in the present moment. I am also convinced that we can more fully restore ourselves to "the open heart," to God's love, when our mortality is acknowledged with compassion, mercy, and awareness.

My hope is that this book will encourage you to talk more openly and freely about death and the issues that surround it. I wish to share with my readers the significance of not waiting to reflect upon death until it is on your doorstep. We will all experience death one day, so the more prepared we are, the better. Therefore, it is never too early, or too soon, to begin to think and talk about and prepare for our life's last adventure.

I also hope that this book will serve as a guide for "letting go." Perhaps it will also help you understand and appreciate this powerful process of transformation that our entire world is moving through; I sometimes refer to the fact that the whole world is on hospice these days! May this book not only assist you to work with your own death or your loved one's death and/or grief; may it also bring you to a deeper sense of the gifts of peace, joy, and love in your life. And may the present, or "being in the now," become the greatest joy of all for you and those you love.

How to Use This Book

This book need not be read straight through, front to back, although you are certainly welcome to do so. I suggest that you open it and read as the Spirit moves you. Please take time to visit the eleven chapters as you are so inspired. There may be one that you are particularly drawn to, or you may wish to simply open the book randomly. Trust that you will find the inspiration or support you need, wherever you are drawn. If you happen to be getting close to your time of death, it may be especially helpful to take a look at Chapters 1, 6, 7, 8, 9 and 11.

It has been said that everything that takes place on hospice is tied to the "center" which is spiritual care, or "spiritual work." My hope is that this book will provide you with spiritual material and resources to help you and your loved one face your fears and questions regarding death, and begin to work through them as much as you can at this phase of your life.

I have grouped the material into eleven chapters. The first four chapters include the spiritual virtues of truth, beauty, love, and joy. The next four include the spiritual processes of trust, reflection, awareness, and hope. Chapter 7 on awareness includes a variety of meditations that can be used for relaxation and help you and your loved ones move more consciously into the present moment. Chapter 9 takes a look at the gifts that our spiritual paths give us, especially at the time of our transition into the next realm. Chapter 10 examines the transforming power that grief work brings to our lives. The eleventh chapter is a collection of resources for healing; I hope that some of these resources may be helpful to you on your personal journey toward healing. Lastly, I have included an annotated bibliography that describes the best books I have found. Each relates to the topics of death, grief, the afterlife, and the spiritual healing and transformation that come about through experiencing great change or loss.

You will notice that I have Japanese/Chinese characters at the beginning and on every subsequent page of each chapter. I use these as a way to include an East-West flavor to my book. Each character represents the theme of that particular chapter. I am delighted that my friend, artist Reiko Mittet, was able to draw (or calligraph) the characters for the book. Thank you, Reiko!

All of the stories I share from my hospice experience in the book are true. However, in order to protect the identity of those I have served, in most cases I have changed the names and some of the details. In just two individual's cases, I have received permissions from their remaining families to share not only their stories, but also some of their writing.

I believe it's true that "There is nothing to fear except fear itself" (Franklin D. Roosevelt). May you be able to see the death that will inevitably come one day in your life's journey, not only as the glorious end to this earthly life, but also as the last true adventure of life!

We Are Always Safe

We are always safe,
It's only change.
From the moment we are born
We are preparing to be embraced by the Light –
Once more…
Position yourself for Maximum Peace.
Angels surround you
And are guiding you each step of the way.
Whatever you choose will be perfect for you.
Everything will happen in
The perfect time-space sequence.
This is a time for Joy
and for Rejoicing.
You are on your way Home
As we all are.

~ Louise L. Hay

Questions Addressed in This Book

1. How might I pray and hold my thoughts as I, or my loved one, approaches death? How can I better trust the process? *(chapters 5, 7, and 9)*

2. What is "nearing death awareness" and how can I be with someone going through this time as death nears? *(chapter 8)*

3. What are some creative responses to the all-too-often asked question, "Why me?" *(chapter 5)*

4. How can I help my loved one work through his or her forgiveness issues before they die? *(chapter 6)*

5.   What is a near death experience (NDE)? How have these experiences transformed people's lives? *(chapters 3 and 8)*

6.   How can I help a spirit who has committed suicide? *(chapter 6)*

7.   What is hospice and how does it work? *(just before chapter 1)*

8.   What is the Hospice Education Institute and how can it help as our family considers using hospice for our loved one? *(chapter 11)*

9.   Where can I learn more about families directing their own family member's funeral in a natural, personalized way? *(chapter 11)*

10. How can music and touch be used effectively as the end of life nears? *(chapter 11)*

11. How can essential oils help a dying person or others in a home where someone is nearing death? *(chapter 11)*

12. How can I cope with the grief I am experiencing since the death of my loved one? *(chapter 10)*

What Is Hospice?

Hospice has its roots in the concept of hospitality. In the Middle Ages, hospices were European monastic communities where weary pilgrims were given respite. In more extreme cases, the pilgrims were offered comfort and care for serious illnesses and even given assistance in dying. One of the oldest hospices was built in Syria in AD 475; an even older hospice was located in Rome almost 2000 ago. It was founded by Fabiola, a disciple of Saint Jerome, for the purpose of caring for pilgrims returning from Africa. If you are interested in studying the origins of hospice, I can suggest two books: *The Hospice Movement* (Stoddard, 1978) and Part I of *The American Book of Dying* (Groves, 2005).

Today, the term hospice has taken on a more specific meaning. A modern hospice is a place of meeting or a waystation, where people can receive assistance in the process of letting go of earthly life. It may be an actual place, not unlike a hospital or a unit in a hospital. More often, it is a team of trained professionals who support the dying person through their last stages of life. The team members usually come to visit the homes of individuals receiving hospice service, to coach and guide them and their loved ones through the dying process.

The key requirement in hospice is that an individual must be considered by a physician to have less than six months to live. It is most important that the dying loved one and his or her family be ready to accept hospice into their lives. Once on hospice, that person must no longer be receiving aggressive curative treatment or diagnostic studies.

One of the main goals of hospice care is to teach and work with the family or network of friends and caregivers so they can take care of and be with their loved one at home, or wherever the loved one lives. It is a co-creative process. Families are able to do so much with a little bit of information and hands-on demonstration. Usually, a registered nurse acts as the case manager, managing the medications and serving as the liaison between the individual on hospice and the doctors. But an entire hospice team can get involved in the process, to assist in various aspects of the care-giving needs. Besides the nurses, this team typically involves a home health aide, a social worker, a spiritual counselor (chaplain), a volunteer, and sometimes a physical or occupational therapist. There is also a consulting physician on the team, as well as a pharmacist and a dietitian.

The following are some frequently asked questions and answers about hospice that I found in a brochure entitled, "You matter to the last moment of your life," published by The National Hospice and Palliative Care Organization. I have not included all twenty questions; I have also made a number of editorial changes.

1. *When does a decision need to be made about when to go onto a hospice program? Who should be involved in this decision?*

    At any time during a life-limiting illness, it's appropriate to discuss all of a person's care options, including hospice. By law, the decision belongs to the person him/herself. Many people in our culture are uncomfortable with the idea of stopping an all-out effort to keep treating disease.

    The person dealing with the illness and their family can bring up and discuss hospice care at any time with any of their doctors, other healthcare professionals, members of the clergy, or friends. For further education and information about hospice, you might contact a local hospice program, the American Academy of Hospice and Palliative Medicine, the National Hospice Helpline (800-658-8898), or The Hospice Education Institute (207-255-8800 or 800-331-1620). You or your physician may also obtain information about hospice from the American Cancer Society or the American Association of Retired Persons. (See also websites listed in the Bibliography at the back of this book.)

2. *Once a person is on hospice, if they show signs of recovery or improve-ment, or if they decide to pursue further treatment, can they return to receiving regular medical treatment?*

    Certainly. If improvement in the condition occurs or the disease seems to be in remission, the person can be discharged from hospice and return to more aggressive therapy or go on about his or her daily life.

If a discharged person later needs to return to hospice care, Medicare and most private insurances will allow additional coverage for this purpose.

3. *What does the hospice admission process involve?*
A hospice staff nurse will contact you and interview you over the phone to get an initial assessment. Then, if it looks as though you are eligible, a hospice RN will likely come to where you or your loved one reside to sign you up for hospice care. Your doctor will be contacted to make sure that he or she agrees that hospice care is appropriate for you at this time. You will be asked to sign consent and insurance forms. These are similar to the forms you sign when you enter a hospital, except the emphasis will be on palliative care (aiming for pain relief and symptom control, keeping the person comfortable, rather than aggressive curative treatment).

4. *Is there any special equipment or changes I have to make in my home before hospice care begins?*
Your hospice provider will assess your needs, recommend any necessary equipment, and help make arrangements to obtain it. Often the need for equipment is minimal at first and increases as the disease progresses. Hospice will assist in any way it can to make home care as convenient, clean, and safe as possible.

5. *How many family members or friends will it take to care for a person at home? Does someone need to be with the person at all times?*
There's no set number. One of the first things a hospice team will do is prepare an individualized care plan that will address the amount of care-giving a person will need. Hospice staff will visit regularly and are always accessible to answer questions and provide support.
In the early weeks of care, it is usually not necessary for someone to be with the person all the time. Later, however, since one of the common fears of people is the fear of dying alone, hospice generally recommends that someone be with the person continuously. Family and friends need to be relied on to give most of the care. Hospice does provide volunteers, when they are available, to help with errands and to provide a half-day break and "time away" for the major caregiver involved.

6. *How difficult is caring for a dying loved one at home?*
It's rarely easy and sometimes can be quite challenging, especially physically and emotionally. At the end of a long, progressive illness, nights especially can be long, lonely, and scary. This is why hospice programs have staff available around the clock to consult with the family and to make night visits as appropriate.

7. *How does hospice help to deal with the pain? And how successful are they in helping to keep the pain to a minimum?*

Hospice nurses and doctors are up-to-date on the latest medications and devices for pain and symptom relief. In addition, physical and occupational therapists assist patients to be as mobile and self-sufficient as possible. There may also be specialists available who are trained in music therapy, art therapy, massage therapy, diet counseling, and other therapies.

Hospice believes that emotional and spiritual pain are just as real as, and sometimes even tied in with, physical pain, so hospice addresses these, too. Grief counselors including social workers and spiritual counselors are available to assist family members as well as patients. Guided imagery and meditation, essential oils, herbal and homeopathic remedies, acupressure, healing touch, and other kinds of healing modalities can be useful to promote relaxation and the reduction of pain. The counselors and therapists may suggest these modalities to you, but if not, you are encouraged to look into them yourself. (See Chapter 11 for more ideas in this area.) Almost always, hospice can help greatly with reducing and even eliminating pain. Using a combination of medicine, counseling, and other modalities of healing, most people are able to attain a level of comfort that is acceptable to them.

8. **Will medications prevent the patient from being able to talk or be aware of what's happening?**

Usually not. It is the goal of hospice to help people be as comfortable and alert as they would like. By consistently consulting with the patient, hospices have been highly successful in reaching this goal.

9. *Is hospice affiliated with any religious organizations?*

Hospice care is not an offshoot of any religion, though its roots are connected to a ritual of hospitality that was offered to pilgrims and sojourners in religious communities in the Middle Ages. While some religious organizations have started hospices, sometimes in connection with their hospitals, these hospices usually serve a broad community and do not require people to adhere to any particular set of beliefs. In fact, it is the goal of the hospice's spiritual counselors and chaplains to encourage and develop the spiritual life of the people we meet, right where they are on their spiritual journeys, and in a way that is the most comfortable and appropriate for them.

10. *Is hospice care covered by insurance? If not, will hospice still provide care?*

Hospice coverage is widely available. Coverage is available through Medicare nationally, through Medicaid in some 42 states, and through most private health insurance policies. To be sure of coverage, families need to check with their employers or health insurance providers. Hospice will help assist families in finding out whether or not their loved one is eligible for any coverage they may not be aware of. Barring this, most hospices will provide care for those who cannot pay, using money raised from the community or from memorial or foundation gifts.

11. Does hospice provide any help for the family after the loved one dies?

Hospice provides continuing contact and support for family and friends for at least a year following the death of a loved one. Most hospices also sponsor bereavement and support groups for anyone in the community who has experienced the death of a family member, a friend, or a loved one. There are also bereavement coordinators associated with most hospices who can point you to other resources that you might be able to use at this emotionally sensitive and exhausting time. There is tremendous opportunity for growth and healing at a time when one is grieving; it is to your advantage to make the most of all the resources available to you. (See Chapter 10 for more information related to grief and loss.)

The following is a poem written by a hospice nurse to a dying patient for whom she was caring. Notice the tremendous love and sense of commitment that is shared in this "pledge."

My Pledge

You are dying.
I know it, and I won't deny it.
I won't give you false assurances or false hope.
But I'll give you the comfort you seek.
I'll hold your hand.
I'll listen without judgment when you cry
  "Why me?"
I'll support you when you cry,
And dry away your tears.
I will be near.
When you want to be left alone, I'll leave.
But when you need me,
I'll be there.
When you are gone
I'll stay by your family.
I'll let them know you died in peace.
And that when they were there you knew it.
And how much you loved them all.
When you are gone, I'll remember
How you helped me.
You taught me so much about life.
When you are gone, I'll remember
How much I loved you.

~ Diane Willett, RN

If you send forth love to others, you will receive in return the reflection of that love; and you will shine a light that will brighten the darkness of the time we live in — whether it is in the sickroom of a dying patient, on the corner of a ghetto in Harlem, or in your own home.

~ Elisabeth Kübler-Ross, M.D.

13

Chapter 1
Truth

Letting Go Is Liberating

Often the test of courage is not to die but to live.

~ Vitrio Alfreri

DEATH IS our greatest teacher. I am reminded daily during my hospice work that none of us gets out of this earthly journey alive. We all must face the fact that we will be leaving our bodies and this planet some day. One of the helpful ways the members of the hospice team assist families in dealing with this reality is that we talk openly about death and dying, using the word "death" and other related words.

In our society we often sidestep the real issue by using euphemisms like "passed on," "passed away," "kicked the bucket," and "gone to heaven." There is a time and place for these phrases, but in order for us to deal with the finality of death, it is important to become comfortable with the use of words like "death" and "dying." Children especially need to be talked with openly and honestly about what death is all about, when the opportunity arises to do so naturally.

Recently I learned of the *memento mori* of the Rule of Saint Benedict. It literally means "remember that you will die" and is an encouragement for us to remind ourselves daily that we are one day going to die. Brother David Steindl-Rast, a

14

practicing Benedictine monk, speaks of this aspect of the Benedictine Rule in his article, "Learning to Die":

When I first came across the Benedictine Rule and tradition, that was one of the key sentences that impressed and attracted me very much. It challenged me to incorporate the awareness of death into my daily living, for that is what it really amounts to. It isn't primarily a practice of thinking of one's last hour, or of death as a physical phenomenon; it is a seeing of every moment of life against the horizon of death, and a challenge to incorporate that awareness of dying into every moment so as to become more fully alive.

~ Brother David Steindl-Rast

This reminds me of some of the reading I have done in Tibetan Buddhism concerning death. The Tibetan Buddhists have much to teach us. One of the insights that looms large in their thinking is the impermanence of all life. In The *Tibetan Book of Living and Dying,* Sogyal Rinpoche writes that he often asks himself, "Why is it that everything changes?" And the answer that comes back to him is, "That is how life is." He then makes the point that, "One of the chief reasons we have so much anguish and difficulty facing death is that we ignore the truth of impermanence. We so desperately want everything to continue, as it is, that we have to believe that things will always stay the same. But this is only make-believe."

He goes on to say that the only thing we can truly count on in life is impermanence, or change. He suggests that we embrace this reality, and regularly ask ourselves a key related question: "Do I remember at every moment that I am dying, and everyone and everything else is, and so treat all beings at all times with compassion?"

In Tibetan Buddhism, all of life is seen as a preparation for the end of life, the final and biggest letting go that each of us must confront. As we work through the small good-byes of our lives, we get ready for the biggest good-bye, the "graduation" we face at the very end. How are you dealing with those small good-byes in your life these days?

We are of the Nature to Grow Old and Die

Here are some wise words from Gotama Buddha that reinforce the Buddhist view of life and death. May you come to honor the awareness of death in your own life.

I am of the nature to grow old.
There is no way to escape growing old.

I am of the nature to have ill health.
There is no way to escape having ill health.

15

I am of the nature to die.
There is no way to escape death.

All that is dear to me
And everyone I love is of the nature to change.
There is no way to escape being separated from them.

My actions are my only true belongings.
I cannot escape the consequences of my actions.
My actions are the ground on which I stand.

~ Shakyamuni Buddha

Living in the Present Moment

The following is a piece by Christian theologian and storyteller Frederick Buechner that speaks poignantly to being in the present moment. It reminds me of the perspective I've been pondering, that life is simply a series of moments, and we really cannot cling to any one moment. As soon as it happens, it is gone. Life is so precious, so fragile, so fleeting, and we are called, as spiritual beings, to pay very close attention to everything that is going on in and around us, each and every moment.

Be Alive

You are seeing everything for the last time, and everything you see is gilded with good-byes. The child's hand like a starfish on the pillow, your hand on the doorknob. Caught between screen and window, a wasp unfolds one wing. With a sick smile, guilt-ridden, the old dachshund lurches off the forbidden couch when you come through the door, his nose dry with sleep, and makes for the pillow by the hot-air register. It is the room where for years Christmases have happened, snow falling so thick by the window that sometimes it has started to snow in the room, brightness falling on tables, books, chairs, the gaudy tree in the corner, a family sitting there snowmen, snowbound, snowblind to the crazy passing of what they think will never pass. And today now everything will pass because it is the last day. For the last time you are seeing this rain fall and in your mind that snow, this child asleep, this cat. For the last time you are hearing this house come alive because you who are part of its life have come alive. All the unkept promises if they are ever to be kept have to be kept today. All the unspoken words if you do not speak them today will never be spoken. The people, the ones you love and the ones who bore you to death, all the life you have in you to live with them, if you do not live it with them today will never be lived.

It is the first day because it has never been before and the last day because it will never be again. Be alive if you can all through this day today of your life. What's to be done? What's to be done?

Follow your feet. Put on the coffee. Start the orange juice, the bacon, the toast. Then go wake up your children and your wife. Think about the work of your hands, the book that of all conceivable things you have chosen to add to the world's pain. Live in the needs of the day.

~ Frederick Buechner

The following is a poem along the same vein. Victory Lee Schouten is a poet on Whidbey Island whom I have come to know through her husband Rob's art. She was inspired to write this piece just after the huge tsunami hit Indonesia and its environs.

Beyond This Breath

Your body must miss him so much.
Beyond the grief, no old age shared,

the small of your back must cry out
for his belly pressed up warm against,

his arm heavy around your hips
anchoring you here
with your children and grandchildren.

Beyond the shock of sudden death,
trying not to think of how scared
he might have been.
Beyond the silence
where his laughter used to live,

your sweet breasts must long
for his familiar hands
to hold their soft weight again.

Your lonely body listens,
impossible to believe
he won't be coming home.

Tonight I rub my man's shoulders,
memorize his spine with fingertips.
Mine. Mine for a breath,
so brief our time.

Just the time it takes
for a kitchen curtain to stir
in the evening breeze.

~ Victory Lee Schouten

✓ **PRACTICE: I could die today**

The following is an exercise I received at a weekend retreat on "Embracing Death as a Spiritual Path," led by Rodney Smith, a teacher of Insight Meditation. I asked him for permission to use this exercise, and he shared that he got it from Wayne Muller, another author I have quoted in this book. (See the end of Chapter 5, "Don't Ask Why.")

Pick a simple daily activity, something you do at least once every day, such as turning on the faucet, turning on a light switch, getting into or out of your car, putting on or taking off your clothes, climbing a stairway, taking a drink of water, or opening a doorway.

Choose one of these activities. Then, for one week, whenever you perform this activity, say to yourself: "I could die today."

Stop for just a moment in the process of this activity and reflect on the truth of the simple phrase, "I could die today."

What if this could be true? It is true, you know. Any one of us could die, any time, any day. What if YOU were to die today?

What feelings arise within when you think this thought? Who comes to mind? What activities? What hopes and dreams? What burdens or responsibilities do you feel liberated from?

Pay attention to what arises within when you say this to yourself every day: I could die today.

Only Kindness Matters

There is a powerful popular song out now that repeats: "Only kindness matters." We live in an information age when people tend to become objects and numbers, especially in hospitals and institutions. And many of us, in our hurry and in compartmentalized cars and cubicles, tend to forget kindness. In the work that I do, the most fundamental thing, the heart of the matter, is being kind and gentle in sharing our human presence with the people and families we serve.

I have met and been taught by many beautiful people while doing hospice work during the last ten years. One person who stands out is a woman who took her spiritual life very seriously. Niah was also a teacher and writer who shared her work openly with me. At age 50 she was dealing with the end stages of breast cancer. Niah let me know that her work could be shared with others, as long as it was not edited in any way. So throughout this book, here and there, you will be reading some inspirational pieces from Niah Kinczewski. I hope that you, too, will come to appreciate her beauty through her inspirational writing. Here is one of my favorites. It echoes the unifying power of kindness.

My Religion

"Please sign here," the nurse looked at me with compassion. "You seem to know the routine...." I nodded affirmatively.

When you enter the hospital for any kind of surgery or even the simplest of procedures, you must fill out numerous admittance forms. Having had many tubes put in my chest (4), a mastectomy on my right side, a bone marrow transplant, and biopsies of several kinds, believe me, I know the routine! But one thing has always bothered me…the space where the patient is asked to put his or her religion. Over and over I write "none." But deep inside, this never seemed quite right.

So I've decided to place the word "kindness" in this space in the future. (If ever there is need. And by the looks of things now, it's a strong possibility.)

I've decided that kindness is what I really believe in. It's as good as any religion. I believe that my priest is compassion. My hymnal is understanding. My church is courage, and my highest emotional and mental peaks thus far that I have reached – these are my daily meditations.

Nature is my companion on this journey – this human visitation to planet Earth, my soul's sojourn. And children have always been the joy of my life, both my own and others that I've taught for 25 years. These souls have been my teachers.

And what have I truly learned in this lifetime?

I have learned that you must take the hand of wisdom and let its light guide you to see the story that you are – for we are all stories, simple or complex. We all have our dramas, our ups and downs. We all experience joy and sorrow. We are all heroes and villains alike. We are all the same with a difference.

When you finally accept what is…you then become teachable. It is then you will learn in earnest, that what you thought was real, wasn't. And when this realization hits you like a ton of bricks, you learn to let go, and finally to forgive. That's really all there is.

~ Niah Kinczewski

Mindfulness of Death

In closing this chapter, I would like to share some words on staying mindful about our deaths, by the Buddha. This is a reminder to us all that even though our physical bodies may be changing and deteriorating over time, our spiritual selves remain intact and vibrant, healthy and whole as ever.

You should train yourself: Even though I may be sick in body, my mind will be free of sickness. That's how you should train yourself. … And how is one sick in body but not sick in mind? There is the case where an instructed noble disciple… does not assume the body to be the self, or the self as possessing the body, or the body as in the self, or the self as in the body. He is not obsessed with the idea that "I am the body" or "The body is mine." As he is not obsessed with these ideas, his body changes and alters, but he does not fall into sorrow, lamentation, pain, distress, or despair over its change and alteration. (Similarly with feeling, perception, mental processes, and consciousness.) This is how one is sick in body but not sick in mind.

~ Shakyamuni Buddha

On each branch of the trees in my garden
Hang clusters of fruit, swelling and ripe.
In the end, not one piece will remain.
My mind turns to thoughts of my death.

~ Seventh Dalai Lama

Chapter 2
Beauty

The Divine Presence Within All Living Things

Every man goes down to his death bearing in his hands
only that which he has given away.

~ Persian Proverb

All art that really draws us to look at it deeply is spiritual. Art accepts
all the sadness and transforms it implicitly, affirming that beauty is
essentially the presence of God.

~ Sr. Wendy Beckett, *The Mystical Now: Art and the Sacred*

By a Plain but Amiable Cat

See what a charming smile I bring,
Which no one can resist,
For I have found a wondrous thing –
The Fact that I exist.
And I have found another which
I now proceed to tell.

The world is so sublimely rich
That you exist as well.
Fact One is lovely, so is Two,
But O the best is Three:
The Fact that I can smile at you,
And you can smile at me.

~ Ruth Pitter

The Beauty of Each Soul Unfolding

I FIND amazing beauty and great strength of the human spirit on a regular basis through the work I do. This very beauty and strength is part of what keeps me going and doing hospice work week after week. Whether it's the people and families I meet through the work as spiritual counselor, or my teammates who persevere in the midst of sometimes great demands and stress, I consistently see how beautiful, how courageous, and how loving the human spirit is.

I have been asked how I manage working with the dying, day after day. "How do you do it? Don't you get depressed?" people ask. But still others know the truth. When they hear what I do, they respond, "Oh, you must be blessed to have such meaningful work." Yes, I am, nourished by the depth of conversation I have with the people and families on hospice.

Many people have an open heart when dealing with such change and vulnerability. They are not prone to chit-chat but want to get to "the heart of the matter." Most people reflect on the true meaning in life, which brings out their beauty and strength. It is a time of deep connections. Of course there are also depressed people, or people who feel victimized. They are typically the more challenging ones. But they have their own beauty; they, too, are often open to new insights and growth during their momentous transition. I learn a great deal about myself when interacting with all the different people. Most of all, I love the variety of people I come in touch with, and the beauty of the terrain I travel.

美

A Clown and a Dragonfly:
The Interconnecting Web of Life

Hospice work has taught me how interconnected every detail of our life can be. One day, as I was heading out to make my hospice visits, I stopped to get some gas. As I was getting ready to pump the gas into my car, a young woman all dressed up as a clown stepped out right next to me. She had short red hair, a painted face, and looked terrific. I asked her where she was "decked out" to go. She said she was headed to a preschool in the Monroe area.

I moved on to pump gas into my car, but when I arrived at the nursing home and entered the room of the woman on our hospice, I remembered that she was a clown connoisseur. Her room was decorated with a large picture of a clown, among other things. We got to talking about clowns and clowning. It turned out that she'd once had a neighbor who was a clown, and who got her clowning with him on some of his trips around town to cheer people up!

On this same morning, I attended a memorial service of one of our hospice people. Lenora, who had just died of a mysterious brain disease, had loved dragonflies. During the service, I was reminded of this when one woman got up and shared how much Lenora had loved rings. Lenora had worn a beautiful dragonfly ring on one of her middle fingers. Later in the service, I decided to get up and share a few words. Among other things I talked about the dragonfly and how it has been known to symbolize "more joy and light." (Ted Andrews' book, *Animal Speak* (Andrews 1995), is a wonderful reference guide for the meaning specific animals and birds have for us when they show up in our lives.)

About an hour later, when I stepped out into the parking lot of the church, there was a beautiful dragonfly waiting to greet me as I walked over to my car. What a lovely "sign" and surprise blessing! Having days such as this one in the midst of hospice work, I have become a firm believer that there are no coincidences, only synchronicities. And truly, we are upheld by an amazing web of life that connects us living beings, one to another.

> A sacred place is where the earth's voice can be heard more clearly.
> Go to these places and listen.
> Once you have heard her, she can reach you anywhere.
>
> ~ Frederic Lehrman, 1988

Compassion Training

Ram Dass coined the phrase "Be here now" through his early book by that name (Dass 1971). He said that all the grief, pain, and suffering we go through in life are "compassion training." Perhaps a way to look at our life's journey – as we all face the possibility and reality of suffering and death – is that we are being trained to have more compassion, both for ourselves and for others.

Why are You People So Nice?

We are all mirrors for each other. And working on a hospice team, I have met kindred souls from all walks of life.

I remember a gentleman who came to our hospice who was dealing with a form of cancer but also struggling with a very challenging family situation. His wife had some dementia. She was abusive verbally and almost totally dependent on him for her care at that point. He had at least one son who was doing his best to be helpful in his own way.

After I had been meeting with Glenn for a few weeks, he interrupted me one day with the words, "Why are you people so nice?" His question took me totally by surprise. I rather awkwardly came up with some response at the time. However, Glenn's words have echoed in my soul ever since, and I am reminded that we never know how we might touch people at any given time. It is most gratifying to recall that we on the hospice team offer our love and compassionate support to those who have had challenging times so near the close of their lives. The joy of being a light-bearer can be felt almost tangibly.

The Wisdom and Beauty of the Children of Our Times

So many special children and young people are helping with the transformation of our world today. One such child was Mattie J. T. Stepanek, who dealt with a rare neuromuscular disorder from age two. He died in June of 2004. Thirteen years old, a living miracle, he inspired all with whom he came in touch. Mattie said that his surviving against the odds helped him focus on what's truly important in life. "It's just made me more determined to work for peace," he stated. "We need to stop fighting over things that don't matter, like land and money."

Mattie began reading books like *Moby Dick* in kindergarten. He lost three siblings to the same disease he had and began to write at age three, as a way to express himself and work through his grief. He published at least four best-selling collections of poetry.

Mattie was awarded the Melinda Lawrence International Book Award for inspirational written works by Children's Hospice International. He was a frequent public speaker and lived with amazing courage and integrity in the face of his own uncertain health situation. His very special mom Jeni has a special place in our thoughts and prayers as she deals with one more loss.

I invite you to take a look at some of the poems that Mattie has written. Some are specifically about welcoming death, such as "Heavenly Greeting" in *Journey Through Heartsongs*; about saying goodbye, such as "On Saying 'Goodbye'"; and about faith, as in "Faith Imagery" in *Hope Through Heartsongs*.

Nothing to Fear

Many adult children of those who have died have shared after their parents died that they are no longer afraid of death. Their dying parent taught and showed them that there really is nothing to fear in the dying process except fear itself. I would like to ask those of you who are facing death at this time: Do you realize what a witness you are as you go through this journey with dignity, courage, and love, not to mention simply being true to who you really are?

Once again, Niah brings home this message through one of her poems.

By Example... Shall You Lead

You cannot change humanity by words alone,
But by example the meaning is clearly shown!

You cannot teach another to love the wicked,
But by example you can demonstrate forgiveness!

You cannot leave off for others,
The temptations of lust and greed,
Yet you can show to them the folly to which these two lead!

You cannot give another human the will to seek himself,
Yet within your eyes, you can indeed,
Speed to him the Light!

The world seems wrought with dos and don'ts,
With the constant twists and turns of those out of control...

It is the steadfast concern within a purified Heart
That will then, make the difference!
It is the unfaltering focus of a higher Mind

That will lead the way to needed change!
Always, it is the few
Who form the many in society.
May those few now be so worthy
As never before in history!

~ Niah Kinczewski

Ministry is a Two-way Street

One of the joys of hospice work is that I frequently receive energy and perspective from the people I serve. I think of the man who had such a strong faith that even though his greedy wife had left him, and he was getting ready to die, he managed to stay amazingly positive in his outlook for most of his stay on hospice.

There was one morning in particular when I went to see him when I was feeling quite low, I don't remember why. However, by the time Jerry and I finished our visit, my perspective had changed, and I was feeling upbeat about my life again. His faith, hope, and beauty had inspired me and made a big difference in my day. You could say that Jerry even affected my whole life somehow, as I'm still remembering his essence and my interaction with him to this day – several years after the fact!

The most beautiful people I have known are those who have known defeat, known suffering, known struggle, known loss, and have found their way out of the depths. These people have an appreciation, sensitivity, and an understanding of life that fills them with compassion, and a deep loving concern. Beautiful people do not just happen.

~ Roy Nichols (historian)

Beautiful Endings – Love Overflowing

The most memorable after-death experience I've witnessed was after the death of a beloved man who had fought the good fight with ALS. He was a remarkable younger man who had shared of his journey freely and openly, with many friends and family. His name was Mark Reiman, a man well known for the hope and inspiration he offered to many ALS patients and their families. In particular, he set out in 1998 to successfully set a Guinness World Record by singing the national anthem in all thirty major league baseball stadiums in a single season! He also sang the Canadian anthem in Toronto and Montreal, singing it in French in Montreal.

I happened to hear about Mark's death shortly after it took place. When I called his wife Julie to see how she was doing, she invited me to come over for a visit. Upon my arrival, I could tell that this would be an interesting visit because there were so many cars parked outside their home. It turned out that quite a few friends and family were with Julie, supporting her when she was going through a huge challenge. You see, Mark had died, but his body was still in the home; and Julie was dreading having to physically and literally let Mark go.

The love in their home was palpable. Friends and family – and relative strangers like me – were being introduced to one another. Hugs and emotions were shared generously. The atmosphere was warm and joyous, not as if there had just been a death, really. At one point Julie shared with me that a few minutes after Mark died her cell phone had rung with the tune that was on the ringer, "Take Me Out to the Ball Game." When she went to pick it up, no one answered, and the caller ID indicated "Mark at home." This means that the call somehow had been made from their home phone! Julie was certain that it was Mark, who was one of the few people who even had her cell number. He was calling her from the other side to let her know that he had made it safely home. In fact, during the last couple of months of Mark's life, Julie had asked him to contact her from the other side, if possible. Mark had looked at her and said, "I'll try, but I don't know what the rules are" in heaven. They had had a good laugh at the time.

Mark had written his first book, *Through the Perilous Fight*, before he died (Reiman 2000). Julie gave me permission to share some of his writing here, so I have picked a piece from a section called "Hope, Part II."

The Wellspring

It is foolish and destructive to separate the health of our body from the health of our state-of-mind. Science is now only scratching the surface of knowledge regarding how the way we think and feel impacts our body's functioning. Hope… positive outlook… optimism – our state-of-mind – is comprised of ideas and ways of looking at the world that can change everything about how we live our lives, and very possibly, how our bodies respond to illness and disease. William James, the famous philosopher and psychologist, originated the doctrine of Pragmatism or Practical Thinking. My favorite quote of William James is, "The greatest discovery of my lifetime is that we can change our lives by changing our attitudes." We can not only make today a great day to be alive; we can also make a difference in the lives of others, and in doing so, in our own life as well.

Hope is a valuable, precious commodity. It is much too rare in the world at large and sometimes almost impossible to find in the lives of those engulfed by serious illness. When doctors must deliver the news that their patient is seriously ill, they want to be "honest" with their patients, but with that no-holds-barred honesty may often quash all chance for hope with their pronouncement that a person has a limited time to live. Don't we all? As opposed to unlimited time to live?

Hope has come to me in many different forms and through many different sources. My friend, Chris, gave me hope when he suggested an alternative treatment idea for my illness. I realized that I had options, that everything hadn't been tried and this wasn't The End. My friend, Jim, gives me hope when his eyes sparkle with another idea for an adventure that seems impossible, but he finds a way to make happen. My wife gives me hope when she tells me that some little task I'm fretting about not being able to do, is "small potatoes" and can be accomplished some other easier way. My spiritual faith gives me hope by reminding me of the Purpose of Life, which is Love. When I can love and I open my eyes, ears and heart to the love of others…and the needs of others…I am renewed in hope.

Hope also helps give me the courage, the strength, and the energy to keep believing and trying. Hope is something that we can offer to others, but like so many other gifts, in order to receive it we must be willing to take a step forward in faith and risk. It's possible that the

thing we hope for will not happen at this time, the way we want it to, or perhaps not happen at all in our lifetime.

I need to keep up my search on this journey and keep my eyes open for not only the cure for my illness, but also the work, the joy, and the adventures that are waiting along the way. I have discovered a truth that became obvious when we began to bicycle a lot and I must try to always remember: the purpose for the journey and the joy of the journey is not in simply reaching the destination, but is in the journey itself. It is in that journey I have found the wellspring of hope.

~ Mark Reiman

We Are All One

Rodney Romney is an American Baptist preacher who has captured the universal vision that "We are all one." His sermons and writings have given me inspiration as I grow and expand spiritually. The following represents the core of his book on spirituality and nature that he has titled *Wilderness Spirituality* (Romney 1999).

Beatitudes for the New Wilderness

Blessed are those who remember who they are,
For they shall come home to the truth of their own being.

Blessed are those who treasure the sacred trust of life,
For they shall be the inheritors of everlasting riches.

Blessed are those who attend to the inner places of solitude pulsating in
their own souls,
For they shall know God.

Blessed are those who confess their pain and brokenness,
For they shall take hold of their healing.

Blessed are those who connect to all things and refuse all sense of
separation,
For they shall become one with God.

Blessed are those who wrestle with their own darkness,
For they shall touch again the light from which they came.

Blessed are those who wait upon God,
For they shall renew their strength and deepen their faith.

Blessed are those who give compassion to the world,
For they shall burst the bonds of suffering and death.

Blessed are those who forgive life for not being all they have wanted it to
be,
For they shall create a new beginning for themselves.

Blessed are those who accept every person as holy and who do not burden
anyone with narrow judgments or stifled love,
For they shall point to that mysterious road that leads back to God.

Blessed are those who realize they have been created by love and for love,
For they shall live in love all the days of their lives.

Blessed are those who rejoice at all times and in all circumstances,
Knowing that God is in everything with eternal joy.
Through them the seed of love will be eternally resown and they shall
stand tiptoe
In the bright kingdom of the moment, awakening the universe with their
astonishing smile.

~ Rodney Romney

And You Thought They Were Just Blossoms

The fleeting beauty of nature teaches us about the fleeting beauty of life – all life. The
following is an article about the Japanese cherry trees that have graced the University
of Washington's main campus for more than 35 years now. I discovered the article
through my daughter's piano teacher who found it in one of her newspapers and
happened to share it with me (Kawamoto, 2003).

For many people in Japan, the cherry blossoms (sakura) that bloom in spring are cause for an annual pilgrimage to parks, historic castles, sacred grounds and other public spaces where young and old gather to experience something that cannot be fully described in words.

Hanami, which roughly translates to "the viewing of cherry blossoms," is an annual obsession there. Dozens of festivals usher in the colorful rites of spring. Television news programs provide daily status reports about precisely where in the country the trees are blooming. The explosion of small pinkish-white flowers begins in the southernmost part of Japan in late March and moves north like an irrepressible wave of awakening beauty.

But that beauty is fragile, brief and fleeting. While celebrating and enjoying *hanami*, sometimes in a state of considerable inebriation, many viewers experience a peculiar contradiction of emotions, especially when the wind blows and a flutter of delicate petals momentarily take flight. They are said to feel complete happiness and complete sadness at the exact same moment: Happiness because the scene is resplendent in a gentle sort of way; sadness because these same blossoms will soon fall to the ground and wither away, existing only as a memory as they are trampled underfoot.

The aesthetic philosophy of *wabi, sabi* has been used to describe this complex fusion of seemingly opposite emotions. To try to define this abstraction in Western terms is to court misrepresentation, but here goes: *Wabi sabi* involves an ethos of perceiving and embracing beauty that is transient, imperfect, nuanced, simple and yet not completely describable. Behind the awe of cherry blossoms in full and radiant bloom is the realization, even at a subconscious level, that death is just around the corner. The force of beauty meets – head on – the force of mortality, and it quite frequently can strike one speechless.

This is the powerful symbolism of cherry blossoms: They transport the viewer from a literal plane to a symbolic one. The message is clear: Savor every morsel. Don't squander your life. Don't give up on your dreams. Don't take anyone or anything for granted, especially time. Appreciate physical beauty but realize it is superficial and fades; symbolic beauty persists in the mind, in the heart (*kokoro*), and through time, as sure as spring will follow winter.

For only a couple of weeks in the spring, the cherry trees on the University of Washington's main campus transform the landscape in the Quad – an expanse of green open space and walkways surrounded by Gothic brick buildings housing classrooms, offices and computer labs – into a spot of peace and tranquility.

For more than 35 years, about 30 Japanese Yoshino cherry trees have stood guard around the Quad perimeter. For most of the year they look like ordinary trees, providing nice shade during the occasional sunny day. In late March and early April, these trees make the Quad anything but ordinary. Pinkish petals begin to peek out from pregnant buds; soon the entire perimeter is awash with this gentle but breath-taking color. Spring has come. Many who walk through the Quad stop in their tracks and stare. Call it depth perception, or seeing through to something real.

These trees are even older than their many years in the Quad may suggest. They were not planted there as saplings but were replanted as adults from another location. In human years they would be considered senior citizens. Trees, like people, do not live forever. It is not clear how many more springs they will continue to bloom. Happily, younger ones are slated to take their place so that future generations can enjoy hanami in Seattle.

The Quad's cherry blossoms provide an ideal setting to contemplate life – and death – or to just read a book or sit with friends. Theses quiet pursuits are a refuge for those who seek inner peace despite the outer turmoil of an increasingly unstable world. It is also ironic and reassuring that these trees are related to a country that was at one time an archenemy to the United States and is now an ally.

The blossoms' physical beauty may be fleeting but the pleasant feelings they conjure remain much longer in the soul. In this sense, wabi sabi is not really a fusion of opposite emotions but rather of complementary ones: The happiness completes the sadness and vice-versa. Contemplate that.

~ Kevin Kawamoto

May there be Love, Truth, Beauty, Trust, Harmony, and Peace
for all living things, everywhere.

~ Melchizedek's prayer

Chapter 3
Love

The Only Real Power

That Love is all there is, Is all we know of Love.

~ Emily Dickinson

When you find the love, you find yourself. The secret is in the love. You are the love.

~ Sidi Muhammad al-Jamal

Sonnet LXXIII of William Shakespeare

That time of year thou mayst in me behold
When yellow leaves, or none, or few, do hang
Upon those boughs which shake against the cold,
Bare ruined choirs, where late the sweet birds sang.
In me thou see'st the twilight of such day
As after sunset fadeth in the west;
Which by and by black night doth take away,
Death's second self, that seals up all in rest.

In me thou see'st the glowing of such fire,
That on the ashes of his youth doth lie,
As the death-bed, whereon it must expire,
Consum'd with that which it was nourish'd by.
This thou perceiv'st, which makes thy love more strong,
To love that well, which thou must leave ere long.

Imagine How Loved You Are

WE ARE so profoundly loved by Spirit. If we only knew how much, our lives would be transformed. I have had the following quote hanging on my office wall for some time now. I found it some time ago in a metaphysical newspaper, but I do not know its origin. Whenever I read it, it serves as an encouragement and reminder of how much I am loved by my Creator. May it remind you that you are greatly loved, too.

Imagine ✓

Imagine that there is a loving being – loving beyond the most cherished mother's love, loving beyond anything you have ever consciously remembered experiencing.

And this being – who loves you unconditionally, blissfully, fully – says to you: "Trust in me, only me. Surrender to me, only me. For I am the one who birthed the real you – your soul. I am the one who is always there to assist you, to nourish you, to hold you in my hands, to catch you when you leap, to support you when you fly, and to provide you with all your needs. All this I can provide for you…if you will allow it…if you will surrender."

And imagine how it would feel to leap in faith – total faith, total trust, total surrender…into bliss.

Imagine leaping while fully releasing the belief that money, possessions, and insurance policies provide security and sustain you.

Imagine leaping when – with both hands – you release your grip on the illusion of this physical world and know, truly know, for the first time that all there is is this loving being, and that you and this being are One.

Imagine this, feel this, be this and you, beloved one, are free.

Ashi – I honor God for speaking to me and I honor myself for being still enough to listen.

Out of the Mouth of Babes!

Healthy and whole children are so filled with love and a beautiful innocence. And in their pure love, joy, and wisdom, they have much to teach us. The following story was shared with me on one of my hospice visits.

Catherine had just lost her favorite cat, Dinah. Catherine's son, Joey, was taking his seven-year-old daughter, Samantha, to visit her grandmother. On their way, Joey specifically told Samantha not to say anything to Grandma about Dinah because it would upset her.

Shortly after they arrived at Grandma's house, Samantha couldn't contain herself. She blurted out: "Dinah died, didn't she?" Grandma responded that indeed, her favorite cat had died. Samantha exclaimed, "Don't be sad, Grandma. One day, you, too, are going to die. And then, you'll get to be with Dinah again!"

May you be blessed with children in your life. And may they bring abundant wisdom into your life. May you attend to them in a good way.

Daddy

A man came home from work late again, tired and irritated, to find his five-year-old son waiting for him at the door. "Daddy, may I ask you a question?" "Yeah, sure, what is it?" replied the man. "Daddy, how much money do you make an hour?" "That's none of your business! What makes you ask such a thing?" the man said angrily. "I just want to know. Please tell me, how much do you make an hour?" pleaded the little boy. "If you must know, I make $20.00 an hour." "Oh," the little boy replied, head bowed. Looking up, he said, "Daddy, may I borrow $10.00 please?" The father was furious. "If the only reason you wanted to know how much money I make is just so you can borrow some to buy a silly toy or some other nonsense, then you march yourself straight to your room and go to bed. Think about why you're being so selfish. I work long, hard hours every day and don't have time for such childish games." The little boy quietly went to his room and shut the door. The man sat down and started to get even madder about the little boy's questioning. How dare he ask such questions only to get some money.

After an hour or so, the man had calmed down and started to think he may have been a little hard on his son, maybe there was something he really needed to buy with that $10.00, and he really didn't ask for money very often. The man went to the door of the little boy's room and opened the door. "Are you asleep, son?" he asked. "No Daddy, I'm awake," replied the boy. "I've been thinking, maybe I was too hard on you earlier," said the man. "It's been a long day and I took my aggravation out on you. Here's that $10.00 you asked for." The little boy sat straight up, beaming. "Oh, thank you, Daddy!" he yelled. Then, reaching under his pillow, he pulled out some more crumpled up bills. The man, seeing that the boy already had money, started to get angry again. The little boy slowly counted out his money, then looked up at the man. "Why did you want more money if you already had some?" the father grumbled. "Because I didn't have enough, but now I do," the little boy replied. "Daddy, I have $20.00 now. Can I buy an hour of your time?"

~ Author unknown

Understanding the Near-Death Experience and How It Transforms

One of the most profoundly loving, mystical experiences a person can have in life is a so-called "near-death experience" or NDE. This typically happens when a person is very ill and close to death. The individual is transported out of his or her body into another reality that is usually blissful and carefree. Dr. Melvin Morse, a well-known pediatrician in the Puget Sound area, is known for talking about and working with children who have had NDE's (see *Closer to the Light*). Many children have not only had these experiences, but they believe that their lives have been categorically changed by their experiences. Dr. Morse has written about this in his work, *Transformed by the Light* (Morse 1992).

I have had the privilege of getting to know a number of people who have experienced NDEs, through both my hospice work and my life at large. One such person I have recently reconnected with here on Whidbey Island is Edmond Nickson. Edmond is a spiritually tuned-in, energetic man in his mid-seventies, who knows "who he is," and knows that he has been and continues to be guided continuously in his life. I am deeply grateful to him for his help in editing this book. In the course of our conversation and work on my book, he agreed to write the following, which tells of his special relationship with the divine as a result of a near-death experience that took place in his very young life. (For more pieces on the NDE and the interconnectedness of all life, see Chapter 8.)

Edmond's Out-of-Body, Near-Death Experience

As I write this in my seventy-fifth year, I feel a great sense of peace and thanksgiving for the message the event gave me. It is my hope that sharing it will reveal to you, the reader, how guided we all are when we truly listen to that wee small voice inside.

I'm nearing my second year of life and I'm flying, floating around the ceiling with a bunch of white objects or lights. What fun I'm having with all these white things. They are so friendly, so loving – whatever they are. Then I look down and see me in a large bed, my mom and dad's bed, I guess – it looks like theirs. My parents are standing

35

beside the bed as they look down at my figure lying there. "Hey, I'm up here, I'm up here," I shout silently. I can't get their attention. They don't hear me, don't see me. I go back to playing with my new friends for a while and then I look down again. Dad has his arm around mom as if to comfort her. Her head is on his shoulder and it looks like she's crying. Then I see a strange man walk in from the bedroom door across the room. Who is he, and why he is here? He's wearing a dark suit or coat and has a long colorful scarf around his neck. I once again go back to playing with the friendly white things floating around me. Words are not spoken, but somehow I tell them that I want to stay and play with them. They tell me without words that "no, you must go back now – you cannot stay here with us," and so I jump down into my body below.

I never shared that story with my parents for fear of ridicule or worst of all, rejection. As the years went by, I began assembling an idea about my sojourn from conversations overheard between my parents. It appears that I was bedridden and in a comatose state over a period of days, perhaps a week, with a high temperature of 104 or more. Mom and Dad were very worried that I would not live through the night and had placed me in their bed to make me more comfortable and to have me close to them. The doctor had told them that he did all he could to get the fever down, but could do no more. My parents then called in a local pastor from the Lutheran church to have me baptized. Mom was a Lutheran. The man had vestments around his neck as he approached the bed. He stood over me, reciting the rite of baptism. Later, I also discovered that my parents and the doctor were suspicious that I had rheumatic fever. If that is true, I was very fortunate to not be left with any serious complications such as a heart murmur – a seeming miracle in itself.

I credit my "childlike" acceptance, utter trusting of the unknown, to that illness. I believe it imparted an unshakable belief in Spirit that goes beyond any logical explanation. There continued to be instances where someone or something watched over me and protected my every move. There is a further reminder of my connection with Spirit through a wonderful ongoing dream during my early youth and into my teens.

I am visited by this bearded man in a white garment. He's very friendly and loving and always takes me flying. It happens almost every night; and I remember how much fun it was. I looked forward to going to sleep, just so I could go flying with him.

And life continued presenting possible, perhaps better stated as impossible, life-snuffing, challenges that revealed how guided, how protected I was.

At about the age of seven, I can't remember the exact age, I was placed under quarantine in General Hospital of Kansas City with diphtheria, scarlet fever, and hives. What I recall the most while I was there is looking out the window one Sunday at my sister, mother, and father visiting me from a hillside across from my room. It is summer and the hospital windows are open so we can shout at each other across the way (no air-conditioning in 1934). I remember noticing and saying to my father how I liked his new white shoes. Funny what commonplace things stick most vividly in the memory. It was so great being able to see and hear them, even though we could not touch or hug. I came out of that illness with no after-effects.

Then, at thirteen I almost drowned by swimming under a floating dock, running out of air, when a commanding voice told me to dive down to get free.

And there was the time my youngest daughter and I were in the family car during a snowstorm. We skidded toward an oncoming car, and miraculously straightened out to pass without a scratch. I recall saying a quick, silent prayer like, "Uh-oh, God, I need some help here."

I could go on recalling incidents throughout my life like these that have made me see how protected, how connected I am. I never took unnecessary risks to test my protection, but when a near accident was derailed, foiled, I became ever more aware of my connection with Spirit.

And the latest most profound gift was given me during a ten-day silent meditation course. Have you ever pondered over your "life's purpose"? I have many times and believe I was led to it during that meditation of 1991. While in a state of deep peace I was shown a vision and given explicit instructions to build a device that would aid in improving the environment of this planet. The name given that instrument was "Harmonichi – the life-force purifier." Today the prototype is being tested by "sensitives" who fully understand and accept Harmonichi's gift to alter, purify, and improve a being's life-force energy. They report outstanding and most gratifying results.

Harmonichi along with my other lessons are constant reminders that there is nothing to fear, and that my life is truly a gift. Every serious or near-death incident where I have come away unharmed has carried a deep message. The first one given while playing with the white lights as a child is still here guiding me. Not a day goes by without my feeling grateful for that early near-death, out-of-body experience and how it has connected me to the Source of all life. Call it God, the Infinite, Allah, Spirit, it is with me constantly.

~ Edmond Nickson

Water and Love

I find the beauty of earth powerfully restorative. One of the best ways for me to bring balance into my life is to go out into Mother Nature and enjoy her beauty, and through it, her overflowing, sometimes overwhelming, love. This remarkable story came to me through a now-defunct newsletter called "The Messenger: News of the Great Tomorrow," published by Nick Bunick, a deeply spiritual man. The combination of a child's love for a fawn and the love and patience of his mother is most moving.

Water Is VERY Important. So Is Love.

It was one of the hottest days of the dry season. We had not seen rain in almost a month. The crops were dying. Cows had stopped giving milk. The creeks and streams were long gone back into the earth. It was a dry season that would bankrupt seven farmers before it was through.

Every day, my husband and his brothers would go about the arduous process of trying to get water to the fields. Lately, this process had involved taking a truck to the local water rendering plant and filling it up with water. But severe rationing had cut everyone off. If we didn't see some rain soon, we would lose everything. It was on this day that I learned the true lesson of sharing and witnessed the only miracle I have seen with my own eyes.

I was in the kitchen making lunch for my husband and his brothers when I saw my six-year-old son, Billy, walking toward the woods. He wasn't walking with the usual carefree abandon of a youth but with a serious purpose. I could only see his back. He was obviously walking with a great effort...trying to be as still as possible. Minutes after he disappeared into the woods, he came running out again, toward the house. I went back to making sandwiches, thinking that whatever task he had been doing was completed. Moments later, however, he was once again walking in that slow, purposeful stride toward the woods.

This activity went on for an hour: walk carefully to the woods, run back to the house. Finally I couldn't take it any longer and I crept out of the house and followed him on his journey (being very careful not to be seen...as he was obviously doing important work and didn't need his mommy checking up on him).

Billy was cupping both hands in front of him as he walked, being very careful not to spill the water he held in them. Maybe two or three tablespoons were held in his small hands. I sneaked close as he went into the woods. Branches and thorns slapped his little face, but he did not try to avoid them. He had a much higher purpose.

As I leaned in to spy on him, I saw the most amazing sight. Several large deer loomed in front of him. Billy walked right up to them. I almost screamed for him to get away. A huge buck with elaborate antlers was dangerously close. But the buck did not threaten him...he didn't even move as Billy knelt down. And I saw a tiny fawn lying on the ground – obviously suffering from dehydration and heat exhaustion – lift its head with great effort to lap up the water cupped in my little boy's hands.

When the water was gone, Billy jumped up to run back to the house and I hid behind a tree. I followed him back to the house...to a spigot where he had shut off the water. Billy opened it all the way and a small trickle began to trickle out.

He knelt there, letting the drip-drip-drip slowly fill his makeshift "cup" as the sun beat down on his little back. And it became clear to me. The trouble he had gotten into for playing with the hose the week before. The lecture he had received about the importance of not wasting water. The reason he didn't ask me to help him.

It took almost twenty minutes for the drops to fill his hands. When he stood up and began the trek back to the woods, I was there in front of him. His little eyes filled with tears. "I'm not wasting," was all he said. As he began his walk, I joined him…with a small pot of water from the kitchen. I let him tend to the fawn. I stayed away. It was his job.

I stood at the edge of the woods watching the most beautiful heart I have ever known working so hard to save a life. As the tears that rolled down my face began to hit the ground, they were suddenly joined by other drops…and more drops…and more. I looked up at the sky. It was as if God Himself was weeping with pride.

Some will probably say that this was all just a huge coincidence. That miracles don't really exist. That it was bound to rain sometime. And I can't argue with that. I'm not going to try. All I can say is that the rain that came that day saved our farm…just like the actions of one little boy saved another living thing.

~ Author unknown

Water, I have been told, is the symbol for the consciousness we are moving toward in our world right now. We are moving from the "two" energy to the "three" energy. This "three energy" is represented by the mystical substance, water. Water is the only substance in the world that, instead of sinking, rises to the surface when it freezes. Even our scientists don't completely understand water and how it works. And water is the miraculous substance that allows us to have life on earth in the first place. Its ability to flow with such flexibility is truly remarkable.

Remember the Power of Touch Through Hugging!

One of our hospice patients gave me the following piece on one of our last visits; she apparently found it on the Internet. She gifted me with it after she had shared that what she missed the most at this time in her life was being touched. It was an important reminder to me not to take the gift of touch for granted, and also never to miss an opportunity to share the gift of touch with the ones we love and the ones who may be missing that gift.

Hugging

Hugging is healthy. It helps the body's immune system; it keeps you healthier, it cures depression, it reduces stress, it induces sleep, it's invigorating, it's rejuvenating, it has no unpleasant side effects, and hugging is nothing less than a miracle drug.

Hugging is all natural. It is organic, naturally sweet, no pesticides, no preservatives, no artificial ingredients and one hundred percent wholesome.

Hugging is practically perfect. There are no movable parts, no batteries to wear out, no periodic checkups, low energy consumption, high energy yield, inflation-proof, nonfattening, no monthly payments, no insurance requirements, theft-proof, non-taxable, non-polluting and, of course, fully returnable.

~ Sharon Lindsey

I'll tell you something, Agnes: We're here for a good time, not a long time. And having a friend like you is as good as it gets.

~ Agnes's friend Marian in the movie *Agnes Brown*

Loving Ourselves

As much as I love serving and caring for others, I have learned through hospice work the importance of taking care of myself. Lovingly taking care of my own needs is most important, for if I do not do this, if I have not filled up my own cup, I cannot reach out to others in a centered, helpful way to fill their cups.

The following is a piece I found in a bereavement newsletter that expresses this exact point. A woman who had lost her husband of forty-plus years wrote it. She was inspired to write this only one year after her husband died. She came full circle, too, as she had been quite devastated when her husband died. Her daughter told me that Helga died not very long after writing this piece, having accomplished her earthly life.

There is a whole universe inside of me.
I am the only one who is always with me,
everyone else walks away.
I am the only one who can give me
emotional support at any time.
I constantly look inside myself, consciously or subconsciously,
for anything I need to make it through each day and night.
It is right there to nourish my emotional well being,
all the love I ever received and am still receiving.
I give of myself freely when I am needed.
Sometimes I can see it, sometimes I need to be asked.
Being by myself, I don't feel lonely anymore,
because I am never alone,
Someone is always with me. I can feel it strongly always.
Although I enjoy being with people,

and rejoice when hearing from my children,
I do not mind being by myself anymore, because I never am.
God is with me all the time, and He surrounds me
with all of my family,
who left to go to the other side.

~ Helga Erika Svensdotter Luederitz

Do not underestimate the power of treating yourself to what you
yourself believe is important.

~ Victoria Moran

Getting the Conversation Started

One of the most gratifying conversations we have with hospice families is about death and dying. Some families, out of awkwardness in discussing death, have not taken the chance to talk to each other about what is really going on, even when a family member is being served by hospice. Sometimes I open up the topic, and this often starts a robust conversation. This takes courage and an open heart, for everyone involved.

Recently, I met with a woman who was being cared for by her daughter-in-law in her own apartment. She was not afraid of dying; in fact, she was hoping that her time was coming soon. We talked about some of the mystical experiences that take place around the time a person dies. Then she shared a mystical experience that she had had after her husband died many years ago. Later, her daughter-in-law joined our conversation and told me that she was reading the book *Final Gifts* (Callanan & Kelley 1992). I encouraged her to read out of the book to her mother-in-law, as there are some very special end-of-life stories in that book. I highly recommend this book to anyone who is involved with hospice.

Another very practical book is *Start the Conversation: The Book About Death You Were Hoping to Find* (Stone 1996), which I also recommend. A good way to start the conversation is to tune into your intuition for the right time, then find your inner courage, and just start talking about death and dying!

It's basically the same thing with children. It may seem more difficult to bring up the conversation with them, but the truth is, they already know what's going on. They might even bring up the topic of death before you do, especially if they sense that you want to talk about it.

If you are wondering how to talk with your children about death, I highly recommend that you view the movie *Stepmom*, with or without your children. This movie, starring Susan Sarandon and Julie Roberts, is about a divorced mother who realizes she is probably going to die of cancer. There are some beautiful scenes toward the end of this film where the mom talks with her children about how they could continue to relate to her after she dies. She invites her young son to meet her in his dreams. What a beautiful way to acknowledge that life goes on, and that we can continue to have a relationship with those we have loved who die. She later encourages her teenage daughter to remember her and "take her with her" to those important events and occasions that will come down the road in her life. This is another beautiful way of acknowledging that their relationship as mother and daughter will go on, only in a different form.

The public library is a good source of books on death and dying. You might go by yourself, but it would also make for a great afternoon outing with your children or grandchildren. There are many books on this topic that could be helpful. One such book, a small but special one, is published by Pilgrim Press: *Water Bugs and Dragon Flies: Explaining Death to Young Children* (Stickney 1982).

Hospice as a Bridge Over Troubled Waters

As one can imagine, hospice workers are called upon to muster a great deal of inner and sometimes outer strength, to help people through a transition that often covers much new and challenging territory for all concerned. Transitions, by nature, are challenging, are they not? Hospice workers are typically people who have faced some of our own inner demons through the work we do. Then, hopefully, we continue to face more of our fears and shadows as we do our work, day after day. Whether we deserve it or not, our hospice families are often very appreciative of us.

Recently, I heard from one of our hospice families who told us that we had been "a bridge over troubled waters" for them. A daughter and husband had been caring for their ailing mother at home for quite some time, and they were burning out. About this time, hospice was able to come in and offer some much needed assistance and expertise. The woman's condition improved, so we let her go off hospice, which does happen sometimes! Her family said they greatly appreciated the assistance we were able to offer. They got the needed expertise and renewed energy to move forward in their journey with their beloved mother.

Hospice is not perfect, but we do offer support and suggestions based on years of experience and specialized knowledge of end-of-life comfort care. I would encourage a seriously ill person or the caring family to look into hospice sooner rather than later. It may be a good idea to bring the topic up with the person's doctor, as doctors sometimes have trouble letting go of their patients, too.

All Is One

Before his recent death, my father lived with his wife in a retirement community where he received extra care because of his dementia and personal hygiene needs. Several times in the last few years, I visited him and my stepmother. I am so grateful for the loving care and attention I found them receiving there.

In the following article by a physician we are reminded that we need to care for one another as if we were caring for ourselves, or for one of our own family members. One day, who knows, we may be the one in need of the same care!

The Golden Rule, Revisited

They lie there, breathing heavy gasps, contracted into a fetal position. Ironic, that they should live 80 or 90 years, then return to the posture of their childhood. But they do. Sometimes their voices are mumbles and whispers like those of infants or toddlers. I have seen them, unaware of anything for decades, crying out for parents long since passed away.

I recall one who had begun to sleep excessively, and told her daughter that a little girl slept with her each night. I don't know what she saw. Maybe an infant she lost, or a sibling, cousin or friend from years long gone. But I do know what I see when I stand by the bedside of the infirm aged. Though their bodies are skin-covered sticks and their minds an inescapable labyrinth, I see something surprising. I see something beautiful and horrible, hopeful and hopeless. What I see is my children, long after I leave them, as they end their days.

This vision comes to me sometimes when I stand by the bedside in my emergency department, and look over the ancient form that lies before me, barely aware of anything. Usually the feeling comes in those times when I am weary and frustrated from making too many decisions too fast, in the middle of the night. Into the midst of this comes a patient from a local nursing home, sent for reasons I can seldom discern.

I walk into the room and roll my cynical eyes at the nurse. She hands me the minimal data sent with the patient, and I begin the detective work. And just when I'm most annoyed, just when I want to do nothing and send them back, I look at them. And then I touch them. And then, as I imagine my sons, tears well up and I see the error of my thoughts. For, one day, it may be me.

One day, my little boys, still young enough to kiss me and think me heroic, may lie before another cynical doctor, in the middle of the night of their dementia, and need care. More than medicine, they will need compassion. They will need someone to have the insight to look at them and say, "Here was once a child, cherished and loved, who played games in the nursery with his mother and father. Here was a child who put teeth under pillows, and loved bedtime stories, crayons and stuffed animals. Here was a treasure of love to a man and a woman long gone. How can I honor them? By treating their child with love and gentility. By seeing that their child has come full circle to infancy once more, and will soon be born once more into forever."

This vision is frightful because I will not be there to comfort them, or to say, "I am here," when they call out, unless God grants me the gift of speaking across forever. It is painful because I will not be there to serve them as I did in life, and see that they are treated as what they are: Unique and wonderful, made in the image of the Creator, and of their mother and me. It is terrible because their society treats the aged as worse than a burden; it treats them as tragedies of time. It seems hopeless because when they contract and lie motionless, no one will touch them with the love I have for them, or know the history of their scars, visible and invisible. I am the walking library of their lives, and I will be unavailable. All I can do is ask, while I live, for God's mercy on them as they grow older.

And yet, the image has beauty and hope as well. Because if I see my little boys as aged and infirm, I can dream that their lives were long and rich. I can dream that they filled their lucid years with greatness and love, and that they knew God and served Him well, were men of honor and gentility. I can imagine that even if they live in their shadowland alone, somewhere children and grandchildren, even great-grandchildren, thrive. I can hope that their heirs come to see them, and care, and harass the staff of the nursing home to treat Grandpa better. I can hope that they dare not allow my boys to suffer, but that they hold no illusions about physical immortality, and will let them come to their mother and me when the time arrives. And best, I can know that their age and illness will only bring the day of that reunion closer.

My career as an emergency physician has taught me something very important about dealing with the sick and injured, whether young or old. It has taught me that the Golden Rule also can be stated this way: "Do unto others as you would have others do unto your children." I think that this is a powerful way to improve our interactions with others, not just in medicine, but in every action of our lives. And it is certainly a unique way to view our treatment of the elderly. For one day all our children will be old. And only if this lesson has been applied will they be treated with anything approaching the love that only we, their parents, hope for them to always have.

~ Edwin Leap, M.D.

The Power of the Words "I Love You"

The following is a true story I heard from a hospice worker.

A dying woman was lying in a bed in a nursing home, seemingly unable to let go of life. Her daughter came to visit and began to repeat in her mind the words, "Go to the Light, Mom," over and over. Suddenly, the mother rose up in her bed and told her daughter to "Stop saying that!"

The daughter was taken aback and wondered what she should do now. After a while, she was guided to repeat in her mind the words, "I love you, Mom." A while later, her mother rose up in her bed again, this time to say, "I love you, too." Then, about an hour later, the mother breathed her last breath.

There is no question that our thoughts, all by themselves, carry a great deal of power.

Cross-Fertilization

I seem to be a born bridge-builder. Perhaps it has to do with the fact that I was conceived in the United States, and then born in Japan? Who knows! Even the main image I used in my ordination paper was that of the bridge-builder.

One of the reasons I enjoy being a bridge-builder is that I can plant seeds and "reframe" things for people so they might possibly begin to shift their thinking. I especially enjoy doing this in the realm of religion. At one hospice visit I was sharing a prayer with the husband of a woman with Alzheimer's. He had just told me that he had become a Catholic recently, after having been an Episcopalian most of his life. He told me that the Catholic way felt more authentic to him. Somewhere in the midst of my prayer I asked that he be given the *chutzpah* (confidence, energy, courage) needed to continue in his caring and attending to his wife. Afterwards he commented, "You're the first Christian minister I've ever heard use that Jewish [Yiddish] term in a prayer." We chuckled together, and I could feel the connection strengthening.

As I continue with hospice work, now in my tenth year, I am becoming a firm believer in the statement, "We are all children of God." We all come from the realm of pure Spirit, and we all one day will return. As a daughter of one of our hospice patients put it, "You cannot enter one room without leaving another." She attributed this statement to the book *A Stranger in a Strange Land* (Heinlein 1961).

It seems important that we come to appreciate and respect one another, and this includes our religions, too. My prayer is that we come to embrace one another in love and joy, whatever our spiritual backgrounds and journeys. My hope is that we learn from one another in gratitude for the diversity that exists on this magnificent planet. And may we bring down the religious barriers by practicing humor, joy, and lightheartedness. Let us be about the creation of more love and acceptance in the world.

Love that springs truly from the nature of the mind is so blessed that it has the power to dispel the fear of the unknown, to give refuge from anxiety, to grant serenity and peace, and to bring inspiration in death and beyond.

~ Christine Longaker

It seems appropriate to share the following story by Harley Moor while thinking about love, tolerance, and opening up to the many different ways of honoring God or our Higher Power. The story comes from Lee Lawson's beautiful collection of stories: *Visitations from the afterlife: True Stories of Love and Healing* (Lawson 2000).

Only Love

My father was a hellfire-and-brimstone preacher in the small town where I grew up. As I started to see his religious ranting as garbage, I saw how he had dominated my life with all of his rules and regulations from God Almighty. He hated anyone who disagreed with him and damned them to hell.

When I was a teenager we started arguing about religion (and everything else), and for the rest of the time that I lived in my parents' house my father and I were almost constantly screaming and cursing each other. When I was a senior in high school I became a raving atheist. We were really at each other all the time. Finally, he threw me out of the house and disowned me, damning me to eternal hell. We despised each other passionately.

I went away to college, overjoyed to be gone and fully intending never to go back. Three years later, I did go back, for his funeral. I didn't want to go even then, but I went to help my mother settle things. In truth, I was glad he was gone.

A few nights after the funeral, while sorting through some of his stuff, I thought I heard someone laugh. I stopped, listened intently, and heard it again, only this time it was right there in the room. I turned around and saw my father sitting there, in his favorite chair, laughing his head off. I realized then that I had never before, in my entire life, ever heard the man laugh. Not once.

"What is so funny?" I demanded.

I will never forget it. "We were both wrong!" he said and howled with laughter. A bolt, just like lightning, shot out of him into me. It was a bolt of pure love. When that happened I had perfect understanding that he was saying that love is the only thing that matters. Nothing else. Absolutely nothing else.

For weeks afterward I felt his searing love shooting through me. At the same time, I was filled with sickening grief and regret that we had wasted our precious time together when he was alive. It took me a few years to come to peace with that.

~ Harley Moor

Becoming a Deep Listener

Perhaps, in the end, the most powerful thing we can do for one another is to be better listeners. By quietly and gently witnessing the one who is getting ready to die, we help them get in touch with themselves on a deeper level, and we become a mirror for them. At a time when a person is losing much of their control in life, hearing them speak is one form of allowing them more control. Through listening to each other, we can also learn a lot about ourselves. A good listener avoids giving unsolicited advice, or judging inadvertently. We might say that "simple acceptance," or being unconditionally loving as the end of life encroaches, is the most profound and meaningful form of spiritual care we can give.

> There is a land of the living and a land of the dead and the bridge is love, the only survival, the only meaning.
>
> ~ Thornton Wilder, *The Bridge of San Luis Rey*

Chapter 4
JOY

Tuning in to Humor and Gratitude

A merry heart doeth good like a medicine.

~ Proverbs 17:22

Work with the dying requires not only great sensitivity and patience but a robust and earthy sense of humor for when you are in the business of caring for those whose bodies and minds are literally disintegrating, tragedy and farce are intertwined.

~ Sheila Cassidy,
Medical Director of St. Luke's Hospice, Plymouth, England

The Helpfulness of Giggles

His Holiness the Dalai Lama has demonstrated the power of lighthearted humor and friendliness toward everyone he meets. He grins and chortles at you as if you were his long-lost friend when you meet him, gazing deeply into your eyes with love. John Cleese once discussed this with him, asking why it is that in Tibetan Buddhism they enjoy laughing so much. The Dalai Lama responded in all seriousness, explaining that laughter is very helpful to him in teaching and indeed in political negotiations, because when people laugh, it is easier for them to admit new ideas to their mind.

~ Geri Larkin

In seminary, when we were learning about preaching, we were taught that it is good to start a sermon with a joke or something lighthearted that makes people laugh. This way, the congregation is put at ease, and the preacher has helped to create an environment that is more conducive to learning.

Laughter Meditation

Have you had a good laugh recently? Remember that feeling of laughing till your stomach starts to hurt a little? It really is good for your soul, you know. Here's a "laughter meditation" you might try with your eyes open or closed. You can do this first thing in the morning, or really any time of the day when you need a change of pace: First, stretch and arch your body like a cat does. Then, after a couple of minutes of enjoying the stretching, begin to laugh. You can start by lifting the corners of your mouth and opening your mouth. Even if you don't feel like it, before you know it, the forced laughter will stimulate the real thing and you will find yourself laughing. This may well change the mood of your entire day!

~ Tanmaya Honervogt

Laughter is such healing medicine. Norman Cousins found healing through humor, laughing more, and taking life less seriously. The following is a magnificent piece related to this idea; and the message comes from the other side that through laughter there is, indeed, absolutely nothing to fear.

Laughter

There alone by the edge of the sea at my grandfather Sam's house, in my dream I looked out upon the deserted beach, seeing nothing around me but the sea in every direction.

Suddenly I was looking deeply into the eyes and soul of my grandfather Sam, who had been dead nearly ten years. Enlivened and filled with joy and radiant energy, Grandfather looked into my eyes and just laughed. He laughed the most joyful, powerful, clear, full-bellied laugh that I have ever heard in my life. Grandfather's explosion of laughter contained all of eternity.

In a state of pure elation – no words were spoken – he communicated an awesome feeling of ecstasy and, with it, the knowledge that there is nothing to fret about. Nothing at all in the universe to fret about. I could feel my heart and solar plexus tingling and vibrating with energy.

His immense joy is the joy that in time will come to everyone. The absolute knowing that this is what awaits me and those I love filled me with an overwhelming gratitude and peace.

Grandfather's laughter chased all of my fears away, existential fears that I didn't even realize that I'd had about death and the afterlife. Allowed somehow to see into the infinite, I experienced it as a state of passionate joy and release. Grandfather let me see eternity in him, and my soul was healed of the collective darkness that we hold when we do not know of the vast continuation of life. We live our earthly lives as deeply wounded beings when we hold the belief that life and love and passion simply end with the death of the body.

I was there with my own body and soul, lucid and awake. It was a vivid and real dream beyond anything that can be called a dream. My body was asleep, while my soul was totally awake. When I arose from sleep, I knew that it had been a visitation of some sort, that my grandfather came to me, to reach me, to leave me with something that would change the very way I journey through life. I have carried it with me every day, and I can feel Grandfather's healing gift as it lightens this sometimes heavily weighted world.

~ William Mann

A smile costs nothing, but gives much. It enriches those who receive, without making poorer those who give. It takes but a moment, but the memory of it sometimes lasts forever. None is so rich or mighty that he can get along without it, and none is so poor but that she cannot be made rich by it. A smile creates happiness in the home, fosters good will in business, and is the countersign of friendship. It brings rest to the weary, cheer to the discouraged, sunshine to the sad, and it is nature's best antidote for trouble. Yet it cannot be bought, begged, borrowed, or stolen, for it is something that is of no value to anyone until it is given away. Some people are too tired to give you a smile. Give them one of yours, as none needs a smile so much as s/he who has no more to give.

~ Author unknown

Here's the first half of a delightful piece by the executive editor of Guidepost magazine, which will make you laugh. May you find many other stories and material in your lives that will keep you laughing, now and throughout this journey of life.

The Miracle of Laughter: Where Humor and Spirituality Meet

I knelt at the altar of the medieval church of St.-Germain-des-Prés in Paris, the afternoon sun filtering through the stain-glass windows. Grace seemed to flow through that light. I experienced a profound peace and sense of holy intimacy. Finally, I rose and made my way toward the exit. I decided to stop in the bathroom before I rejoined my friends in a nearby café. When I was through I dried my hands and pulled at the door. It didn't budge. I couldn't get out of the bathroom.

I peeked through a crack. Nuns and monks bustled back and forth. I rapped gently on the door. No response. I pounded. Harder. "Help!" I yelled. "I'm trapped." I heard mutterings outside, the sound of a key rattling in the lock. More commotion. Finally, with a mighty heave, a short, stout monk who looked like Friar Tuck fell through the doorway. "Madame," he gasped, catching his breath and leaning against the sink, "we have never had such excitement here."

"I'm so sorry," I kept saying. I just wanted to get out of there as fast as I could. A little too fast, as it turned out. I tripped over a tourist's camera case, bumped into a stroller, and set the baby inside it wailing. By the time I reached the street, the church was in an uproar.

So much for my transcendent spiritual experience. Except when it was all over, I couldn't stop laughing.

A lot of people think that all our profound spiritual moments have to be serious – calming, centering, elegant. But is that really true? One Christmas Eve during a difficult time in my life, I found myself concentrating so intensely during the service that I gave myself a dreadful headache. The time for the Gospel reading arrived. The minister stood and read from Luke. He got to the part about the Baby Jesus wrapped in swaddling clothes and declared that the baby was "strapped in waddling clothes."

I couldn't really help myself. I tried not to laugh, I really did. I buried my face in my hands. Maybe people thought I was in deep spiritual contemplation. Instead I was trying to compose myself and stop thinking about "waddling clothes." By the time I finished giggling, my headache was gone. I felt clearer than I had in months. The minister's mistake made that Bethlehem manger feel even more grounded in reality, the heavenly and earthly closer together. In the catharsis of my laughter, I found peace.

~ Mary Ann O'Roark

The Bittersweet Nature of Life

The following excerpt (Hilbert 1979) is simply one of the most beautiful stories I have ever read about life and death. It seems to capture the joy and sorrow, the bittersweet nature of life. It also shares the magnificent innocence of a child. May the deep emotion in this story touch you and remind you of the fleeting yet joy-filled nature of everyday life.

A Sandpiper to Bring You Joy

She was six years old when I first met her on the beach near where I live. I drive to this beach, a distance of three or four miles, whenever the world begins to close in on me. She was building a sandcastle or something and looked up, her eyes as blue as the sea.

"Hello," she said. I answered with a nod, not really in the mood to bother with a small child. "I'm building," she said.

"I see that. What is it?" I asked, not caring.

"Oh, I don't know, I just like the feel of sand."

I thought that sounded good and slipped off my shoes. A sandpiper glided by.

"That's a joy," the child said.

"It's a what?"

"It's a joy. My mama says sandpipers come to bring us joy." The bird went gliding down the beach.

"Good-bye joy," I muttered to myself, "hello pain," and turned to walk on. I was depressed; my life seemed completely out of balance.

"What's your name?" She wouldn't give up.

"Robert," I answered. "I'm Robert Peterson."

"Mine's Wendy...I'm six."

"Hi, Wendy."

She giggled. "You're funny," she said.

In spite of my gloom I laughed too and walked on. Her musical giggle followed me.

"Come again, Mr. P.," she called. "We'll have another happy day." The days and weeks that followed belonged to others: a group of unruly Boy Scouts, PTA meetings, and an ailing mother. The sun was shining one morning as I took my hands out of the dishwater. "I need a sandpiper," I said to myself, gathering up my coat. The ever-changing balm of the seashore awaited me. The breeze was chilly, but I strode along, trying to recapture the serenity I needed. I had forgotten the child and was startled when she appeared.

"Hello, Mr. P," she said. "Do you want to play?"

"What did you have in mind?" I asked, with a twinge of annoyance.

"I don't know, you say."

"How about charades?" I asked sarcastically.

The tinkling laughter burst forth again. "I don't know what that is."

"Then let's just walk." Looking at her, I noticed the delicate fairness of her face. "Where do you live?" I asked.

"Over there." She pointed toward a row of summer cottages. Strange, I thought, in winter.

"Where do you go to school?" I asked her.

"I don't go to school. Mommy says we're on vacation." She chattered little girl talk as we strolled up the beach, but my mind was on other things. When I left for home, Wendy said it had been a happy day. Feeling surprisingly better, I smiled at her and agreed.

Three weeks later I rushed to the beach in a state of near panic. I was in no mood to even greet Wendy. I thought I saw her mother on the porch and felt like demanding she keep her child at home.

"Look, if you don't mind," I said crossly when Wendy caught up with me, "I'd rather be alone today." She seemed unusually pale and out of breath.

"Why?" she asked.

I turned to her and shouted, "Because my mother died!" and then thought, "My God, why was I saying this to a little child?"

"Oh," she said quietly, "then this is a bad day."

"Yes," I said, "and yesterday and the day before and – oh, go away!"

"Did it hurt?" she inquired.

"Did what hurt?" I was exasperated with her, with myself.

"When she died?"

"Of course it hurt!" I snapped, misunderstanding, wrapped up in myself. I strode off.

A month or so after that, when I next went to the beach, she wasn't there. Feeling guilty, ashamed and admitting to myself I missed her, I went up to the cottage after my walk and knocked at the door. A drawn looking young woman with honey-colored hair opened the door.

"Hello," I said. "I'm Robert Peterson. I missed your little girl today and wondered where she was."

"Oh yes, Mr. Peterson, please come in. Wendy spoke of you so much. I'm afraid I allowed her to bother you. If she was a nuisance, please, accept my apologies."

"Not at all – she's a delightful child," I said, suddenly realizing that I meant what I had just said.

"Wendy died last week, Mr. Peterson. She had leukemia. Maybe she didn't tell you." Struck dumb, I groped for a chair. I had to catch my breath.

"She loved this beach; so when she asked to come, we couldn't say no. She seemed so much better here and had a lot of what she called happy days. But the last few weeks, she declined rapidly." Her voice faltered, "She left something for you…if only I can find it. Could you wait a moment while I look?"

I nodded stupidly, my mind racing for something to say to this lovely young woman. She handed me a smeared envelope with "MR. P" printed in bold childish letters. Inside was a drawing in bright crayon hues – a yellow beach, a blue sea, and a brown bird. Underneath was carefully printed:

A sandpiper to bring you joy.

Tears welled up in my eyes and a heart that had almost forgotten to love opened wide. I took Wendy's mother in my arms. "I'm so sorry, I'm so sorry, I'm so sorry," I muttered over and over, and we wept together.

The precious little picture is framed now and hangs in my study. Six words – one for each year of her life – that speak to me of harmony, courage, and undemanding love.

A gift from a child with sea-blue eyes and hair the color of sand who taught me the gift of love.

~ Mary Sherman Hilbert

The Enchanting Power of Music

Music is such a universal and powerful "heart language." I had the special opportunity to meet Deforia Lane, a music therapist from Ohio, while attending a workshop on the subject of music therapy. (Zondervan published Lane's autobiography and video called *Music as Medicine* in 1995.) She shared some creative ways in which she uses music of all kinds to promote healing and relaxation for patients in the hospital where she serves. She helped me to reflect on what a "heart opener" and healer music can be, all by itself.

Especially at the time of death, music seems to have the power to open people up to its process. In the video called *Chalice of Repose,* the following story is shared.

A vital man in his forties is dying. He is married with two young sons. His wife is terribly grief-stricken as he is close to death. The harpist from the Chalice of Repose Project comes to share her music with the dying man who is in great physical pain. His wife is sobbing, reminding him that he promised not to leave them. After a period of hearing the music, the young dying man raises his arms from his lying position, as if to greet someone in front of him. His grieving wife notices this, and changes her behavior. All of a sudden, she is able to let him go on his way. Shortly after she gives him the permission and encouragement to go, her husband takes his last breath, peacefully. (See the section on Therapeutic Music in Chapter 11 for more information about Music-Thanatology, its history, and how it works.)

Sometimes I break into song with my hospice people. Especially when words are hard to come by, or if the person is unable to speak and I am strongly guided by my intuition, I may quietly sing one of my favorites, like "Amazing Grace" or "How Can I Keep from Singing," an old hymn which is special to me. Sometimes I sing in Japanese, too. If it's a tune people recognize, something simple like "Jesus Loves Me, This I Know," they recognize what I'm singing, even when I'm singing in Japanese.

I have heard of groups of people, choirs even, singing to dying friends. What a beautiful way to send a loved one off into the next realm! Many loved ones of the dying have told me of their singing to their beloveds as they prepare to die. This may be one of the most healing things you can do for your dying friend or family member. Sit near them, let them know how much you love them and, if you wish, how much God loves them, too. Then, start singing one of your or their favorite songs. Our voices and the sound of music can convey so much love and reassurance. They help us all relax, breathe more deeply, and reduce stress, too. In all of this, it goes without saying that we need to keep in mind first and foremost the desires and wishes of the person we are singing for; we need to be certain that we are not putting our own religious beliefs and musical preferences ahead of those of the dying person for whom we sing or play music.

Don't Take Things Personally!

I am learning to take seriously Don Miguel Ruiz's words, "Don't take anything personally." Most of the people we work with in hospice are pleasant and special to work with. However, we do sometimes have families and individuals who consistently play the victim role; families who are stuck in the angry, sorrowing aspects of grief; and people who are practically impossible to please. In these cases especially, it is so important not to take what is happening personally. There is a great deal going on at the time we interact with these folks and we usually have very little to do with it except we happen to "show up" at a certain time. Then we sometimes end up the "lightening rod" for that individual or family system to vent their rage or grief. I have learned and encourage you, also, not to take anything personally that comes up in your relationship with one who is dying, or with those who are supporting you through your dying process. At the same time, I invite you to learn from even the most challenging of situations.

One important lesson learned while working with such a challenging family was this: Do not respond immediately when someone questions your actions or words. I was initially angry and upset when I heard what a family member had told my supervisor about what I had said. I let the weekend pass and was grateful for the time to mull over the situation before responding. The pause gave me time to settle myself down, pray about the situation, and clarify my own feelings before responding. I've heard this wise suggestion: Always count to ten before responding to a statement that brings up a lot of emotion. Sometimes, it's best not to respond at all.

Then, after a challenging situation in which you've worked hard not to take things personally, it may be well to remember the Buddhist adage that all of life is actually an illusion. Just as it's important not to take anything personally, it's also important not to take anything – or anyone, including yourself – too seriously!

Note: The above is the second agreement in Don Miguel Ruiz's "Four Agreements" from *The Four Agreements: A Toltec Wisdom Book* (Ruiz 2000). These four agreements are (1) Be impeccable with your word; (2) Don't take anything personally; (3) Don't make assumptions; and (4) Always do your best.

Death is Not What We Think It Is

One day I met a brother of one of our hospice patients who brought a beautiful piece to read to his dying brother. This piece reminds us to take death more lightly, for it may not be the big deal we make it. And – who knows? – after reading it, you may decide to read it to a loved one yourself.

Death is nothing at all. It does not count. I have only slipped away into the next room. Nothing has happened. Everything remains exactly as it was. I am I, and you are you, and the old life that we lived so fondly together is untouched, unchanged. Whatever we were to each other, that we are still. Call me by the old familiar name. Speak of me in the easy way which you always used. Put no difference into your tone. Wear no forced air of solemnity or sorrow. Laugh as we always laughed at the little jokes that we enjoyed together. Play, smile, think of me, pray for me. Let my name be ever the household word that it always was. Life means all that it ever meant. It is the same as it ever was. There is absolute and unbroken continuity. What is this death but a negligible accident? Why should I be out of mind because I am out of sight? I am waiting for you, for an interval, somewhere very near, just around the corner. All is well. Nothing is hurt; nothing is lost. One brief moment and all will be as it was before. How we shall laugh at the trouble of parting when we meet again!

~ Henry Scott Holland

Just to be is a blessing. Just to live is Holy.

~ Rabbi Abraham Joshua Heschel

The Profound Power of Gratitude

Just as laughter and humor can be a great medicine, so can gratitude. I once heard that gratitude is the hallmark of a true Christian. I would like to expand that thought to: Gratitude is the hallmark of any spiritually centered person, whatever religious or spiritual path he or she may be on. And gratitude, along with expressing creativity, can be another way to move us swiftly out of fear.

Remembering to give thanks every day, not only for what we eat, but for all the blessings of our lives, is a meaningful practice. We might begin with our health, abundance of all kinds, meaningful work, the beauty of Mother Earth, and all of the various and wonderful people in our lives, not to mention the miracle of being alive! I once heard a spiritual teacher say that it's good to give thanks on a daily basis with the words: "Thank you for my life; thank you for my life's work."

Gratitude has also been known to promote health and healing. Sharon Huffman has said that "feelings of gratitude release positive endorphins throughout the body, creating health." The following inspirational story of a real-life experience is recorded in a book of stories about the powerful effects of gratitude (Ryan 1999). I have paraphrased it here.

Josephine was diagnosed with a malignant brain tumor in her fifties. She was to have surgery a few days afterward. During the time that she waited for the operation, she sat on her porch, swinging in a swing, giving thanks for all the wonderful blessings in her life. She wrote a letter of gratitude to each member of her family, asked them to gather around her, then went into the hospital. On the night before her surgery was scheduled, she suddenly became aware of "what looked like a beautiful woman with long, flowing hair smiling at me and radiating light. She said she was an angel who felt my love and she had come to reassure me that everything was OK; that I would have plenty of time to fulfill my life's purpose." The angel then added these words before parting: "Always remember that it was your love and your appreciation that brought healing to you." As it happened, the tumor had disappeared. Josephine was sent home from the hospital that next day with no operation performed!

Recent scientific research has indicated that positive thoughts and emotions, such as gratitude and love, affect our health in a good way. Dr. Masaru Emoto of Japan has even made the discovery that positive thoughts and prayers can affect water crystals! (See movie *What the Bleep Do We Know!?* or the book, *The Hidden Messages in Water* (Emoto 2004).) They also help to strengthen the immune system, which in turn helps the body to recover from illness and heal more quickly. Endorphins are released into the bloodstream through a strong immune system, and this contributes, among other things, to a relaxed and healthy heart.

Blessings of a Grateful Heart

Just before the second edition of this book went to print, I heard this inspiring story from a lovely woman I met at a conference sponsored by Second Journey, an organization dedicated to mindfulness, service, and community in the second half of life. Shirley is a skilled architect and also a deeply spiritual woman with a keen interest in healing. She gave me permission to share her words here.

Very few spirits are as sweet, gracious and grateful as that of my friend Amy's mother, Sherry. She was the picture of gratitude and how it purifies the soul. If there was one word to describe her life, it would be gratitude. She lived everyday and every moment in gratitude. On the very sad occasion of her funeral, I was honored to assist her husband through the service while Amy tended to the guests. I felt deeply honored to be in the position of witnessing a very special and personal farewell between two worlds, separate from the occasion of the event.

That night, I was awakened three times by a vision of words, no sound, no background, no voice, only the words, "Blessings of a Grateful Heart." In the morning, I immediately called Amy to let her know the message from her mother; and together we tried to make sense of it. There was nothing to figure out; it was a clear message from an obvious source, without a doubt. Three simple words had so much message and meaning; it was truly a communication beyond the limitation of words. We both felt the sweet "thank you," the important message of what she had taught us and the message she wanted to send as her last words to her friends and family.

Amy sent this message in her thank-you notes: "Blessings of a Grateful Heart." It was a message from heaven. These words continue to be a blessing in our everyday lives as we remember that our worlds are connected and that our loved ones are with us always.

~ Shirley Tomita

As we count our blessings, we literally bathe ourselves inwardly in good hormones. And... a sense of appreciation... will make us feel better!

~ M. J. Ryan

I know God will never give me more than I can handle;
I just wish He didn't trust me so much.

~ Mother Teresa

信

Chapter 5
Trust

Healing into Wholeness

And dying you will leave your body as effortlessly as a sigh.

~ Psalm 121:8 (Stephen Mitchell's translation)

Death is absolutely safe! Like taking off a tight shoe...

~ Emmanuel

I MET one of my finest teachers on dying when I was just beginning this work ten years ago. I met this plucky woman on our hospice unit. Janet was at the end of a battle with lung cancer. She had not had an easy life. Her husband had committed suicide after their divorce, and she had raised their children on her own. Janet's spiritual journey had somehow given her the faith to face death squarely.

At the time when I met her, Janet had decided to stop eating, though she continued to use oxygen and drink fluids. On one of our first visits, Janet shared that she was "looking forward to the last adventure of life." I was deeply moved by her words. Janet had come to a remarkable place of peace about dying, and was looking at her unknown future with hope and courage, rather than fear. Janet offered me a wonderful gift through her "reframing" that helped me deal with my fears surrounding death – and all kinds of change, for that matter.

Another gentleman I met on hospice was told he had a very serious illness. Adding to this burdensome news, he was also dealing with his only daughter's recent loss of her home to a fire. But his strong faith was holding him steady. In the midst of our talking about what loomed ahead, he shared the following: "I don't believe the Lord would close one door without opening another."

It's All About "Trust, Trust, Trust"!

As I share with courageous people who have positive attitudes toward death, I realize how important it is for those on our hospice, and their family members, too, to stay relaxed and open-minded. The more they honor and trust the process, the better it works. When the person stays relaxed, there is less pain. Some refrains to engender trust include: "Let go, let God," "Go with the flow," "infinite trust," or simply, "trust."

Here's a wonderful piece on trust and the dying process by the Dutch priest, Fr. Henri Nouwen, who lived life fully and prayerfully, often moving toward his own fears and spiritual questions. I recall his class lectures on "Ministry and Spirituality" at the Yale Divinity School. I biked out there twice a week to hear him because his lectures were an inspiration, an enchanting sermon each and every time. My cup was filled by his deep spirituality.

Over the years Fr. Nouwen got to know the Flying Rodleighs, trapeze artists who performed in the German circus Simoneit-Barum. When the circus came to Freiburg some years ago, friends of Fr. Nouwen invited him and his father to see one of their shows. Fr. Nouwen writes of how he became totally enraptured watching the artists move through the air like elegant dancers.

The Catcher Will Always Be There for You

The next day, I returned to the circus to see them again and introduced myself to them as one of their great fans. They invited me to attend their practice sessions, ...and suggested I travel with them for a week in the near future. I did, and we became good friends.

One day, I was sitting with Rodleigh, the leader of the troupe, *of trapeze artists* ✓ in his caravan, talking about flying. He said, "As a flyer, I must have complete trust in my catcher. The public might think that I am the great star of the trapeze, but the real star is Joe, my catcher. He has to be there for me with split-second precision and grab me out of the air as I come to him in the long jump. ...The secret...is that the flyer does nothing and the catcher does everything. When I fly to Joe, I have simply to stretch out my arms and hands and wait for him to catch me and pull me safely over the apron behind the catchbar."

"You do nothing!" I said, surprised.

"Nothing," Rodleigh repeated. "The worst thing the flyer can do is to try to catch the catcher. I am not supposed to catch Joe. It's Joe's task to catch me. If I grabbed Joe's wrists, I might break them, or he might break mine, and that would be the end for both of us. A flyer must fly, and a catcher must catch, and the flyer must trust, with outstretched arms, that his catcher will be there for him."

Trust God When Rodleigh said this with so much conviction, the words of Jesus flashed through my mind: "Father, into your hands I commend my Spirit." Dying is trusting in the catcher. To care for the dying is to say, "Don't be afraid. Remember that you are the beloved child of God. He will be there when you make your long jump. Don't try to grab him; he will grab you. Just stretch out your arms and hands and trust, trust, trust."

~ Henri J. M. Nouwen

We Know Not the Hour...

Dying, in so many ways, is like birthing. One way is that we never know the exact hour it will come. And this can be one of the most baffling aspects of the dying experience. It's our reminder that we are not ultimately in control of life and death. I have worked with some people on hospice for months, even years, and with others who have been on hospice for only days or even hours. Some people I have met have been oh, so ready to die, and yet it has taken them agonizing weeks or even months before they are allowed to exit the earth. And many would like to have much more time, but their bodies are simply not able to keep going.

In most cases, the dying person seems to know when his or her time is getting close. In fact, I believe the person facing death knows best when death will come. One gentleman on our hospice actually seemed to "time" his death. With the family gathered informally around his deathbed, he took his last breath just as the last grandchild finished reading the letter he had written for him.

I often encourage a person to think about and visualize how he might like to die. Would he simply like to go in his sleep? Or would she like her loved ones, or perhaps a particular loved one, with her, holding her hand – or looking into her eyes – as she dies? As we visualize and pray about this, it can become a reality in our lives. I have recently heard it said that if the word "imagination" had existed in Jesus' time, he might have used it in lieu of the word "faith." If we can imagine it, we can help make it happen!

Incidentally, there have been a number of occasions when I have heard of the dying spouse taking one last look at his or her beloved before taking that last breath, as if to say, "I love you," one last time. A story like this always moves me deeply.

信

As Gently as a Leaf Falling off a Tree

We have all observed a tree losing its leaves in autumn. Last fall I purposely paused to look at a large maple tree. Most of the leaves had already turned a beautiful yellow. I was amazed by the gentle way in which these leaves naturally let go of their attachment to the branches. In the right amount of time, a leaf dries up and "ages" so that eventually it very naturally lets go. When the time is right, or when the wind blows hard enough to disengage it, the leaf slowly and gently drifts to the ground.

Is this not a simple but apropos image for our own deaths? In the right way, at the right time, we, too, each have a time to let go! The key is to stay relaxed, at peace with the whole process. Let go of any fear, and tune in as much as possible to the love, the joy, and the peace.

The metaphysical journal, *Sedona: Journal of Emergence!*, published an article by Mary Fran Koppa, entitled "What to Do When You Realize You Are Dying," which contains some very valuable information that I share with my clients regularly. Here is the gist of that article in my own words:

Recommendations for the Time When Death Draws Near

The first thing you are encouraged to do when you realize that you may be in the dying process is to know or accept that you will be "transitioning" to a much higher vibration. The reality you are moving toward is more important than this one, so it's best not to waste energy trying to resist the dying process.

Next, how you conduct yourself during this dying process will help determine your "destination" on the other side. Therefore, it is recommended that you:

1. Remain centered in God and God's love
2. Remain humble
3. Avoid blaming others
4. Forgive everyone and everything, especially yourself
5. Last, but not least, stay relaxed – at peace with the whole process!

It is also recommended that you take as little medication as possible, because drugs tend to change your energy fields and can even lengthen the dying process. Strive to convince those around you, through your behavior, that you want to take a minimum of drugs.

If you are dying alone, it's best if you do not fall into a "victim mentality." There is a reason you are going through the process by yourself – and you're never actually alone, right? God loves you more than you will ever know, and it's okay to die – to move on.

信

"Don't Worry about Me; Pray for Me"

My mother was a tremendous inspiration to me as she dealt with her cancer, and then later her death sixteen years ago. I will never forget one of our last visits when she was still able to drive me to the train station to send me off. After I got onto the train, we stood together at the train car doorway. She looked me straight in the eye and said, "Don't worry about me; pray for me." Over the years those precious words have stayed with me; I share them regularly with my hospice people. The following words by Rev. Schuller echo my mother's words.

Faith Is… Replacing Worry with Hope

> Do not worry about your life. … Which of you by worrying can add one cubit to his stature? … Your heavenly Father knows that you need all these things!

Matthew 6:25–32

Our Bible text today is one of the most beautiful prescriptions for the traveler on the road to faith. It comes from our Lord Jesus Christ. According to His definition, faith is replacing worry with hope.

Somebody said, "Worry is like a rocking chair: It gives you something to do, but it doesn't get you anywhere."

Worry doesn't put a twinkle in your eye, a whistle on your tongue, or a happy gait to your walk.

You are the manager of your moods, with the responsibility and the freedom to manipulate your emotions. You can elect to go out today with worry or step forth with hope.

Many Christians have tried this therapeutic experiment: They write down what they're worried about in their daily diary. They pray about it and turn it over to God. A year later they see how beautifully the Lord took care of the situation, or with the passing of time, discover that it was actually incredibly inconsequential!

Hope is a phenomenon. Faith replaces worry with hope, and no psychiatrist knows what it is. We only know what it does to people. It makes gray skin pink, dull eyes sparkle, and releases healing forces in the body itself!

Affirmation: Today I'm going to walk the walk of faith. My faith will take action as I replace worry with hope.

And what's hope? Holding on, praying expectantly!

Good-by, worry! Hello, hope!

~ Robert H. Schuller

信

Watch for Diamonds

The Buddhist approach to life and death can be helpful in the area of trust. Buddhist thinking has much to do with appreciating, accepting, and observing things as they are. I have had the privilege of following a daily e-mail course that shares some Buddhist concepts in a succinct manner. Here is one of the lessons from that course, based on Charlotte Joko Beck's words.

The paths of our lives seem to be filled with difficulties and challenges. However, the longer we practice our spiritual path, the more we realize that those "sharp rocks" on our paths are "in fact like precious jewels; they help us to prepare the proper condition for our lives." These rocks are different for each one of us: "One person might desperately need more time alone; another might desperately need more time with other people. The sharp rock might be working with a nasty person or living with somebody who is hard to get along with. The sharp rocks might be your children, your parents...."

Various health or career-related issues might be your sharp rock. The challenges, the sharp rocks are everywhere and all around us on our paths. What makes the difference after years of spiritual practice, however, is recognizing in a new way "that there are (actually) no sharp rocks – the road is covered with diamonds."

The Road of Life

Someone along the way shared with me this piece from a Christian perspective. I like it and want to share it here with you.

The Road of Life

At first, I saw God as my observer, my judge, keeping track of the things I did wrong, so as to know whether I merited heaven or hell when I die. He was out there sort of like a President. I recognized His picture when I saw it, but I really didn't know Him.

But later on when I met Christ, it seemed as though life were rather like a bike ride, but it was a tandem bike, and I noticed that Christ was in the back helping me pedal.

I don't know just when it was that He suggested we change places, but life has not been the same since.

When I had control, I knew the way. It was rather boring, but predictable.... It was the shortest distance between two points.

But when He took the lead, He knew delightful long cuts, up mountains, and through rocky places at breakneck speeds, it was all I could do to hang on! Even though it looked like madness, He said "Pedal!"

I worried and was anxious and asked, "Where are you taking me?" He laughed and didn't answer, and I started to learn to trust.

I forgot my boring life and entered into the adventure. And when I'd say, "I'm scared," He'd lean back and touch my hand.

He took me to people with gifts I needed, gifts of healing, acceptance, and joy. They gave me gifts to take on my journey, my Lord's and mine.

And we were off again. He said, "Give the gifts away; they're extra baggage, too much weight." So I did, to the people we met, and I found that in giving I received, and still our burden was light.

I did not trust Him, at first, in control of my life. I thought He'd wreck it; but He knows bike secrets, knows how to make it bend to take sharp corners, knows how to jump to clear high rocks, knows how to fly to shorten scary passages.

And I am learning to shut up and pedal in the strangest places, and I'm beginning to enjoy the view and the cool breeze on my face with my delightful constant companion, Jesus Christ.

And when I'm sure I just can't do anymore, He just smiles and says… "Pedal."

~ Author unknown

Never Underestimate the Power of Prayer

Praying is so important, for it is much easier for Spirit to intercede on our behalf if we ask. We must give permission, if you will, through prayer. Worrying is not helpful – a waste of our precious time and energy. If you happen to be a worrier, I encourage you to pray rather than worry. Use your imagination and pray for success! This will work, if you simply train yourself to cancel out the negative and believe in (imagine!) the possibility of good, if you are trusting that success is a given.

One day I went to visit a woman who was not dealing with her death and dying process in an open way. Her daughters were eager to talk more openly with Anne about the process, but she was a traditional woman. She also had a very close friend who had been deeply hurt by a recent loss in his life. For a combination of reasons, Anne had chosen to keep her thoughts about her impending death to herself.

I met privately with the daughters first. We talked about some of their challenges, hopes, and fears. Then their mother joined us, and we gently shared some words about what was likely to be coming in the near future for her. We closed our time together with a prayer for Anne, her family and friends, and for the whole process.

After my visit, the family called a priest to talk with their mother. During his visit, he asked Anne if there was anything that was still "unfinished" in her life. Anne

信

mentioned a brother whom she had not been in communication with for years. This brother suffered from some form of dementia. They prayed about this before the priest left. The following day, the woman got a phone call from her brother! She then died peacefully, several days after reconnecting with this brother.

The following story came to me through my pastor at the Richmond Beach Congregational (U.C.C.) Church, via a friend of hers. It is a moving testimony to the mysterious power of prayer.

A True Story on Transcontinental Prayer

A missionary on furlough told this true story while visiting his home church in Michigan: "While serving at a small field hospital in Africa, every two weeks I traveled by bicycle through the jungle to a nearby city for supplies. This was a journey of two days and required camping overnight at the halfway point. On one of these journeys, I arrived in the city where I planned to collect money from a bank, purchase medicine and supplies, and then begin my two-day journey back to the field hospital. Upon arrival in the city, I observed two men fighting, one of whom had been seriously injured. I treated him for his injuries and at the same time witnessed to him of the Lord Jesus Christ. I then traveled two days, camped overnight, and arrived home without incident.

"Two weeks later I repeated my journey. Upon arriving in the city, I was approached by the young man I had treated. He told me that he had known I carried money and medicines. He said, 'Some friends and I followed you into the jungle, knowing you would camp overnight. We planned to kill you and take your money and drugs. But just as we were about to move into your camp, we saw that twenty-six armed guards surrounded you.'

"At this I laughed and said that I was certainly all alone out in that jungle campsite. The young man pressed the point, however, and said, 'No sir, I was not the only person to see the guards. My five friends also saw them, and we all counted them. It was because of those guards that we were afraid and left you alone.'"

At this point in the sermon, one of the men in the Congregation jumped to his feet and interrupted the missionary and asked if he could tell him the exact day that this happened. The missionary told the congregation the date, and the man who interrupted told him this story: "On the night of your incident in Africa, it was morning here and I was preparing to go play golf. I was about to putt when I felt the urge to pray for you. In fact, the urging of the Lord was so strong, I called men in this church to meet with me here in the sanctuary to pray for you. Would all of those men who met with me on that day stand up?"

The men who had met together that day stood up. The missionary wasn't concerned with who they were — he was too busy counting how many men he saw. There were twenty-six.

When I pray, I never ask for anything, because I don't even know why things are the way they are. How could I ask for them to be different? The only thing I ask is: "Help me understand better what's happening so my actions will come out of more wisdom."

~ Ram Dass

Why Pray?

A patient of Dr. Larry Dossey's was dying from cancer. The day before his death, Dr. Dossey sat at the man's bedside with his family. The man knew he was short on time, and he chose his words carefully, using only a hoarse whisper. He was not religiously oriented, but he let Dr. Dossey know that he had begun to pray frequently in recent days. When Dr. Dossey asked him what he prayed for, the man responded: "I don't pray for anything; how would I know what to ask for?" Dr. Dossey was somewhat surprised by this response, and pushed the man with the following question: "If prayer is not for asking, what is it for?" The man reflected, "It isn't 'for' anything... it mainly reminds me that I am not alone."

According to Dr. Dossey, Jiddu Krishnamurti is said to have once asked a small group of listeners what they would say to a close friend who is getting ready to die. Their answers included assurances, words about beginnings and endings, and various expressions of compassion. Krishnamurti stopped them short. "There is only one thing you can say to give the deepest comfort," he said. "Tell him that in his death a part of you dies and goes with him. Wherever he goes, you go also. He will not be alone."

Pray About Everything

One of my hospice patients had a Stephen Minister, like a deacon from his church, who came to visit him regularly in his home. One day this person brought my patient a copy of *The Message,* a contemporary rendering of the Bible. This is how I came to learn about this edition of the Bible by Eugene H. Peterson, a Presbyterian minister who has served in Canada and Michigan, among other places. His version speaks in a down-to-earth way to young people – in fact, to people of all ages. I find it one of the most refreshing renditions of the New Testament; I read it to my hospice people regularly. The following is one of my favorite passages, which I often share on my first visit with people of the Christian tradition.

Celebrate God all day, every day. I mean, revel in him! Make it as clear as you can to all you meet that you're on their side, working with them and not against them. Help them see that the Master is about to arrive. He could show up any minute!

Don't fret or worry. Instead of worrying, pray. Let petitions and praises shape your worries into prayers, letting God know your concerns. Before you know it, a sense of God's wholeness, everything coming together for good, will come and settle you down. It's wonderful what happens when Christ displaces worry at the center of your life.

Summing it all up, friends, I'd say you'll do best by filling your minds and meditating on things true, noble, reputable, authentic, compelling, gracious – the best, not the worst; the beautiful, not the ugly; things to praise, not things to curse.

Put into practice what you learned from me, what you heard and saw and realized. Do that, and God, who makes everything work together, will work you into his most excellent harmonies.

~ Philippians 4:6–9

"I Love You, God!"

My clients are the best teachers. One day I was praying with a bereaved widow and giving one of my rather long and all-encompassing prayers. Then the widow began with a very simple, heart-strong prayer that included the words, "I love you, God." I was so moved by her simple prayer. It was a good reminder that our prayers need not be complicated or sophisticated. Prayer is most powerful when simple, direct, and from the heart. These are no doubt the prayers that God hears most clearly.

House of Confidence in the Future

I recently received a newsletter from Bethel, a unique town in Germany created exclusively for handicapped persons. Everything in Bethel is built around people who are differently able-bodied. They can live there, work there, and spend their whole lives there. I know about this place because my father used to send our used stamps there, even when I was very young. Then, one summer, we were able to physically visit this town, as my family took a trip through Europe on our way back to the U.S. from Japan. I remember, even as a young person, being very impressed by this unique place.

In the newsletter, one of the pastors in Bethel was telling about a relatively new hospice-home there. He mentioned that the name of the home is Haus Zuversicht, meaning "House of Confidence in the Future." What a special name for a hospice. Pastor Friedrich Schophaus shared in this newsletter about a homeless man who came to Haus Zuversicht. Before he died, this man shared with the staff that his stay at their hospice-home had been the happiest time of his life.

All I have seen teaches me to trust the creator for all I have not seen.

~ Ralph Waldo Emerson

Banishing Fear

The longer I live, the more aware I am of the significance of letting go of our fears. The more focused our fear, the more we can actually manifest that fear. I'll never forget the words from a gentleman whose wife was dying of breast cancer. He said to me one day, in confidence, "You know, her greatest fear was that she would get breast cancer."

Another woman I worked with had a fear of losing her mind. On my second visit with her when she was feeling confused, we began to talk about how she could use prayer to help her with her fears. After praying the Lord's Prayer together, I commented that she might recite the Lord's Prayer the next time she began to feel confused and fearful about her life situation. Then she mentioned that she could use the twenty-third Psalm, as well. She knew what I was talking about.

A bit later I quoted to the same woman, "Be still, and know that I am God." Then she responded with, "Be still, my fluttering heart." I remember saying with excitement, "That's it! That's the perfect phrase for you!" We each know deep within what works best for us. The challenge is to go deeper and deeper within to find our own answers.

Two Wolves

"A fight is going on inside me," the elder said to the boy. "It is a terrible fight and it is between two wolves. One is evil – he is anger, envy, sorrow, regret, greed, arrogance, self-pity, guilt, resentment, inferiority, and ego. The other is good – he is joy, peace, hope, serenity, humility, kindness, benevolence, empathy, generosity, truth, compassion, and faith. This same fight is going on inside you, and inside every person."

The grandson thought about this for a moment, then asked his grandfather, "Which wolf will win?"

The elder simply replied, "The one you feed."

~ Cherokee children's story (found on the Internet)

Healing Takes Many Forms

I have learned that I, too, must "trust the process" when I am working with my hospice clients and families. The following story helped me in this process as I recalled it while working with a man who had physically and verbally abused his wife and children. Unfortunately, his wife had already died, and dementia had overtaken him by this time, and there was no way that his children would be able to work through and heal the damage done – at least, not in this lifetime and not directly with him.

The Healing Heart

I watched as the urn containing my mother's ashes was placed alongside those of her husband and two-year-old son.

Two weeks after her death, my mother was standing just a few feet in front of me, radiant and filled with a joyful contentment I'd never seen in her when she was alive. A brilliant light surrounded her body. She appeared to be in her early twenties, young and beautiful. Her hair was the natural blond color of her youth, before the silver-gray clouds of loss and sorrow swept across her life.

As we embarked on a journey together, my mother reached out to me, her arms wide open with pure love. Her love permeated the air around us with a sweet fragrance of flowers. Hesitant at first, frozen in a moment of our bitter past, I could not help remembering that when she was alive, her conditional affection, tangled up with critical, abusive words, had wounded me painfully and left deep and painful scars.

Even as I wondered if I would be safe responding to her embrace, I had no doubt about the hunger in my heart. Since the age of eight I had longed for her closeness, for my mother's love. It seemed just seconds before my reluctance melted, and suddenly, I had no more need to protect myself or anxiously hold back out of fear. With a new trust and understanding emerging between us in that timeless moment, I felt total peace in my emotions. Peace was a freedom I'd so seldom experienced with her when she was alive.

The next sensation I felt was indescribable, as her arms surrounded me in an embrace filled with the most exquisite, unconditional love I have ever felt from another person. Instantly, her love incinerated years of emotional pain, anger, and fear like a fire clearing deadwood from land soon to be planted with spring flowers. Saturating every cell of my being was my mother's love, unconditionally.

In our embrace of forgiveness, there healed a lifetime of critical words and my childhood terror of abandonment. My mother and I were one, merged into love. Nothing mattered except being in that embrace. I was consumed in infinite love, the kind of love that lifts the sun in the morning and makes it shine and ignites the stars at night into brilliance.

In returning to me after her death, my mother gave me the greatest gift a person can receive in any realm. She gave me the opportunity to forgive her after so many difficult years between us. Only in forgiveness can I move away from the wounding and pain that consumed my life.

Where once there was a tangle of deadwood, now wildflowers grow.

~ Cheryl Fuller

"Why Me?" – The Oft-posed Question

Sometimes the question "Why me?" is paramount in my patient's or their family member's thoughts. This is a difficult question. But since so many ask it, let's deal with it here. Some people have the wisdom to turn this question around and say, "Why not me?" (in a world where suffering is inevitable). Others seem to want a definite answer; this creates more of a challenge.

A man I greatly admire is Dr. Bernie Siegel, an oncologist who has been on the cutting edge of a movement to help doctors and their patients bring spirituality into the healing process. Here's a beautiful story he shares in relation to this question.

Understanding Why

When I was a young boy, several of my friends became seriously ill, and one was hit by a car while bicycling to my house. When they all died, I said to my father, "I wish I were God so I would understand why God made a world where terrible things happen. Why didn't God make a world free of diseases, accidents, and problems?"

He said, "To learn lessons." I didn't like that answer and asked my rabbi, teacher, and others. They said things like, "God knows." "Why not?" "Who knows?" "That's life." "To bring you closer to God." Some were honest enough to just say, "I don't know." This didn't leave me satisfied or enlightened. When I told my mother what they said, she answered, "Nature contains the wisdom you seek. Perhaps a walk in the woods would help you to find out why. Go and ask the old lady on the hill who some call a witch. She is wise in the ways of the world."

As I walked up the hill I saw that a holly tree had fallen onto the path. As I tried to push it aside the sharp leaves cut my hands. So I put on gloves and was able to move it and clear the path. A little farther along the path I heard a noise in the bushes and saw a duck caught in the plastic from a six-pack. I went over and freed the duck and watched him fly off. None of this seemed enlightening.

Farther up the hill I saw five boys lying in a tangled heap in the snow. I asked them if they were playing a game and warned them the cold weather could lead to frostbite if they didn't move. They said they were not playing but were so tangled they didn't know which part belonged to whom and were afraid they'd break something if they moved. I removed one of the boy's shoes, took a stick and jabbed it into his foot. He yelled, "Ow." I said, "That's your foot. Now move it." I continued to jab until all the boys were separated, but still no enlightenment.

As I reached the top of the hill I saw, in front of the old woman's cabin, a deer sprawled on the ice of a frozen pond. She kept slipping and sliding and couldn't stand up. I went out, calmed her, and then helped her off the ice by holding her up and guiding her to the shore. I expected her to run away, but instead she and some other deer followed me.

信

I wasn't sure why they were following me, so I ran toward the house. When I reached the porch and felt safe, I turned, and the deer and I looked into each other's eyes before I went in the house.

I told the woman why I had come. She said, "I have been watching you walk up the hill and I think you have your answer."

"What answer?"

"Many things happened on your walk to teach you the lessons you needed to learn. One is that emotional and physical pain are necessary, or we cannot protect ourselves and our bodies. Think of why you put on gloves and how you helped those boys. Pain helps us to know and define ourselves and respond to our needs and the needs of our loved ones. You did what made sense. You helped those in front of you by doing what they needed when they needed it.

"The deer followed you to thank you – their eyes said it all – for being compassionate in their time of trouble. What you have learned is that we are here to continue God's work. If God had made a perfect world it would be a magic trick, not creation, with no meaning or place for us to learn and create. Creation is work. We are the ones who will have to create the world you are hoping for – a world where evil is to fail to respond to the person with the disease or pain, whether it be emotional or physical. God has given us work to do. We will still grieve when we experience losses, but we will also use our pain to help us know ourselves and respond to the needs of others. That is our work as our Creator intended it to be. God wants us to know that life is a series of beginnings, not endings, just as graduations are not terminations, but commencements."

~ Bernie Siegel

Here's another perspective on the question, "Why me?"

Don't Ask Why

Some people once brought a blind man to Jesus and asked him, "Rabbi, who sinned, this man or his parents, that he was born blind?" They all wanted to know why this terrible curse had fallen on this man. And Jesus answered, "It was not that this man sinned, or his parents, but that the works of God might be made manifest in him." He told them not to look for why the suffering came but to listen for what the suffering could teach them. Jesus taught that our pain is not punishment; it is not one's fault. When we seek to blame, we distract ourselves from an exquisite opportunity to pay attention, to see even in this pain a place of grace, a moment of spiritual promise and healing.

~ Wayne Muller

While reading the June, 2004 issue of the Unity publication *Daily Word*, I came across one more perspective on how we can respond to the existential question, "Why does suffering come into my life?" The Rev. Bob Barth, who has a brother with Down Syndrome, and more recently a wife who was diagnosed with fibromyalgia, says that he has found comfort in the words that he has been given through prayer. He shares these words with people who ask the "why" question. "I really don't know why – other than that one of two things is going to happen. You are going to be blessed, or you are going to give a blessing. And both can happen simultaneously."

✓ There is NO THING that is absent from God's good!

~ A Unity affirmation

The Three Temptations at the Time of Death

There is a drawing I have seen from the Middle Ages. A dying man lies on a bed. Surrounding him are at least five demons; there are also angels and "good" spirits watching over him behind the demons. The demons are offering the man three different crowns; the dying man holds one and the demons hold the other two. I have been told that this painting represents the three temptations at the time of death:

1. to numb the pain;
2. to give in to fear;
3. to give in to impatience.

These are interesting concepts to consider when we look at our own deaths. How can we best deal with our pain, both physical and non-physical, without denying its presence? How can we develop our spiritual lives so that we can keep fear from trampling us? And how can we stay patient, if we are eager to hurry up and get it over with? The three "demons" offer some food for thought as we contemplate the gifts of trust and faith.

After the first printing of this book, I met a bookseller in Olympia who found my book very intriguing as he worked out some of his doubts about the afterlife. He turned out to be a poet, and he sent me this moving piece that he had just written in honor of a man he had befriended on death row, on the day the man's life was to be terminated.

August 23 – For Robert Shields, 1975–2005

On the way to Otto's one last time,
I pass Kerry from Browsers' Books –
"Hi Craig, it's always nice to see you."
She can't know how sweet that sounds
    today.
I sit at one of our booths, Robert,
while the radio guitar gently weeps
and I read the first book I sent you,
after Long Hair David gave me your letter
asking for Tolstoy's *Kingdom of God*,
back in the winter of '98.
You've got eight hours left to live.

More old music, *Jumpin' Jack Flash*,
too much coffee one more time.
All those years of letters here –
I can't come back when you're gone.
This book inspired Gandhi,
gave birth to Non-Violent Resistance.
This is the book you wanted then
and that's why I answered,
and here we are.
I'm finally reading it now,
while you wait for your last meal.
I feel self-conscious sitting here,
watching myself acting out
my easy role in your hard story,
writing out the minutes of this day.

Home to the dishes and laundry,
then I force myself to watch
the end of *Dead Man Walking*,
the details of what they'll do to you.
Roll over Tolstoy, nothing's changed
except the cold technology.
It's still what they did to Jesus,
and they do it in his name.
How's that meal, did they get it right?
Their tiny act of Christian charity!

After all our "Bush and baseball" letters,
it figures that the Mariners
are playing in Texas tonight.
By the time they throw the first pitch,
your radio will be silent.
And Bush is in Texas too,
hiding at his toy cowboy ranch
from the mothers' camp for peace,
the daughters of Tolstoy, Gandhi, King.
And you've got six more hours
in your cell in Texas hell.
As you've said so many times,
"It's just another day in paradise."

The last words you wrote to me
echo across the summer miles –
"Until we meet again."

It's down to two hours
as I stumble on the trail,
approaching my own edge
while I stare in wonder at yours.
You've taken such a rough road
and you have passed the test,
Houston Chronicle be damned.

The clouds have finally lifted,
the light pours into the glistening forest,
let's imagine that it's just for us.
(Like you always say,
"What's **really** going on?")
You can do this, Robert,
just aim for the light.
One more hour to go,
we'll both just aim for the light.
There's something right here with us,
something kind, beyond time.
That's all we need, and all we know.

~ Craig Oare

So we do not lose heart. Even though our outer nature is wasting away, our inner nature is being renewed day by day. For this slight momentary affliction is preparing us for an eternal weight of glory beyond all measure, because we look not at what can be seen but at what cannot be seen; for what can be seen is temporary, but what cannot be seen is eternal.

~ II Corinthians 4:16–18

Listen with inward ear
to the music of her wisdom
teaching all creation.
With inward eye
visualize her brilliant name,
flowing across your heart
in letters of molten gold.

~ Ramprasad (Bengali poet)

Chapter 6
Reflect

Life Review and Dealing with Unfinished Business

May you have the commitment to heal what has hurt you,
to allow it to come close to you and in the end, to become one with you.

~ Words of itinerant monk Fintan
(Celtic end-of-life wisdom, *The American Book of Dying)*

PERHAPS THE most significant listening I do as spiritual counselor is to hear people's life stories. There is often much to reflect on when one knows one's life is ending. There is much that yearns to be witnessed and also confessed. Sometimes things feel unfinished, and there may be ways to help bring healing or closure. I would invite you to be a good friend to your beloved and hear him or her out. Listen deeply and speak from your heart. Your heart will be your best guide. The following material has been shared with me so I pass it along with the hope that it may enrich your listening as your friend faces great change. He or she may look to you for guidance on working through an issue of forgiveness or letting go. May you find the wisdom to be there for your beloved and live the questions with him or her.

Saying Goodbye

I happened to come across this in a local newspaper while compiling this book. It beautifully describes how we might deal with the yet "unpolished stones" of our lives. And I find the term "bed of life" delightful.

√ My "Bed of Life"

When I die do not call it my "deathbed," call it my "bed of life." Let my body be taken to help others lead a fuller life. Burn what is left of me and scatter the ashes to the winds to help the flowers grow. If you must bury something, let it be my faults, my weaknesses and all my prejudices against my fellow man. Give my sins to the devil, give my soul to God. If, by chance, you wish to remember me, do it with a kind deed or word to someone who needs you. If you do all I have asked, I will live forever.

~ Author unknown

One of the positive things about a person being on hospice for a period of time is that they have some time to say goodbye and take care of unfinished business before dying. My role as spiritual counselor sometimes involves assisting people to reflect on what they might like to do, and how, as they prepare to let go of life. The following are some reflective questions and ideas that we can use when helping people think about how they wish to place the finishing touches on their lives. From Ira Byock, a hospice physician, I picked up the following "Five Things" that need to be spoken before any significant relationship is complete.

Five Things

These are probably the most basic thoughts that you'll want to convey to your beloved ones before you leave them, or before your beloved leaves you. Don't wait until the last minute to share your deepest feelings, like why and how you appreciate and love them.

1. Forgive me.
2. I forgive you.
3. Thank you.
4. I love you.
5. Goodbye. (God be with you.)

省

Some Questions for Life Review

Here are some questions you and your loved one may wish to ponder. Your death need not be imminent to reflect on these thoughtful queries by Frederick Buechner (Buechner 1988), a beloved Christian author and theologian.

1. If you had to bet everything you have on whether there is a God or whether there isn't, which side would get your money and why?

2. When you look at your face in the mirror, what do you see in it that you most like and what do you see in it that you most deplore?

3. If you had only one last message to leave to the handful of people who are most important to you, what would it be, in 25 words or less?

4. Of all the things you have done in your life, which is the one you would most like to undo? Which is the one that makes you happiest to remember?

5. Is there any person in the world, or any cause, that, if circumstances called for it, you would be willing to die for?

6. If this were the last day of your life, what would you do with it?

The following are are some additional questions that might be asked when one is approaching the end of life or moving through some significant changes in life.

1. What is still unfinished in your life? What one thing do you wish to accomplish yet, and how can you take one step toward finishing it today?

2. How has life changed you? What were some significant spiritual turning points ← in your life?

3. How do you best experience God? How would you define, or symbolize God? What does the divine look like to you?

4. Have you had a negative experience with any religion or religious experience? If so, how did you deal with it? Have you been able to let it go? What would help you find deeper peace around this experience?

5. What are your spiritual needs at this time? Would anything help you grow spiritually? Would a community of people help? More solitude? Do you need spiritual guidance?

6. How can you bring meaning to the rest of your life and/or to your current suffering?

7. What do you believe happens when you die? What about after you die?

8. What is your greatest fear? What brings the greatest comfort to you? What is most satisfying?

Leaving a Tape or Video for Your Family Members

I remember hearing a story on the radio about a grandfather who had left a tape recording of his voice for his grandson. I believe he had been a harmonica player, so he left some of his harmonica playing on the recording, as well. This made me think about the power of voice and how it conveys the "texture" of a person. It made me wonder what it would be like to hear my mother's voice again. I have wished that I had a tape recording of her speaking to me, perhaps sharing some of her words of wisdom or some of her life stories with me.

I sometimes suggest to my hospice people that they think about leaving a recording of some kind for their descendants and loved ones. Even if they do not feel the importance of it at the time, their loved ones will relate to it later. Consider leaving some words of wisdom, stories or lessons from your past, or some special memory that you sense your family might enjoy learning about later. The above life review questions might aid you in reflecting on your life. Or just simply let them know how much you love them and what you have specifically appreciated about them. Your gesture and efforts may be appreciated in times to come more than you will ever know.

Forgiveness: A Key to Letting Go

Christine Longaker wrote a book, published in 1997, called *Facing Death and Finding Hope*. I am convinced that it is through facing our death, preparing for our death, that we do find the deepening peace of God, also God's hope, and even joy.

Until very recently, at least during this last century or so in Western culture, talking about death was almost taboo. We procrastinate about making preparations for our actual death. Even when people are actively dying, some choose not to deal with the reality of death.

However, many of the people I visit with on hospice are very interested in facing their deaths. And some share with me their personal struggles to let go. For many, it is the thought of leaving their loved ones here on earth that is the most difficult. "I haven't been able to face that one yet," some will say when I ask them about preparing to leave a beloved spouse or deeply cherished children and grandchildren.

Once in a while the people I meet get to the heart of the matter very quickly, perhaps because they know they have very little precious time left. I recall meeting with a family in which the wife of a beautiful man and mother of some special daughters was dying. Rebecca loved God and the natural world very much. But she was struggling deeply with the fact that she and her husband had not attended church during the later years of their life together. I helped Rebecca refocus her love for God and encouraged her to forgive herself for not attending church. She was reminded that it's how we live our lives that truly serves God. How we have loved God, ourselves, and our neighbors throughout our lives is truly the important question, not how often we have attended a house of worship.

I was looking forward to meeting with this family again because they were so delightful, but Rebecca developed some physical complications, and my next visit a couple of weeks later ended up being with her grieving family. I participated in a lovely memorial service in a beautiful garden next to their home. As sad as I was not to see Rebecca again, I instinctively knew and was grateful that she probably had released her guilt about not having attended church in those last few years of her life.

> Out beyond fields of wrongdoing and rightdoing, there is a field.
> I will meet you there.
>
> ~ Rumi

On Being a Non-judging Presence

For those of us who work with the dying and their families, it is especially important that we withhold judgment. Everyone is on his or her own timeline, and on his or her own spiritual journey, one that is fitting for his or her particular process. Here is a poignant statement about judgment from an exceptional book by Glenda Green, *Love Without End: Jesus Speaks* (Green 1999).

> The long era of judgment has been man's darkest night, but that will end soon when the last judgment has been made. The last judgment will be the judgment against judgment itself. At that time, human consciousness at last will rise in splendor like a valiant bridegroom to join his bride, the Sacred Heart. This is the Holy Wedding which has been the dream of prophets. After this marriage occurs, there will be peace on Earth. In the meantime, it is your right to seek a betterment of life in all the ways that are available to you. Enjoy every opportunity for positive change. Make the most of every day.
>
> ~ Jesus, through Glenda Green

How this rings true for me! Especially in these times of great transformation, and when we work with those who are experiencing the greatest change ever in their personal lives, may we withhold judgment. Instead of judging, let us sit with our friends, our family, our beloved ones, with an open, non-judging heart, whenever and however we have the chance to do so. Change and growth, especially spiritual growth, seem to be at the heart of the matter these days. It is critical that we be patient and nonjudgmental with everyone, especially ourselves. The following is a story that helps illustrate this point.

Judgment

There was an old man in a village, very poor, but even kings were jealous of him because he had a beautiful white horse. Kings offered fabulous prices for the horse, but the man would say, "This horse is not a horse to me, he is a person. And how can you sell a person, a friend?" The man was poor, but he never sold the horse.

One morning, he found that the horse was not in the stable. The whole village gathered and they said, "You foolish old man! We knew that some day the horse would be stolen. It would have been better to sell it. What a misfortune!"

The old man said, "Don't go so far as to say that. Simply say that the horse is not in the stable. This is the fact; everything else is a judgment. Whether it is a misfortune or a blessing I don't know, because this is just a fragment. Who knows what is going to follow it?"

People laughed at the old man. They had always known that he was a little crazy. But after fifteen days, suddenly one night the horse returned. He had not been stolen; he had escaped into the world. And not only that, he brought a dozen wild horses with him.

Again the people gathered and they said, "Old man, you were right. This was not a misfortune, it has indeed proved to be a blessing."

The old man said, "Again you are going too far. Just say that the horse is back. Who knows whether it is a blessing or not? It is only a fragment. You read a single word in a sentence – how can you judge the whole book?"

This time the people could not say much, but inside they knew that he was wrong. Twelve beautiful horses had come.

The old man had an only son who started to train the wild horses. Just a week later he fell from a horse and his legs were broken. The people gathered again, and again they judged. They said, "Again you proved right! It was misfortune. Your only son has lost the use of his legs, and in your old age he was your only support. Now you are poorer than ever."

The old man said, "You are obsessed with judgment. Don't go that far. Say only my son has broken his legs. Nobody knows whether this is a misfortune or a blessing. Life comes in fragments and more is never given to you."

It happened that after a few weeks the country went to war and all the young men of the town were forcibly taken for military enlistment. Only the old man's son was left, because he was crippled. The whole town was crying and weeping, because it was a losing fight and they knew most of the young people would never come back. They came to the old man and they said, "You were right, old man – this has proved a blessing. Maybe your son is crippled, but he is still with you. Our sons are gone forever."

The old man said again, "You go on and on judging. Nobody knows! Only say this: that your sons have been forced to enter into the army and my son has not been forced. But only God, the total, knows whether it is a blessing or a misfortune."

~ Author unknown

Do Not Judge Death

One of our hospice nurses attended a conference for hospice caregivers, and she later shared this piece from a thoughtful book written from the Taoist perspective on caring for the dying.

Do Not Judge

Death can be very painful.
Do not waver in your attitude of allowing.

Death can be very exhausting.
Do not waver in your attitude of allowing.

Death can be very ugly.
Do not waver in your attitude of allowing.

Childbirth can be very painful, exhausting, and ugly.
Yet a beautiful child can still be born.
So it is with dying.

Do not judge the death by the dying!
Do not judge the dying!
Do not judge death!
Do not judge!

Be prepared for anything.
Allow for anything.
Accept anything.

There is no other way.

~ Doug Smith

A friend of mine sent me the following beautiful quote from Archbishop Desmond Tutu via e-mail. The universal concept that we are integrally interconnected with each other, that whatever we do to another we actually do to ourselves, unites us one with another, around the whole world. It reminds me that walking the road of forgiveness is always in our best interest, no matter how challenging the pain.

Ubuntu – Our Interconnectedness with All Living Beings

Ubuntu is very difficult to render into a Western language. It speaks of the very essence of being human. When we want to give high praise to someone we say, *"Yu, u nobuntu"*; "Hey, so-and-so has **ubuntu**." Then you are generous, you are hospitable, you are friendly and caring and compassionate. You share what you have. It is to say, "My humanity is caught up, is inextricably bound up, in yours." We belong in a bundle of life. We say, "A person is a person through other persons." It is not, "I think therefore I am." It says rather: "I am human because I belong. I participate, I share." A person with **ubuntu** is open and available to others, affirming of others, does not feel threatened that others are able and good, for he or she has a proper self-assurance that comes from knowing that he or she belongs in a greater whole and is diminished when others are humiliated or diminished, when others are tortured or oppressed, or treated as if they were less than who they are.

~ Archbishop Desmond Tutu

"Am I Dead Yet?"

It has been said that dying is not unlike birthing. This is true in more ways than one. For instance, sometimes a person dies much more quickly or sooner than expected, just as a pregnant woman suddenly is ready to give birth much sooner than expected. On the other hand, sometimes a dying person's spirit is willing, but the body has not caught up with their spirit's will – not unlike a pregnancy that goes on and on.

When my aunt died some years ago, the staff of the nursing home where she was staying said that toward the end, my aunt was totally ready to die. She would wake up from her sleep asking, "Am I dead yet?" Then the staff would have to let her know that she was still here on earth. Alas! I have worked with people on our hospice in the same predicament. They are so ready to go, but it's just not time yet, for whatever reason. In these situations, perhaps their bodies are simply not finished with their physical processes yet.

At times like these I like to share a passage from "The Letter to the Romans," in *The Message* version of the New Testament, Chapter Eight, where Paul reminds us that we are all, including creation itself, waiting to be released from this dense physical reality. This is true in our day, perhaps more than ever before.

That's why I don't think there's any comparison between the present hard times and the coming good times. The created world itself can hardly wait for what's coming next. Everything in creation is being more or less held back. God reins it in until both creation and all the creatures are ready and can be released at the same moment into the glorious times ahead. Meanwhile, the joyful anticipation deepens.

All around us we observe a pregnant creation. The difficult times of pain throughout the world are simply birth pangs. But it's not only around us; it's within us. The Spirit of God is arousing us within. We're also feeling the birth pangs. These sterile and barren bodies of ours are yearning for full deliverance. That is why waiting does not diminish us, any more than waiting diminishes a pregnant mother. We are enlarged in the waiting. We, of course, don't see what is enlarging us. But the longer we wait, the larger we become, and the more joyful our expectancy.

Meanwhile, the moment we get tired in the waiting, God's Spirit is right alongside helping us along. If we don't know how or what to pray, it doesn't matter. [God] does our praying in and for us, making prayer out of our wordless sighs, our aching groans. He knows us far better than we know ourselves, knows our pregnant condition, and keeps us present before God. That's why we can be so sure that every detail in our lives of love for God is worked into something good.

~ Romans 8:18–28

Some Tools for Working on Forgiveness

Forgiveness is our key to letting go. It is the key to staying in the present moment. It is the key to living a full life. I have learned this, sometimes the hard way, in my own life. The following are some tools that might assist you in letting go of some of the burdens you may be carrying around. I have also found hypnosis (*Gifts for the Soul*, Clark, 1999-2001), "Scripting" (*Feelings Buried Alive Never Die*, Truman, 1991, 2003), and the Radical Forgiveness Ceremony (*Radical Forgiveness*, Tipping, 2002) to be helpful in my own forgiveness process. You may want to take a look at the websites and books related to these topics in the back of the book, as well.

A Blessing/Affirmation

Developing a forgiving attitude at the end of life is critical. The more we can find peaceful resolution in our relationships, the better. There are multiple ways we can work on developing this forgiveness. Here is a phrase I have found helpful to assist us in letting go of people who are holding us to them because of what they have done to us.

"I bless and release _____, with love, for his/her/their greater good. So be it."

It is helpful to repeat this phrase out loud, at least three times, whenever the person or people come into your consciousness and you start to feel uncomfortable.

May Peace Prevail on Earth!

Another phrase that can be repeated to extinguish our negative thoughts is the simple phrase, "May peace prevail on earth." The founder of The World Peace Prayer Society, Masahisa Goi, says that not only is this phrase the key to forgiveness, but also, by repeating and praying these words over and over, we begin to develop peace and stability in our souls, which has a positive effect on the life around us. Goi says: "When you pray for world peace, the connection between you and humankind naturally becomes clear to you, and at the same time, without even thinking about it, you are causing great waves of brilliant light to spread through the universe." (Global Link, Spring 2003)

A Course in Miracles

When Columbia University professor Dr. Helen Schucman began hearing a voice, she wrote down what she heard. She eventually identified the voice that she was hearing as none other than Jesus, delivering a message of compassion and forgiveness for the modern world. The book, called *A Course in Miracles,* is a three-volume set that includes a Text, Workbook for Students, and Manual for Teachers. The basic message is that the way to universal love and peace, in other words "remembering God," is by letting go of guilt and forgiving others.

The way we overcome fear and guilt is through miracles, which are defined as "expressions of love." Miracles, according to the Course, can also be defined as a shift in perception from fear to love. The Course uses traditional Christian language, but it expresses a nonsectarian spirituality. The introduction explains: "The course does not aim at teaching the meaning of love, for that is beyond what can be taught. It does aim, however, at removing the blocks to the awareness of love's presence...your natural inheritance. The opposite of love is fear, but what is all-encompassing can have no opposite."

At this time, worldwide, there are more than half a million copies of the Course in circulation. It has been translated into nine different languages, and eleven more translations are in progress.

A Forgiveness Meditation

For the full text of this meditation, I invite you to see Stephen Levine's book, Healing into Life and Death, *pages 98–101 (Levine 1987). Here, I will simply give you a flavor of his guided meditation.*

Begin by thinking about what the word "forgiveness" means to you. What is forgiveness, anyway? What would it mean to bring forgiveness into your life, your mind?

Begin by slowly bringing into your mind, into your heart, the image of someone for whom you have some resentment. Gently allow a picture, a feeling, a sense of them to gather there. Gently now invite them into your heart just for this moment.

Notice whatever fear or anger may arise to limit or deny their entrance, and soften gently all about it. No force. Just an experiment in truth that invites this person in.

And silently in your heart say to this person, "I forgive you."

Open to a sense of their presence and say, "I forgive you for whatever pain you may have caused me in the past, intentionally or unintentionally, through your words, your thoughts, your actions. However you may have caused me pain in the past, I forgive you."

Feel for even a moment the spaciousness relating to that person with the possibility of forgiveness....

It is so painful to put someone out of your heart. Let go of that pain. Let them be touched for this moment at least, with the warmth of your forgiveness.

"I forgive you. I forgive you."

Allow that person to just be there in the stillness, in the warmth and patience of the heart. Let them be forgiven. Let the distance between you dissolve in mercy and compassion....

Now gently bring into your mind, into your heart, the image, the sense, of someone who has resentment for you. Someone whose heart is closed to you.

Notice whatever limits their entrance and soften all about that hardness. Let it float.

Mercifully invite them into your heart and say to them, "I ask your forgiveness." ...

How unkind we are to ourselves. How little mercy. Let it go. Allow you to embrace yourself with forgiveness. Know that in this moment you are wholly and completely forgiven. Now it is up to you just to allow it in. See yourself in the infinitely compassionate eyes of the Buddha, in the sacred heart of Jesus, in the warm embrace of the Goddess.

Let yourself be loved. Let yourself be love.

And now begin to share this miracle of forgiveness, of mercy and awareness. Let it extend out to all the people around you. ...

Whole world floating in the heart. All beings freed of their suffering. All beings' hearts open, minds clear. All beings at peace.

May all beings at every level of reality, on every plane of existence, may they all be freed of their suffering. May they all be at peace.

May we heal the world, touching it again and again with forgiveness. May we heal our hearts and the hearts of those we love by merging in forgiveness, by merging in peace.

~ Stephen Levine

I encourage everyone to keep working on issues of forgiveness and letting go of the past, especially of resentment and bitterness. Therapeutic massage can be helpful, so can essential oils, and a host of other tools. Feelings of anger and resentment can literally get "housed" in our bodies and cause blockages, and in time, illnesses, when we hang onto ill or negative feelings for long periods of time.

Not Clinging to Your Loved One

On occasion, for some unexplainable reason, the dying person can have trouble letting go into the unknown. Sometimes this is related to the fact that they are not sure that it's okay for them to let go, especially considering the needs of their family members. This is why hospice team members sometimes find themselves encouraging family members to specifically say their goodbyes to their dying loved one, and also let them know that they have their permission to move toward death and what lies ahead.

If you have not yet done so, and you sense that the time is right, I invite you to say goodbye to your loved one. If it is your family member who is dying, and you feel at all comfortable saying so, give them your permission to "let go." You might encourage them to "move toward" or "merge" with the Light and Love of God, when that time comes. Embolden them on their way, however you might do that. Trust that your loved one is very open at this time, and is ready to hear you say what you sense is the right thing to say.

Also, it may be helpful not to be at your dying loved one's side all the time. Some families get very caught up in being present with their loved one every minute, perhaps in part because they want to be with them at the exact moment of their death. However, it's possible that your love for them could be holding them to the earth. When a person is very close to the time of death, they have one foot in this world and their other foot in the next realm. They are likely to need some "space." In fact, some people literally need to be alone so that they can "let go."

One of our hospice specialist nurses kindly advises families who are spending every waking minute with their loved one that they need to let their beloved be alone at least five minutes out of every hour. In light of that consideration, if your family is making sure to have someone with the dying person at all times, you may want to revisit your decision with your beloved. It may behoove you, and your loved one, to spend at least some periods of time apart – as difficult as this may seem. Consider it a way of preparing for what lies ahead. You might also consider it one way of taking care of yourself at this critical time. And if you absolutely want to be with your loved one when they die, you may want to make this as clear as possible to them and all their caregivers before the actual time of death, making sure that they know your wishes and that this is what they desire as well. Clear communication is so important, especially as the end of life draws near.

When Your Loved One is Not of Sound Mind

I had one visit with a woman who knew she had been married to her soulmate. Grace had cared for James for many years, while he struggled with Alzheimer's Disease. Grace knew that it was time to let him go, and James had been referred to our hospice. However, Grace had not really said "goodbye" to him yet. I suggested during our first visit that she might want to do this sooner rather than later.

A week or two later, Grace told me that she had taken my advice. As difficult as it was, she had plucked up her courage and told her beloved goodbye in her unique way. Grace told me that she was grateful that she had said her farewell, for sure enough, within about 24 hours, James was able to let go and move into his last adventure of life!

It is not always so clear-cut or easy. In another situation, I was working with a woman who was dealing with the last stages of cancer and who also had dementia. Julia was able to converse relatively clearly and seemed to know what was going on much of the time. One day, I gently brought up the subject of her death. Julia agreeably engaged in some conversation with me at the time. Later, however, her daughter-in-law told me privately that Julia had asked her about what I had said. She had not been comfortable with my bringing up the subject of death she said, as she did not want to think about death. I realized then that it would be best not to bring up the subject again unless Julia brought it up herself.

Just as with grief, I'm learning that everyone in our culture has a different way of coping and dealing with this sensitive subject, especially when there is no obvious mental clarity. All the more then, the issue of facing death must be dealt with lightly, gently, and with an open, caring heart, not to mention our heightened intuition.

Relying on our developing intuitions and prayer (spiritual practices) to intentionally guide our way on this delicate issue will no doubt bring us the best assistance.

> Funny how you'll plan every aspect of every trip except the most important one you'll ever take!
>
> ~ Found on the National Hospice website www.nhpco.org

"Every Death is a Birth"

Miracles can and do happen – even at the very end of our lives. Death, like a rebirth, holds the potential for tremendous healing. I have witnessed and heard about many such healings through my hospice families, and here is one I read about. It took place in a hospital room, as a Jewish mother was preparing to die. Her daughter, Joan Borysenko, and her grandson witnessed a most sacred and healing process during their last night with this powerful spirit. To read the entire piece, I invite you to find a copy of *Experiencing the Soul* (Rosen, editor, 1998) and read chapter 21.

Joan writes that between the time it took for her and her mother to go from the hospital basement up to the seventh floor, they "got a lot of work done." Her mother had lived through the Holocaust, among other horrors, and she tended to cope with life by not facing her pain. She point-blank asked her daughter, "Look, I know that I've made a lot of mistakes. Could you forgive me?"

These "blessed words" allowed Joan to open her heart and allowed her to see the pain she had been holding onto. Then she was able to look at her mother and say plainly, "I'm sorry, too. I've made a lot of mistakes. Can you forgive me?" And Joan reflects, "In the sacred place, the gateway of death, the words that are spoken carry a tremendous capacity for healing. And there was a tremendous moment of forgiveness that just passed through our eyes at that time."

After they got up to the hospital room and everybody had said good-bye to Joan's mother, Joan and her son Justin stayed with her through the night. Justin was 20 then, and very close to his grandmother who had raised him. He dearly loved her and it was easy for him to tell her what a difference she had made in his life. He began to sing to her, too, including the song "Some Enchanted Evening," a very special piece for her personally. At one point she looked up with tears and said, "Do you think Grandpa will be waiting for me?"

Around midnight, after the doctor asked if she would like a little morphine and she took it, Joan and her son began "the vigil," sitting on either side of her bed. Around three o'clock in the morning, as they sat waiting and meditating, Joan experienced the following mystical vision:

I felt luminous, light-filled, and I felt that I was giving birth to the entire world in the form of a baby – I've given birth twice, and know that point of giving birth to life that can feel like a death. During this vision, I realized that birth was no great picnic for the baby either – that the baby is also dying, and that every death is a birth and every birth is a death. I was equally present in the vision both as the baby and as the mother.

Joan goes on to describe moving into the consciousness of the baby and feeling herself being "born" as she moved through a tunnel and then out into a tremendous realm of light. It felt as if her soul had been bare: All her flaws were seen, but she could still somehow experience the purity of her soul. At this time, much about her relationship with her mother became clear to Joan – that they were a part of "a circle of death and birth that went on forever."

When Joan came out of the vision, she saw that the entire room was filled with luminous, mystical light; everything "was all molecules of light dancing. I looked across at my child, at Justin, and Justin was weeping. His face was suffused with light, and he looked up at me and he said, 'Mom, the room is filled with light. Can you see it?' I said, 'Yes, I see the light.' And he said, 'It's Grandma. She's holding open the door of eternity for us so that we can have a glimpse. It's her last gift.'"

Then Justin looked at his mother with eyes so filled with love that Joan could sense the light that began in his heart and moved through his eyes. He acknowledged how grateful Joan must be to her mother, which allowed Joan to see that he had had the same experience as she had. Then, Justin concluded with the following profound statement: "You know, she was a very great soul. And she embodied to take a role that was much smaller than the wisdom in her soul, and she did it as a gift for you so that you'd have something to resist against."

Joan concludes her story by sharing what a great gift his statement was because through it she knew that he was forgiving her for what she had not done for him as a mother.

Final Gifts

The following is a story of healing at a time just before death, and of how a young woman was reconciled to her father, from whom she had been separated for most of her life. The story comes from a very special book called *Final Gifts* (Callanan & Kelley 1992). I highly recommend it if you want to know more about hospice – and about the "visions" some dying persons experience – from a spiritual and emotional point of view.

Theresa

Theresa, twenty-two, was dying of bone cancer. She was the younger of two children, abandoned by their father when she was five. Though he lived nearby, the father had had little contact with his son and daughter over the years, and had contributed nothing toward their upbringing. Theresa lived with her mother, who took care of her; her brother, who lived nearby, visited frequently and did what he could to help.

During my first visit, Theresa and her mother described the father as "that man," not "my father," or "my ex-husband." I asked if Theresa wanted to see him. She said that since they had no relationship she didn't feel any need to do so.

Theresa's biggest problems were pain and weight loss. As often happens with young people, Theresa's pain required fairly large doses of pain medicine. We tried other pain-relieving techniques also: Theresa found meditation and music particularly helpful, and we instituted a regular schedule for those.

The weight loss was difficult for her mother to see. Theresa was five feet seven, and had always been slim. But now she ate very little and refused all dietary supplements. As she became weaker and spent more time in bed, her mother had to turn her from side to side every few hours to prevent bedsores.

Four months after admission into our program Theresa was dying. Her pain became increasingly severe; the dosage of her pain medicines had risen accordingly. We thought her physical pain was controlled, but still she moaned. We asked what the matter was, but couldn't get an answer; her speech was difficult to understand. Several times her mother asked me how Theresa could still be alive.

But one day, mixed in among a jumble of words, she said, "Dad."

We wondered if she wanted to see her father. We asked her, but her response was unintelligible, a few words lost in another moan. Her mother felt it was worth a try. She telephoned the father and explained what was happening.

That afternoon Theresa's brother picked up the father and brought him to the apartment.

He went into the bedroom, sat beside Theresa, held her hand, and told her he was there. He said no more. He looked shaken and upset, but also stiff and uncomfortable. After a few minutes he stood.

"I can't take this," he said, leaving the room and saying an awkward farewell.

But Theresa's moaning stopped, her agitation eased, and she died quietly a few hours later. No one can say that her estranged father's visit was what Theresa needed for a peaceful death. But the only circumstance making that day different from those preceding it was his presence. Her mother and brother feel that in some way Theresa needed something from her father, and that after his visit she was able to let go and die.

~ Maggie Callanan and Patricia Kelley

Setting Goals: A Way to Keep on Living

When a person has a clear reason to keep living, he or she often can muster the strength to stay alive in order to reach a certain goal. I think of one older man on our hospice who was particularly close to his granddaughter. He made the goal to live to see his granddaughter get married. Not only did he make it to her wedding, almost one year later, but he lived at least another couple of months after the wedding, as he pondered what his next goal might be!

Another woman with breast cancer on our hospice lived for many months so she could attend her son's wedding. She not only attended his wedding in another state but also enjoyed a separate reception that was planned in the Seattle area about one month later. She finally died a month or two after the reception had taken place. At the time of her death, she seemed to have deeper peace and acceptance about dying than she had had earlier in her hospice stay.

I have noticed that some people even make it a point to keep setting one goal after another as a way to have something that keeps them desiring to stay alive. Marty had a young grandson she was watching grow, day by day. She treasured every moment she spent with him and every picture that was a testament to his growth. She was also in the process of mending a long-term relationship with her husband through her illness. Finally, Marty did succumb to death, but it was not without a determined fight, strong faith, rich humor, and a powerful and loving connection to the earth.

Talking with Those Who are Not Spiritually Oriented

The title "spiritual counselor" is used for my role so that all kinds of people might feel comfortable talking with me. I do not consider it my job to convert people to any kind of belief at the end of their lives. However, I do encourage the people I talk with to have an open mind about what might lie ahead. Of course, everyone is entitled to their own belief or non-belief systems.

Through my work, I have come to see that it's very possible that what we believe at the time of death may be exactly what we get! Therefore, the more open we are about the possibilities in our future, the more possible they may be. I wonder, for those who believe that there is nothing after this life, could it be that they will see nothing – at least for a period of time? The power of imagination is greater than we know. Perhaps there is great truth in the bumper sticker I once saw that read: "Don't die wondering." In this regard, I would encourage you to talk as openly as possible with those with whom you do not see eye to eye on spiritual matters. Preaching or striving to convert is not the answer, but we can share openly and honestly, from the heart, about what has been meaningful to us. And we can agree to disagree, in a loving way, respecting and honoring one another and our individual perspectives in the process.

Unresolved Deaths, including Suicide

Sometimes, things cannot be resolved in this lifetime, and people die under very challenging circumstances. At times, families and loved ones have to deal with suicidal deaths. Such moments are some of the most difficult to live with afterward. Author and medium James Van Praagh suggests in his book *Talking to Heaven* (Van Praagh 1997) that our thoughts and prayers are the best way to get through to such spirits. First of all, we can send thoughts to those who have committed suicide to remind them to "stop wasting their energy by trying to get back into the physical world. They must realize that they have passed out of the physical body." (page 103) Our thoughts are the only way we can communicate with those who have left the earth, and apparently in some cases of suicide, as sometimes in other sudden deaths, the victim does not realize that they have actually died and left their physical vehicle behind. Secondly, we can send them thoughts of love, peace, joy, forgiveness, and light. We can help to bring comfort to their spirits and allow them to become more aware of their new situation.

I have learned that visualizing the violet flame encompassing all things purifies them. You might imagine sending or placing the purifying violet flame around the soul of your loved one. Or you could visualize any negativity, either your own or your loved one's, in the violet flame, allowing the negativity to purify and dissolve into pure white light. You could also envision taking your loved one to a beautiful place, like a magnificent garden, or beautiful healing waters where they can bathe, or someplace where you know they will find peace and comfort. You can then imagine them in this peaceful spot whenever you think of them, knowing and trusting that they, too, can and will find deep peace over time.

Most of all, it's important that the surviving loved ones not blame themselves for what happened, or keep pondering the "what if" scenarios, or second-guessing why the death occurred in the way that it did. Even though guilt is almost unavoidable after a suicide, it is a crippling emotion, and it robs people of their confidence. So by all means, find creative ways to release any guilt you might be carrying around because of the suicide of a loved one. What has happened cannot be changed, and it is not your fault. Let go of the past, and move into the future with abiding confidence and love; this is what your loved one would want for you, too.

Inspiration Through Music and Poetry

Mary Black is a very special singer. Recently, while listening to "The Best of Mary Black, Volume 2," I heard this magnificent song, with words by Steve Cooney. I encourage you to listen to it. Would that I could play it for everyone I know who makes the journey to the other side, just before they go. I initially thought that this was a song written by a parent to a young person getting ready to die, but after a long search I discovered that it was written as a love song for the end of a relationship. It clearly came from a most generous and loving heart.

Bless the Road

Remember when we walked on hills of heather
Singing weaving mystical rings
Now in a while my precious child
You will unfurl your wings
And I'll have lost what I believed
Had promised everything
But before you go my friend, my kind companion
Listen to this song I sing

Then go in peace and grow in grace and goodness
Know that you have nothing to fear
And dry your eyes my little one
And let there be no tears
Send me a dream from away beyond
I promise I shall hear
Oh beautiful beloved soul companion
Thank you for those beautiful years

And heaven hold and watch your way forever
May your every dream come true
Forgive all wrong, always be strong
And do what you must do
You stand before this open door
And you must now go through
My precious friend, my own my sweet companion
Bless the road that carries you

~ Steve Cooney

THE LAST ADVENTURE OF LIFE

I think most of the spiritual life is really a matter of relaxing –
letting go, ceasing to cling, ceasing to insist on our own way,
ceasing to tense ourselves up for this or against that.

~ Beatrice Bruteau, from Radical Optimism

Chapter 7
Awareness

Cultivating the Art of Meditation

Now is the only time there is. Pain, grief, depression, guilt and other forms of fear disappear when the mind is focused in loving peace on this instant.

~ Gerald G. Jampolsky, M.D.

The Power of Meditation

MEDITATION CAN benefit us in all aspects of our daily lives. It can bring us a sense of calmness and centeredness. It can help to raise our consciousness (see *Integral Psychology*, Wilber, 2000). It can also heighten our sense of intuition. It is particularly a helpful tool in developing our awareness when we are preparing for death. In my experience, a person who is comfortable with meditation has an easier time with death. Learning to go inward in our very outward-oriented culture is one of the most profound ways we can develop spiritually.

As a beginning experience for my clients interested in meditation, I encourage them to practice deep belly breathing. First, sit in a comfortable position, with your spine as straight as possible. (Lying down is okay, too.) Close your eyes and put your hands on your stomach. Now take some slow, deep breaths through your nose. As you notice the bottom of your lungs filling with air, you will also be aware that your stomach expands. After inhaling, pause briefly, then exhale slowly, through your nose, if possible, and allow your stomach to deflate and your chest and shoulders to let go

THE LAST ADVENTURE OF LIFE

of any tension in your body. Again, pause briefly, and then repeat this exercise for a total of 10 or 12 breaths. When finished, keep your eyes closed and breathe normally for a while, allowing your breath to regain its natural rhythm before opening your eyes. This kind of deep breathing can be a helpful tool for relaxation and a good beginning point for someone who is not used to the concept of meditation.

There is a wonderful CD to use for practice meditating with the breath, called "Meditations on The Present Moment," by Thich Nhat Hanh. Mr. Hanh is a Vietnamese Zen master who has written extensively on peace and mindfulness. This excellent CD contains eight guided meditations to help a person fully appreciate the miracle of breath and life. Two books I recommend for beginning meditators are *How to Meditate*, by Lawrence LeShan, and *Wherever You Go There You Are*, by Jon Kabat-Zinn.

Recently I was introduced to a special teacher of "Mindfulness Meditation" at Swedish Hospital in Seattle. A physical therapist by trade, Carolyn McManus has come to appreciate mindfulness through her own experience with back pain. She also has books and CDs available at www.carolynmcmanus.com. Please utilize any of these resources as another way to cope with your pain or stress. Meditation practice is also an excellent technique for developing a deeper sense of tranquility in your life.

Radical Ignorance – Understanding the Mystery

One of the most meaningful and thoughtful devotional newsletters I have received over the years is *The Daybook: A Contemplative Journal*, published by Marv and Nancy Hiles of the Iona Center. (Unfortunately, it is no longer being published, although they now publish another newsletter called *The Way Through: A Contemplative Companion*.) I found the following in their Daybook:

The basic fact that we dwell in the midst of a reality we cannot understand has been my fulcrum. If we would get to the roots of our troubles, we must come to terms with our radical ignorance. We shall never master life as though it were a mathematical problem. We shall always need to cast ourselves upon its waters, as pilgrims living by faith. The leading masters of the spiritual life show us why we always depend on the mystery and how we may come to love our constant dependence. What I have loved in contemplation is the relief it offers. My mind clatters along, hour after hour. Entering into the cloud of unknowing finally stops my mind. I need no longer pay attention to all its images, questions, snappy sayings. I can take on ballast and move down to the bottom of my self. What is going on at the top becomes secondary, almost unimportant. That I am, not independently but by the grace of the mystery, steps forth as the primary wonder. When I simply abide in this wonder, calling it the creative love of God, I feel warm and fed in spirit. I have found my place in the scheme of things. I sense no further questions. There is nowhere else I need to travel. Momentarily, I live at the omega and the alpha, the end that is the beginning.

~ John Carmody

So to yield to life is to solve the unsolvable.

~ Lao Tsu

Daily Inspiration for Peace

The Unity Church has a beautiful devotional booklet, *Daily Word*, that shares inspiration for each new day. This is one of their pieces that touched me deeply.

Breathe and Smile

Affirmation: Returning to the simple truth of my divine nature, I appreciate life anew. ✔

Babies instinctively know how to appreciate life in the moment. Remembering the simple and pure expression of a baby's smile, I know there is divine joy in simply being.

As I quiet my mind, I become aware of the here-and-now moment. I breathe deeply, relaxing as I exhale. Then I smile, enjoying the miracle of being alive. I appreciate anew my surroundings, taking in every vibrant sight and sound.

I enjoy consciously being a part of life, instead of being distracted by my mind's endless list of things to do. For now, breathing and smiling are the only things on my "to do" list; in these moments of renewal, simply being alive with the spirit of God is enough.

I pause now, aware of my nature as a living, breathing child of God, and I smile as I enjoy life at the purest level of being.

"Let the peace of Christ rule in your hearts." Colossians 3:15

~ Daily Word

The following reminder to bless everyone and every situation helps me remember that once we find that everything and everyone can be blessed, we are on our way to finding peace in our hearts. In the process of getting permission to reprint this piece here, I discovered that Mr. Pradervand now has a book out by the same title (Pradervand 1993).

The Gentle Art of Blessing

On awakening, bless this day, for it is already full of unseen good which your blessings will call forth; for to bless is to acknowledge the unlimited good that is embedded in the very texture of the universe and awaiting each and all.

On passing people in the street, on the bus, in places of work and play, bless them. The peace of your blessing will accompany them on their way and the aura of its gentle fragrance will be a light to their path.

On meeting and talking to people, bless them in their health, their work, their joy, their relationships to God, themselves, and others. Bless them in their abundance, their finances. Bless them in every conceivable way, for such blessings not only sow seeds of healing but one day will spring forth as flowers of joy in the waste places of your own life. As you walk, bless the city in which you live, its government and teachers, its nurses and street sweepers, its children and bankers, its priests and prostitutes. The minute anyone expresses the least aggression or unkindness to you, respond with a blessing: Bless them totally, sincerely, joyfully, for such blessings are a shield which protects them from the ignorance of their misdeed, and deflects the arrow that was aimed at you.

To bless means to wish, unconditionally, total, unrestricted good for others and events from the deepest wellspring in the innermost chamber of your heart: It means to hallow, to hold in reverence, to behold with utter awe that which is always a gift from the Creator. He who is hallowed by your blessing is set aside, consecrated, holy, whole.

To bless is yet to invoke divine care upon, to think or speak gratefully for, to confer happiness upon – although we ourselves are never the bestower, but simply the joyful witnesses of Life's abundance.

To bless all without discrimination of any sort is the ultimate form of giving, because those you bless will never know from whence came the sudden ray of sun that burst through the clouds of their skies, and you will rarely be a witness to the sunlight in their lives.

When something goes completely askew in your day, some unexpected event knocks down your plans and you too, burst into blessing: For life is teaching you a lesson, and the very event you believe to be unwanted, you yourself called forth, so as to learn the lesson you might balk against were you not to bless it. Trials are blessings in disguise, and hosts of angels follow in their path. To bless is to acknowledge the omnipresent, universal beauty hidden to material eyes; it is to activate that law of attraction which, from the furthest reaches of the universe, will bring into your life exactly what you need to experience and enjoy.

When you pass a prison, mentally bless its inmates in their innocence and freedom, their gentleness, pure essence and unconditional forgiveness; for one can only be prisoner of one's self-image, and a free man can walk unshackled in the courtyard of a jail, just as citizens of countries where freedom reigns can be prisoners when fear lurks in their thoughts.

When you pass a hospital, bless its patients in their present wholeness, for even in their suffering, this wholeness awaits in them to be discovered.

When your eyes behold a man in tears, or seemingly broken by life, bless him in his vitality and joy: For the material senses present but the inverted image of the ultimate splendor and perfection which only the inner eye beholds.

It is impossible to bless and to judge at the same time. So hold constantly as a deep, hallowed, intoned thought that desire to bless, for truly then shall you become a peacemaker, and one day you shall, everywhere, behold the very face of God.

~ Pierre Pradervand

The Importance of Planting the Seed

Clark Strand, an author, teacher, and former Buddhist monk, has written an article called "Planting the Seed" (Strand 2002). His writings, based on Jesus' parable of the sower, emphasize two essential truths about our spiritual practices. First, they often start small; it's actually better that we not be too ambitious in the beginning. Second, they work best when we can take a leap of faith to "trust the process," rather than focusing on the goal or the outcome.

A common mistake when embarking on our spiritual path is deciding that we have to change everything at once. We're much better off starting with just one thing, like chanting or meditating for 20 minutes each day, or perhaps only two or three times a week. I recall when my daughter was still very young, and I was having trouble meditating on any regular basis. My spiritual director at the time advised me to give myself permission to meditate just two times a week. This was probably the best advice she could have given me, as I was able to make this happen. And gradually, my practice grew, without my feeling overburdened by a goal I could not live up to.

Staying focused is the most important aspect of our spiritual path, suggests Strand:

Our job is very simple. We must plant the seed and tend our garden. That is all. Eventually the harvest will come.

How does it come? That is a great mystery. Even Jesus made no attempt to explain it.

All we know is that it happens naturally, provided we do the work. Each of us holds within us the seed of the kingdom of heaven. That kingdom can be different things to different people. But in every instance, the growing requirements are the same: a clear focus and a little persistence... It is the nature of any seed to grow and of any garden to flower and yield its fruit.

As for the question, "What kind of practice is best for you?" it's best if you choose something you are drawn to practicing. Mr. Strand advises: "Don't make your selection on the basis of which one promises the best results. Do what you love and you'll love doing it. It won't feel like a burden at all."

Learning to Be

One of the challenges for people getting ready to die is to learn to be instead of do. Our culture, our society, teaches us well how to "do," but we have more trouble with simply "being." Here is a Tibetan perspective on the power of being at the time of the great transition (LeShan 1986).

The Way to Do Is to Be

There is a Tibetan chant for the dying, in which the loved ones say over and over again, "Nothing to hold to, nothing to do." What this symbolizes is the idea of moving from Doing to Being. It seems to me that this process ought to be part of all living – that one can become accustomed to Being long before it becomes a task related to dying, and that we spend too much of our lives doing, achieving, competing, "keeping busy." Being is not passive; it is as much an act of choice as those things categorized as doing. It is really focusing all our attention on one thing at a time and not doing anything else. It can be playing a game of tennis....

It's being fully present at one's life, without claims or expectations of results. Until the moment of dying, life takes precedence. It will, I believe, be helpful to contemplate how we will face our own deaths, but right now we are alive! The Talmud says that when a wedding procession and a funeral procession meet at a crossroads, the wedding procession has the right of way. While facing the inevitability of our mortality, we still need to focus our energy, our caring, on life.

~ Eda LeShan

Some people think that meditation needs to take a lot of time and energy. This is not necessarily the case. The following meditation practice can be done in five minutes or less, once one begins using it on a regular basis.

A Meditation for Busy People

Four steps to follow to realize the presence of God when there seems no time to meditate. It can be done anywhere and only takes five minutes!

1. Use a mind-sweeper to clear your thoughts. Sweep away all negative, fearful, or unforgiving thoughts. [Takes one minute.]

2. *Relax your body through and through. Start at the top of your head and let relaxation flow down over your body in a stream of white light or sunshine. [another minute]*
3. *Let yourself feel the Love of God that is within you until Love fills your whole being. Envision yourself embraced by Divine Love. [with practice, takes only an instant]*
4. *Be still and KNOW that you are in the presence of God. See every cell of your body glow with pure Love and Light. [two minutes]*

Take the thoughts and feelings of this experience with you as you go about your daily activities. When you practice clearing your mind, relaxing your body, feeling God's Love and Light, and listening in the quiet several times each day, you are building a heightened awareness of Who You really Are. You will look around and see how beautiful and full of Love the world truly is. You will hold the true nature of your fellow sojourners along life's way.

~ *Daily Word*

There are many simple meditations that you can use to help you relax and stay focused. One such meditation I appreciate comes from Stephen Levine, a student of Dr. Elisabeth Kübler-Ross, in his book *Healing into Life and* Death (Levine 1987). It can be read slowly to a friend or silently to yourself. It begins by sending love and compassion to oneself. Then it moves on to share love and compassion with another person. Finally, it shares love and compassion with all living beings. I believe that this is the true way of love. We begin with loving ourselves, and then that love naturally extends to others. It has the effect of healing all living things. If you wish to refer to the whole text, it can be found on pages 23–27 of Levine's book; I have simply paraphrased it below.

A Simple Loving Kindness Meditation

> May I dwell in the heart.
> May I be free from suffering.
> May I be healed (whole).
> May I be at peace.
> May my heart flower.
> May I know the joy of my own true nature.
> May I be healed into this moment.
> May I be filled with love.

After focusing on yourself and your own healing and softening, using these words with the breath for a period of time, then focus on someone for whom you feel loving kindness. Picturing this loved one in your heart, with each in-breath whisper to them, "May you dwell in your heart. May you be free from suffering. May you be healed. May you be at peace."

Continue to send love and healing to your beloved one for a period of time, using these or similar words, combined with your breath. Then, as you sense the healing and peaceful nature of your loved one in your heart, begin to make a shift toward this entire world that yearns "so to be healed, to know its true nature, to be at peace." And in your heart, whisper with each in-breath and out-breath, "May all beings be free of suffering. May all beings be at peace." … "May all sentient beings, to the most recently born, be free of fear, free of pain. May all beings heal into their true nature. May all beings know the absolute joy of absolute being."

Picture the entire world like a blue/green jewel, floating in your heart, embraced by your peace and loving kindness. Each in-breath draws in the compassion that heals the world, that deepens the peace we all hope for. Each out-breath feeds the world with the mercy and love, the warm care and patience that stills the mind and opens the heart. "May all beings dwell in their heart. May all beings be free from suffering. May all beings be healed. May all beings be at peace."

Keep your breathing slow and easy, stay comfortable in your body, and continue this process until it feels like it is complete for now, for this particular healing through a simple, loving kindness meditation.

Tonglen

There is a Buddhist practice called Tonglen which is a practice of taking on, through compassion, the various mental and physical sufferings of another being, and then giving that being, through love, happiness, and well-being, peace of mind and healing, or wholeness. This practice is something we can do for someone who is dying, as well. There are five basic points to follow if you are interested in trying this meditation, and they can be found in detail in *The Tibetan Book of Living and Dying*, pages 205–206 (Sogyal Rinpoche 1993). Here are the points, very simply put:

1. Sit quietly and bring your mind home, allowing compassion to be born in your heart.

2. As clearly as possible, imagine in front of you someone who is suffering. Then, imagine their sufferings as a great mass of hot, black, grimy smoke.

3. Now, visualize this mass of black smoke dissolving with your every in-breath, into the very core of your self. There you see it purifying your negative karma.

4. Imagine that the heart of your enlightened mind, your bodhicitta, is fully revealed. Then, on every out-breath, imagine that you are sending out its brilliant, cooling light of peace, joy, and ultimate well being to your friend in pain. Its rays are purifying your friend's karma.

5. Through this process, feel a strong conviction that all of your friend's negative karma has been purified. Experience a deep, lasting joy that this person has been totally freed of suffering and pain. Continue steadily with this practice while breathing normally.

Practicing Tonglen for a friend or loved one has the capacity to open you up to the wider "circle of compassion." We can then take on the suffering of all beings, and relate to them our happiness, joy, wholeness, and peace of mind. This is the special goal of Tonglen, and in a sense the whole path of compassion, deep understanding, and wisdom.

As I am writing about this healing practice of Tonglen, I discover while holding my beloved black cat, a small growth on her body. I practice my version of Tonglen with her, praying for her, and sending her God's love and pure light, visualizing her complete and total healing. I am visualizing more from my Christian tradition and metaphysical learning. I cannot help but reflect that all healing practices we engage in, whatever their tradition, are operating on the same principle of the power and dynamic of love, mercy, or compassion. Yes, love works; may we think it, see it, and feel it with our whole beings.

Guided Meditations

The following are some guided meditations and methods that you might use with your friends and loved ones. Please take your time to browse through them to see which one might be best to use. Or, you might try using a variety of them and see which one fits best for you and your loved one. Some people may even appreciate the variety, depending on their mood and situation. Once you settle on one or two that you especially like, if you think you will use them often, you may wish to have your loved one tape-record them for you.

The first is a piece from Unity's *Daily Word* which reminds us to "Be still, and know" where the power truly lies.

Be Still and Know

Affirmation: In an awareness of God's presence, I experience absolute peace.

Relax: Sometimes I need to tell myself, "Relax." And then I let a time of quiet meditation take me to a peaceful state of mind.

I begin by closing my eyes and imagining a fluid-like warmth slowly flowing from the top of my head down and over my whole body. All tension melts away from my muscles. As

I take a deep breath, I feel totally alive. Releasing that breath, I feel totally alive. Releasing that breath, I am aware only of God's presence.

I continue to breathe in and out in slow, steady breaths. Here with God, I have moved past being simply relaxed; I am at peace. I linger here in God's presence, no longer aware of my body or my surroundings. When I am ready, I will go back to my day relaxed and peaceful.

"Be still, and know that I am God! I am exalted among the nations, I am exalted in the earth." Psalm 46:10

~ Daily Word

The following is a meditation I first heard from Drunvalo Melchizedek. At the time, he said that it was the most powerful meditation we could be using on the planet today. My version of it below is based on material from *Something in This Book Is True* (Frissell 2003).

Heaven and Earth Meditation

Begin by taking some very deep breaths and getting comfortable in your body. As you take these deep breaths, scan your body and see if there are any places where you have tension or pain. Breathe deeply into any areas of stress or tension and see any stress leaving your body with the out-breath. Imagine bringing light and love to your entire body with your deep, healing breaths.

Now, as you continue taking deep, loving breaths, close your eyes and visualize a tube of light that begins about one hand-length above your head and stretches to about one hand- length below your feet. See the two ends of the tube open. Breathe life through your tube from above and below, and let it meet in your heart area. From there, it will radiate into a sphere around your body. The flow will be continuous on the inhale and the exhale; just allow it to surround you and energize you for a minute or two.

I invite you now to bring your attention to Mother Earth. You might visualize a favorite place you enjoy in Nature and feel your love for the Mother, for the trees, the birds, the animals, the water, and anything else that comes to mind. Gather these feelings of love into your heart; you might see your love as a colorful sphere of light. After your love for the Mother is gathered into your heart, send it down to the center of the Earth, knowing even as you do so that the Mother will be responding by sending her love and energy back to you. Wait until you can feel this energy back from Mother Earth.

Now place your attention on Father Sky, on all life in the cosmos, where inspiration comes from. Feel your love for all the stars and galaxies, and all life in the heavens. Sense the love you have for the Father; you might imagine looking into a night sky. Then take all of your love for the Father and gather it into your heart area. Now see that love as a sphere of light and send it up to Father Sky. As you send your love to the Father, know that Father Sky will be sending his love back to you as well. Then wait until you actually feel the love of the Father returning to bless you. I've heard it said that it can be helpful to visualize a column of golden light coming down over your torso as a way to help organize the energy coming up from Mother Earth.

Now, visualize the love of Mother Earth and the blessings of Father Sky mixing and blessing you and the aura around your body; you might see the different colors of energy blending around your body. And know that now the holy trinity is mystically present in you – the Mother, the Father, and the Holy Child. This means that something very special can take place.

Visualize the tube that stretches through your body again. Now place your attention on the opposite ends. Open up the ends even further, and allow all life everywhere to enter from both ends, to enter into your heart, and to radiate as light all around you. Open up the ends, and allow God/dess All That Is to come in and to form a sphere around your body.

Now as you experience your whole being to be blessed, and as you slowly allow the sphere around you to expand, gradually visualize the energy moving out toward your neighbors and local community. You might think of someone to whom you'd like to send this loving, joy-filled energy. Visualize sending it to that person, or family, or community of people who could particularly benefit from it. Then keep letting the energy expand, allow it to get bigger and bigger, moving out into the world faster and faster. If you can, in the end, let it expand uncontrollably, throughout all dimensions and in all directions. Allow it to return back to all life, everywhere, blessing and bringing peace and delight wherever it goes.

May peace prevail on earth. May peace prevail among all religions, too.

I don't know the source of the following meditation, but I like it and want to share it here.

A Centering Meditation

Close your eyes and begin relaxing your body by taking a really deep breath. Breathe in relaxation. Breathe out stress and tension. Feel yourself slipping back into your deeper self. Feel relaxation travel throughout your body as you continue deep and rhythmic breathing. You may notice anywhere in your body that does not allow the flow of breath. Imagine that you are bringing light and love to that part of your body.

Your breathing is becoming slower and more relaxed now. Breathe in and fill up your lungs with the breath of light and love. Release on your out-breath any of the stresses and harsher thoughts and feelings you do not want. If you are carrying any burdens, imagine a box next to you in which you can place these burdens until after the meditation.

Imagine that over the top of your head there is a beautiful, white light with gold specks in it. It is brilliant light. Feel the top of your head open to receive this light. Breathe in this brilliant light, light that is golden/white and sparkling. Feel your body unwinding now. Releasing. You are SO comfortable. Feel your arms and your legs growing very comfortable. Relax your body even more. Allow more light to enter into your whole body, creating even more of a flow in your body. Allow that feeling of relaxation in your body to continue to deepen as you center now on your emotions.

Imagine a feeling of peace. Deep, quiet peace. A feeling of serenity. Of letting go and trusting. A feeling that you are loved and protected. And your emotions are growing very calm, very still, becoming like the clear mountain lake that reflects the trees and the sun. Feel and see the green and blue colors of a still and renewing nature scene: the lake, the beautiful trees, the sunlight filtering through the branches. You can relax here in this image. Unwind. Let go. Your emotions are becoming so quiet, so still, that you can hear the faint whispering of the Spirit as it speaks to your heart: "Trust, do not be afraid. Be at peace."

Calmer and clearer. Silent. Peaceful. A calm, quiet spirit. And now let your mind grow clear. To do this, you may wish to imagine that you are bathing in beautiful, crystal-clear water. The water washes your thoughts from your body. You can feel the water cleansing your mind. Refreshing you. Imagine, with each breath out, the water helping you to release the heavier thoughts in your body that are unloving or fearful. Breathe out these thoughts with each gentle wave of the water. Let them release. Feel the sunlight with the water and allow yourself to let go as much as you can into perfect peace and love.

Feel the harmony now in your being – an alignment of your physical, emotional, and mental centers.

Rest now at this place. You are being revitalized from the inside out. Like in a blanket of love, wrap yourself up in the light and love of God until you feel totally at peace. Stay in this place for the next few minutes. Let yourself absorb the love that is all around you and within you. Receive.

Begin to become aware of your breathing again. Focus on your breath. Become aware of the room you are in. How you are sitting or lying. Be aware of your body. Remember the peaceful experience you have just gone through and give thanks for it. When you are ready, slowly open your eyes.

Comeditation (Advanced Meditation)

I would like to introduce you to an ancient form of deep relaxation and breathing called comeditation (or co-meditation). It's a method I often have wanted to use with my clients for I know it will bring great benefit to those who are anxious or troubled in any way. This is an "advanced" meditation, so I do not recommend that beginners be the guide for this one.

Comeditation, or "shared breathing," is a method that has been developed through Tibetan Buddhism to relieve psychic suffering. It has been practiced for centuries by Tibetan priests and physicians to help clear and calm the minds of dying persons. Through "cross-breathing," which are special sounds uttered by the guide as the dying person exhales, the dying person is helped to enter a meditative state, which calms the fear and the racing mind that often accompanies illness and death. The technique has been found to be particularly beneficial for people suffering from AIDS.

One does not have to have meditated before to be on the receiving end and to enjoy the benefits of comeditation. Neither is a particular religious belief required. It is a physiological approach that uses the body to affect the mind.

You can begin comeditation with some traditional relaxation exercises. Start with the toes and continue upward to the top of the head, helping your loved one visualize his or her entire body being in a totally relaxed state. Your loved one is to lie comfortably with the eyes closed; he or she only needs to listen and breathe.

After beginning with some guided relaxation, you might say something like: "All you need to do is listen carefully to my voice and follow your breathing. Let's begin with the great sound of letting go, the sound of 'ah.' Just make the 'ah' sound on your next exhalation. Let go of everything else from your mind."

After several repetitions of the 'ah' sound, start counting out loud, slowly, from one to ten, synchronizing each number to your loved one's exhalation. This synchronized counting will allow your loved one to sink deeper into a meditative, relaxed state. At some point, invite your loved one to visualize the numbers you are counting as "clear, white," and "going out over your feet into the horizon." Remind the person that "thinking is not necessary," and to simply focus attention on the numbers being spoken by you.

Occasionally you might interject phrases like "breathing and counting, counting and breathing"; "clear mind, peaceful heart." Remind the person that it is okay to "let go" of their current earthly reality. Let him or her know that drifting off to sleep is okay, too. "The mind talks, but the body knows," is a good statement to use. You can invite your loved one to imagine moving into a "vast, boundless ocean of light." Say, "Picture yourself in the center of this light, and on each exhalation envision merging with this great light." Add a phrase such as, "in your mind's eye, you see only light."

You can practice comeditation for any length of time, but 30 minutes might be a good guideline to begin with. After such a period of comeditation, a person's respiration can drop to as low as one or two breaths per minute. As we slow down the mind, we slow down the breathing; it's as simple as that. Comeditation can introduce people to a state of comfort and even bliss before their death. It can be like a road map to give people an idea of where ultimately they will be going. It is an ancient Tibetan method for helping people to let go of their fear of death. It also is helpful because when a person is in a place of deep relaxation, the breathing slows down, and in turn the need for oxygen lessens as well. As people relax, they also tend to reduce the amount of pain they may have.

Dick Boerstler, a specialist in comeditation, uses this method especially with persons who are troubled, having difficulty breathing or sleeping, having pain, or when a caregiver is feeling distraught and having a sense of being overwhelmed. Once you have helped a person move to a deep place of relaxation through comeditation, you can also have the person visualize a problem-free, smooth procedure, or death, or whatever the person may be having to face at that time. This will inevitably have a positive effect on the challenges being faced.

In conclusion, let me share a story about a nurse who used comeditation at the time of a death in a hospital in the Boston area. This nurse was caring for a patient in the ICU whose physical systems were shutting down; the machines were not able to keep up, and she sensed that death was encroaching. She began counting with this patient, and his breathing and blood pressure returned to their normal state. "He was in a peaceful state before he died," the nurse stated. "That's what's so wonderful about comeditation. It doesn't call attention to itself; you can just let it happen."

Meditations to Help Prepare for Dying

I have found the most specific meditations for the actual time of death in Dr. Bruce Goldberg's book *Peaceful Transition: The Art of Conscious Dying and the Liberation of the Soul* (Goldberg 1997). As the meditations are rather unique, I thought it important enough to get his permission to share some of them here.

General Meditation Script

Focus all of your attention on your breath. Concentrate on the mechanics of breathing, not the thought of the breath. Note how it comes and goes. As the breath enters and leaves the nostrils, feel the expansion and contraction of the lungs.

Focus on the awareness of breathing. Remove all other thoughts and feelings from your awareness. Observe all other thoughts and feelings from your awareness. Observe this natural life process. Do not try to change it. Merely be with it. Let yourself receive the changing sensations that accompany this process.

As you inhale and exhale, one breath at a time, let it happen by itself. If it is deep, let it be deep. If it is slow, let it be slow. If it is shallow, let it be shallow.

If you sense the mind is interfering with this process, just focus on the inhalation and exhalation. Be one with your breath. Nothing else matters.

Observe the uniqueness of each breath. Observe, don't analyze. Note the changing sensations. Be one with your breath.

Ignore all other functions of the body. Remove all thoughts from your mind. You are the breath. Be one with your breath.

You are now floating with the universe. As the wind carries a feather, you are being carried by your breath.

Notice how the distracting thoughts fade. How they become meaningless. All that matters is that you breathe. You are your breath. Be one with your breath.

Let go of the body. Feel as if you have no body. You are weightless, as is your breath.

You are floating in the universe. You are at peace with the universe. You are one with the universe.

Notice how relaxed you are, now that you are free of the confines of the body. You are totally one with the universe.

There is nowhere to go. Nobody is expecting you. You have no schedule or deadline. You are free. Enjoy this moment, for you are one with the universe.

Be quiet. Do not cough or make any movement or sound. Just be still and merge with the universe. You are consciousness.

Let go of all fear and doubt. Let go of all thoughts. Do not try to control your being. Just be free and one with your consciousness.

You have no body. You have no limitations. You are one with your consciousness. You are one with the universe.

Let each moment occur by itself. Observe it and enjoy these intervals of time. Do not resist this merging with your consciousness.

You are now nothing but consciousness. You are the universe.

Play soft, healing music (that is pleasing to the person) for 15 minutes.

Now it is time to return to your body. Again, concentrate on your breath. Now note the other functions of your body. Slowly open up your eyes and do what you feel is important at this time.

Before-Death Meditation Script

Now you are about to enter a very special journey. This is an experience that you have already prepared for many times. You have consciously died many times.

This time your preparation is guided by your Higher Self and your Masters and Guides, with your complete awareness. You are perfectly safe.

See the white light around you, protecting you so that there is no need to be concerned. Be one with the white light. You are the white light.

You are able to maintain your connection with your Higher Self at this time. You are able to keep this connection as we simulate your soul's crossing into spirit and leaving the physical body. This is conscious dying. You are always safe and protected.

You can and will be able to communicate with your Higher Self. It may be by telepathy. You can also hear sounds from the earth plane. You are protected and safe.

Look back at your physical body. Do not be concerned about it. It may be dead but you are not. You are spirit. You are soul. You are immortal. Be one with your Higher Self. Be one with your perfect energy. You are your Higher Self. Observe the death process. Remember, you are conscious. You have died consciously. You are protected by the white light. You are perfectly safe. Your Higher Self is with you.

Leave behind all earth-plane baggage. Leave behind all fears, pain, worries, and insecurities. Immerse yourself in the protective white light coming from your Higher Self. Be one with your Higher Self.

Listen to your Higher Self. It will guide you on a fantastic journey shortly. Be open to its instructions. Have no fear. You are protected. You are perfectly safe.

Do not cling to your old physical body. Do not cling to your Higher Self either. Be empowered. Be confident. You are an evolved soul and with your Higher Self.

You are now on your way to the soul plane. Feel yourself being drawn up to the soul plane. Feel the presence of your Higher Self advising you, protecting you.

Note the changes in colors and sounds as you move toward the soul plane. See how well you have adapted to this trip. See how you avoided the disorienting forces of the lower planes. See how easy it is to do this. Be one with your Higher Self.

As you enter the soul plane observe how peaceful and organized it is. It is warm, yet efficient in helping you choose your destiny. Note how your Higher Self is with you always.

See how the selection process is done. Note how your Higher Self assists you in this choice. See the presence of your Masters and Guides as you are presented with choices on this, the soul plane.

Do not be concerned if you must return to the earth plane. Do not be concerned if you must reincarnate. You will be reborn consciously as you have died consciously. You will have a better and more spiritual life.

If you must return to a physical body, this conscious rebirth will result in a spiritually evolved lifetime. It will be more fulfilling and more joyous than the life you just lived. Your Higher Self will assist you in this conscious rebirth. Be one with your Higher Self.

Play soft, soothing music for 15 minutes.

Now is the time to return to your body. Again, concentrate on your breath. Now note the other functions of your body. Slowly open up your eyes and do what you feel is important at this time.

~ Bruce Goldberg

Every man goes down to his death bearing in his hands only that which he has given away.

~ Persian Proverb

Chapter 8
Hope

Reflections on the Afterlife and the Interconnectedness of All

The soul of man
is like unto water:
from heaven it cometh,
to heaven it riseth,
and then again
to earth it returneth,
forever interchanging.

~ Johann Wolfgang von Goethe

WE HAVE come to believe, in our materialistic culture, that if you can't see it, it doesn't exist. However, the truth is that everything is energy; and nothing really goes away, especially a human spirit. When we die, we simply transform. This is why it gives me such pleasure to read the following passage to some of the dying people I work with. I know that hearing it helps them to recall that death is not something to fear, but rather something they can look forward to, especially when they have found a connection with the divine (God/Goddess/All That Is) while on earth.

Near-death experiences are experiences many individuals have had, during a time of actually being clinically "dead." People who have had NDEs almost universally have a powerful moment in time that transforms their lives. Afterward, they often no longer fear death and have a profound sense of their purpose in life, and a deeper wisdom to focus on the present moment. (For more information on these experiences, I highly recommend Dr. Melvin Morse's book, *Transformed by the Light* and Betty Eadie's *Embraced by the Light.*)

There is So Much More than Meets the Eye...

Working with hospice has taught me how much more there is to life than the physical – what we can see and touch and experience with the five senses. Truly, we are multi-dimensional beings capable of connecting with much more than many of us are currently aware of.

An experience comes to mind about a man I was privileged to meet on hospice several years ago. Michael was 50 and had been living with a heart defect since birth. Many times those around him thought he might be dying; this time, he knew he was dying. And being the spiritual person I found him to be, he was very eager to meet and discuss those beliefs. It was gratifying that his perspectives turned out to be similar to mine. He had lost his faith in the Lutheran church early in life due to some hypocritical adults, but fortunately, he had kept his spirituality intact and was very much his own person in his faith and beliefs.

While exchanging beliefs with Michael and his delightful wife, I discovered that they had visited with a woman who could receive information from their spirit guides. They each had had sessions with her that gave them great clarity and assistance. After Michael died, which was barely two weeks after I had met him, my birthday was coming up; so I decided to treat myself to a reading with the woman who received information from the spirit guides.

The session with her was quite an experience – definitely the first of its kind for me. First, Michael came through to thank me for the bereavement support I had been offering his wife. He then proceeded to share some wisdom concerning a delicate situation I was having with a colleague. It was all very helpful.

Next, to my great surprise, my mother began coming through. Her first words were something like, "Long time no talk!" Indeed, she had come to me through some wonderful dreams since her death eight or nine years ago, but we had never been able to communicate like this. The reader then asked me, "This is rather private, but did you ever have a miscarriage? I'm getting something about a miscarriage." I responded that I had not, but I remembered my mother had. She replied, "Let's go with that."

Well, the next thing that came through from Mom was, "I've met my son." I was truly amazed, and even rather taken aback, because I realized that the little one whom my mother miscarried years ago must have been a boy-to-be; in my family we had only three girls! Mom proceeded to explain that unborn children will "grow up" on the other side, in a manner parallel to the way we grow up on earth. She told me a little bit about how my brother looks now. Then she shared with me that he's one of my guides who helps me in the bereavement work that I do. Was I ever astounded to discover this shocking fact! To think that my own brother, unbeknownst to me, had been helping me do my work from the other side! In a sense, one could say that my

115

life and work from that day on have never been quite the same, knowing that I have such intimate support from the spirit side of our world. It brings tears to my eyes even as I write this. Now I am looking forward to meeting my brother one day "in spirit," at the time of my transition to the next realm. Truly, there is so much more than meets the eye in this mystery-filled world.

The End is the Beginning

The following story has come to my attention many times, through many people. It is a story with tremendous popularity because it reminds us that the end of this life is actually the beginning of something much better.

Keep Your Fork... the Best Is Yet to Come!

There was a woman who had been diagnosed with a terminal illness and had been given three months to live. As she was getting her things in order, she contacted her pastor and had him come to her house to discuss certain aspects of her final wishes. She told him which songs she wanted sung at the service, what scriptures she would like read, and what outfit she wanted to be buried in. The woman also requested to be buried with her favorite Bible.

Everything was in order and the pastor was preparing to leave when the woman remembered something very important to her. "There's one more thing," she said excitedly. "What's that?" came the pastor's reply. "This is very important," the woman continued. "I want to be buried with a fork in my right hand."

The pastor stood looking at the woman, not knowing quite what to say. "That surprises you, doesn't it?" the woman asked. "Well, to be honest, I'm puzzled by the request," said the pastor. The woman explained, "In all my years of attending church socials and potluck dinners, I always remember that when the dishes of the main course were being cleared, someone would inevitably lean over and say, 'Keep your fork.' It was my favorite part because I knew something better was coming…like velvety chocolate cake or deep-dish apple pie. Something wonderful and with substance! So, I just want people to see me there in that casket with a fork in my hand, and I want them to wonder 'What's with the fork?' Then I want you to tell them: 'Keep your fork…the best is yet to come.'"

The pastor's eyes welled up with tears of joy as he hugged the woman goodbye. He knew this would be one of the last times he would see her before her death. But he also knew that the woman had a better grasp of heaven than he did. She knew that something better was coming.

At the funeral people were walking by the woman's casket and they saw the pretty dress she was wearing, her favorite Bible, and the fork placed in her right hand. Over and over, the pastor heard the question "What's with the fork?" And over and over he smiled.

During his message, the pastor told the people of the conversation he had with the woman shortly before she died. He also told them about the fork and about what it symbolized to her. The pastor told the people how he could not stop thinking about the fork and told them that they probably would not be able to stop thinking about it either. He was right. So the next time you reach down for your fork, let it remind you ever so gently that the best is yet to come…and remember to keep your fork.

~ Author unknown

The Airport: An Image for the Time of Death

The wife of one of the people I worked with on hospice had a wonderful image. She said death was like an airport, where some are going to say their goodbyes – hugging and kissing their loved ones as they send them on their way. At the same time, there are those who are being greeted because they are arriving home, enjoying the hugs and joys of reuniting with those they love on the other side. This image of the airport made me think of the following well-known piece.

Parable of Immortality

I am standing upon the seashore. A ship at my side spreads her white sails to the morning breeze and starts for the blue ocean. She is an object of beauty and strength. I stand and watch her until at length she hangs like a speck of white cloud just where the sea and sky come to mingle with each other. Then someone at my side says: "There, she is gone!"

Gone where? Gone from my sight – that is all. She is just as large in mast and hull and spar as she was when she left my side and she is just as able to bear her load of living freight to the destined port. Her diminished size is in me, not in her. And just at the moment when someone at my side says: "There, she is gone!" there are other eyes watching her coming, and other voices ready to take up the glad shout: "Here she comes!"

And that is dying.

~ Henry Van Dyke

Nearing Death Awareness – A Universal Phenomenon

While growing up in Japan I used to hear the phrase *omukae ga kuru,* which means "your 'welcoming' (or "welcome wagon") comes." This referred to the spirit or spirits, typically those who are known and loved by the dying person, who come to the dying one, usually just a few days, hours, or moments before the person is ready to make the journey to the other side.

Doing the work of helping people "cross over," here in the United States, I learned that this "welcome" is not just a Japanese or Buddhist experience. Often, dying people are greeted and welcomed by those they love who have already made their transition to the other side. I have been told that this is known as the "nearing death awareness" phenomenon.

Once, on our hospice unit, we were caring for a man who had taken very good care of his mother at the end of her life. Now it was his turn to be making the passage across to the other side. Just a few days before making his transition, he began to experience his mother coming to him from the next realm to say "hello." Altogether he had three visitations from her before he died. He shared these incidents with the hospice team, and we were all grateful to know he was comforted and guided through his last adventure of life.

The following is a story around this "meeting others" theme that I found in a book by two hospice nurses. *Final Gifts* (Callanan and Kelley 1992) is a "must read" for all those who do hospice work. We also recommend it to many of our families.

Martha

Martha was in her early sixties, dying of uterine cancer which had spread throughout her pelvis. A widow, she'd lived for many years with her daughter and family.

Martha's experience with unseen people was not very dramatic, but her reaction was typical. She wasn't at all surprised or upset by it, and was even able to express her pleasure at seeing what no one else could see.

Several weeks before she died, Martha said to me, "Do you know who the little girl is?"

"Which little girl?" I asked.

"You know, the one who comes to see me," she said. "The one the others can't see."

Martha described several visitors unseen by others. She knew most of them – her parents and sisters, all of whom were dead – but couldn't identify a child who appeared with them. That didn't bother her.

"Don't worry," she told me, "I'll figure it out before I go, or I'll find out when I get there. Have you seen them?"

"No, I haven't," I said. "But I believe that you do. Are they here now?"

"They left a little while ago," Martha said. "They don't stay all the time; they just come and go."

"What is it like when they're here?" I asked.

"Well, sometimes we talk, but usually I just know that they're here," Martha said. "I know that they love me, and that they'll be here with me when it's time."

"When it's time...?"

"When I die," Martha said matter-of-factly.

~ Maggie Callanan and Patricia Kelley

Preparing for an Approaching Death

Many people on our hospice appreciate knowing about the physical signs that come as death nears. When a person moves into the final stages of the dying process, at least two dynamics are at work: one physical, and one spiritual and emotional. The physical piece is typically an orderly and gradual series of physical changes which are not medical emergencies and do not require medical interventions. These physical changes are normal. They are the natural way in which a body prepares itself for death. One of the best responses is to increase a person's comfort and to reassure them as much as possible.

Another dynamic of the dying process is taking place on the spiritual-emotional-mental plane and is a process of getting ready to release from all physical attachments. This process also has its own path, and may include whatever is unfinished of a practical nature. Here, it is best if you can engage with your family member in whatever way is helpful to take care of any unfinished business in the person's life. Usually it's best to let the dying person take the lead.

The experience of death can take place when the body completes its natural process of shutting down, and the spirit completes its natural process of reconciling and finding the inner peace needed to move on. These two processes need to happen in a way that is appropriate and unique to the values, lifestyle, and belief system of the dying one.

The following are some of the signs and characteristics you can watch for as your loved one moves closer to the moment of death. Most hospices have information like this that they share with their families routinely.

Signs of Approaching Death

Decreasing social interactions: Usually, as death nears, the dying person is less socially engaging. However, although talking may decrease, most dying people have a need for the continued calm presence of people who are important to them, and people who can simply sit with them quietly, holding their hands, singing or humming quietly to them, or simply being a loving, reassuring presence.

Changes in consciousness and unusual communication: During the last week and certainly the last days of life, the dying person often has one foot in this world and one foot in the next. Some people may mumble, have odd or jerky movements, or see things and people that others do not see. Whatever the reason for them, these behaviors are normal and natural during the dying process. People can sometimes become totally unresponsive in the days before death, but remember, they can still hear you, so be careful what you say and how you talk in their presence!

Confusion and/or disorientation: Confusion and sometimes disorientation can be caused by the biological changes that take place through the dying process. It is important that you are open and accept people as they are. Speak softly, clearly, and truthfully (though there is no need to try to make them see your "reality"). They may not be as confused or disoriented as they seem.

Restlessness: Repetitive motions like picking at the bed sheets may become apparent. A person can find it difficult to get comfortable, and they may exhibit signs of continual restlessness. At times such as these, it's best if you can respond and speak to the person in a quiet, natural way. You might lightly massage the forehead, hold a hand, read to the person, or play some soothing music that you know the person likes.

Decreasing intake of food and fluids: As death nears, a person will gradually lose his or her appetite and drink less, desiring little or no food and/or fluid. The body will naturally conserve energy this way. It is important not to force a person to eat or drink, even though it is so natural for us to want our loved ones to keep eating. This is likely to only make the person more uncomfortable, and might even cause unnecessary nausea and vomiting. Eventually, the swallow reflex weakens, and it becomes difficult for the person to swallow almost anything.

Circulation changes: Toward the very end of the dying process, you will notice that the person's circulation decreases, and the arms and legs become cool. The fingers and toenails may become purplish or blue. Usually, these are signs that death is near. It is not necessary to pile blankets on a person at this time.

Breathing pattern changes: The dying person's regular breathing pattern is likely to change. Sometimes the breaths can come very infrequently – a shallow breath with a period of no breath from five to thirty seconds, even up to a full minute (called "Cheyne-Stoking"). The person can also have periods of rapid, shallow, panting breaths. These patterns are common, and are indicative of decreasing circulation in the internal organs. It might bring comfort to elevate the person's head or to turn the person on his or her side. Again, you might hold a hand, and speak gently to them.

Physical pain: Pain is usually not part of death. Sometimes, however, there can be a sudden increase in pain. Should this occur, contact a nurse at once, and appropriate medicines can be administered. Almost all pain can be reduced to a tolerable level.

Other changes: Seizures, choking, or bleeding are rare but can occasionally occur at the end of a person's life. Again, whenever you have a question about something that's taking place with your loved one, call hospice and talk to a nurse who can advise you on how best to handle the situation. Also, make sure that you call the hospice line when you feel death has occurred, or if you are at all uncertain whether or not death has occurred.

Saying goodbye and/or giving permission

These are often the great gifts you have to give your loved one before death. A dying person will often keep holding on until he or she can be certain that those who are left behind will be all right. Therefore, whenever you feel that you need to give permission to "let go," or whenever you feel the person is ready to die and you are ready to let go, it's time to give permission and to say, "Goodbye."

You may want to lie in bed with the loved one, and then say everything you need to say. It may be as simple as sharing the words, "I love you." You may wish to retell some special memories you have shared with the person. It may include some words of appreciation, or some words of apology. Just tune into your intuition, say a prayer, perhaps, and let yourself be guided through this process. Any kind of closure you feel is best for you and for your loved one will help make the final release more smooth and possible. And do not be afraid to shed tears. Tears express your love and will help you let go more easily.

After death occurs

People and families desire to handle the time of death and events that follow in their own unique ways. The goal of hospice is to help you be as prepared as possible. Death is not an emergency. Nothing need be done immediately. It is a sacred time to be with someone. Your physical and emotional well-being is important. Some suggestions:

- Remember that the body can stay with you and your family as long as that is desired and needed. Bathing and dressing of the body can be done at this time, if you wish.

- It's good to call the hospice office to notify them of the death. A staff person can help you with phone calls to doctors, the medical examiner, and/or the funeral home, so don't hesitate to ask for their assistance. A nurse is usually available to provide telephone support. A home visit might even be possible, if you request and need it.

- It may be helpful to have a friend or family member(s) come to be with you. They may appreciate being invited and included in your "circle" at this time, too.

Signs of death can include:
- No breathing
- No heartbeat
- No response to communication
- Eyes fixed on a particular spot
- Eyelids slightly open
- Jaw relaxed and mouth slightly open.

The Sacredness of the Moment of Death

Many people have observed and written about the sacredness around the time of death. Death is not unlike the time a human being is born. Often I am not with the people I work with on hospice when they die, but I do usually hear about their time of death. It is a time that loved ones often choose to talk about later and is a moment filled with awe and unexplainable mystery.

When Niah Kinczewski finally died, she was in her sister's home, where her niece, Amanda, had taken part in her care. Amanda wrote the following poem as an expression of her witness to this mystery.

The Journey

It was an oddly natural thing –

her arms outstretched
as we changed the sheets
soiled
and stale with
the last remains of
her efforts to sully
this deathbed she hated,
with anything
indelibly
staining
that she could –

and one moment the
stench of reality filled me
with this reeking knowledge
of our physical frailty –
this loosely contorting
body of pain and –

I flew with her then,
over clouds
I convinced her were
her bed
that lifted away
all the agony of her fight

122

and replaced all with light
and motionless
we became clouds
that were actually molecules
of moisture collected
scintillating and hovering
in one giant formation
yet gliding
amidst the panoply
of sky
and ever much a part of
the gloaming
I promised
in that moment
we would be
if we
allowed ourselves
to be.
But it was all so naturally
not odd or even sad –

though emotions
and losses
all scurried to find their places
as the funeral home was called
and the soiled sheets were balled
up to be washed
clean –

I felt the very presence of her
being
one moment
in a recognizable place –
the next moment
unseen
possibly hovering above us
or drifting out to space –

I felt the empty stare
to be no longer her own
as the body –
where she had lain for days

appeared suddenly vacant
and strangely all one colour –
very white
and dull –

when what before was full
now seemed empty

naturally

it wasn't odd at all
but for my own curiosity
which turned me automatically
into some keen observer –
my eyes voraciously
grazing her body –
that just lay there
all still
and indifferent-like,

like
nothing I had ever seen,
like nothing I could have ever dreamed
to see
when just hours before
it was the two of us
on that journey

through the clouds
within the clouds
as the clouds –

but she
(naturally)
just never returned
to that body

and suddenly,
sitting beside her,
I was
alone.

~ Amanda Sasnett Roebuck

123

The following piece is by a friend who helped my daughter and me find a place to live on Whidbey Island. As we became better acquainted, she shared with me a profoundly mystical experience she had had at the time of her father's death. She agreed to write about her experience for this book.

A Blessing in Disguise: In Memory of My Father and Best Friend, Daniel Alspektor

It was February 1997 when Dad and I sat in the dark on his bed in the ICU. That was the night he was admitted with a 104 temperature. We were told that when this happened, he should be checked into Emergency, as this would be a sign his immune system was failing. You see, Dad was diagnosed about eight months prior with myelodysplasia. After he had a spinal tap, the doctors explained that this disease is the failure of his stem cells to produce mature red blood cells. The doctors weren't sure of the cause, so they kept giving him blood transfusions, and then expensive shots in the hope that his blood volume would increase. It did – for a while. Unfortunately, due to a heart bypass operation in the early seventies, before blood screening was as thorough as it is today, Dad had also contacted Hepatitis B after the surgery.

Now, Dad's blood volume had dropped again after rebounding for a few weeks, so his oncologist felt it would be better to start him on chemotherapy. He was in danger of developing acute leukemia, and now it would be a matter of days or weeks before we would have to say goodbye. Then, he decided he didn't want to go to the hospital, although we thought it best that he get checked. Sadly, we didn't know everything that he had been told by the doctors. He knew that it would be the beginning of the end for him, but he didn't have the heart to tell us. He agreed to go. While we waited for him to be admitted, he read the newspaper and made a few jokes. Then he confessed he was really scared.

Earlier, when Dad was admitted, I showed the admitting ER nurse all the medications he was on and actually gave them to her, including his nitroglycerin pills all neatly packed in his toiletry case. Later that night I discovered they had left the nitro off his medication list, which meant the nurse caring for him didn't have any. Mom and I slept in the waiting room and were awakened by the nurse telling me that my father was complaining of chest pains and wanted his nitro, but that she didn't have it and it wasn't on the med list. I told her he did have it and to call the doctor. She offered to give him some aspirin or something, and then said he calmed down and went back to sleep; we went back to the waiting room and eventually fell asleep on a row of chairs. Again we were awakened, but this time by the loudspeaker blaring, "Code Blue!! Code Blue!!" I ran down the hallway, my heart pounding, and saw my dad at a distance receiving CPR and having a defibrillator applied to him. Before I could reach him, I was physically stopped by a security guard telling me I couldn't go to him! I cried, "But if he is dying, I want to hold

望

his hand!" He wouldn't let me pass. A short while later, they were wheeling him into the elevator saying he was okay, it was a false alarm, but he was being taken to ICU.

When we arrived at his ICU room, the man who had been my father earlier that evening had changed. His head hung down and his eyes had lost that sparkle of life. What had happened!? The nurse's aide had mistakenly diagnosed Dad as having a heart attack, but actually he had had a panic attack because he couldn't get his nitro pill from the nurse. He told her that would have eased his chest pain. It was only later, after he died and after I gathered his belongings, that I found his nitro pills had been left in his toiletry case, next to his bedside the whole time.

As Dad and I sat in the dark on the side of his bed that first night in ICU, with his limp neck and head resting on my shoulder, I sunk into the most intense state of despair, helplessness, and loneliness I have ever known. But as the black night surrounded both of us and tears streamed down my face, a miracle happened that I will try my best to describe. A sensation of expansiveness, and then a blissful euphoria consumed my body. The sensation was beyond any I have ever known and I felt an infinite almost electric connection to the entire universe. Next, I somehow received the following message, "There is no such thing as heaven and hell. This is where we all go. Heaven and hell is on earth," came into my head. In this state, my sadness completely and suddenly lifted, and I knew without any doubt that Dad would be okay. In fact, I actually felt happy, full of grace and peace. During this experience, I didn't have a visual image, nor did I hear the words audibly, but I was definitely spoken to. I wasn't even asking this question, and though I am not a joiner of any religion, I am spiritual. That morning and for the next twenty-four hours, everything looked so ancient, very dense and heavy, but I felt as though I were floating, not even touching the ground as I walked through the halls of the hospital. Was Dad's spirit allowed to pass through me so I would know where he was going? I don't really know the answer to that. Afterwards, I stayed by his side while he fought to live for the next six days. He didn't say much to me directly anymore. Maybe he was trying to protect me by not letting me inside his thoughts.

During some of those last few days in the hospital, I was still in that state of grace, and I wanted to console my family and let them know everything would be all right. But their grief at the thought of losing my father was inconsolable. As we sat in the ICU waiting room, we got to know another family whose young father was in a coma due to an anesthesia mistake made during knee surgery. I encountered their teenage daughter on her way to check on her father, and I had an impulse to take her hand. I looked her in the eye and said, "Go to him and hold his hand. Something wonderful might happen."

The next day she found me and without either of us describing our experiences, she said "It happened to me, too," and she smiled. I was still in this unexplained euphoric state and tried to tell my brothers about what had transpired. The more I spoke about the experience, the more the sensation of being in a state of grace faded, until I was entirely planted on the ground and once again engaged in the physical world with all its weight and sadness. Yet, even though this occurred almost eight years ago, I cannot doubt what I experienced or forget about it, and it has certainly changed my attitude about death. I will always be grateful for the magnificent blessing I received that night, to have been given this glimpse of another dimension of our reality that is infinite and unites us all.

~ RoseAnn Alspektor

After-Death Communications

In the hospice bereavement follow-up work, I hear many mystical stories from the bereaved. One such story in particular stands out from the others. I was speaking with the wife of a man who had died on our hospice. She was telling me about how she and her family were doing. I asked her, as I often do, if she had had a sense of her husband's presence around her. She proceeded to relate the following story.

One of her children had a young son who was one-and-a-half years old. This grandson was in bed one morning with his parents, shortly after his grandfather had died. He had not yet been told of his grandfather's death. Suddenly, he raised one of his arms and said, "Bye-bye, Grampa! Bye-bye!" It would seem this little boy was somehow able to see his grandfather, who perhaps was waving his goodbye to him from the other side. This was also a way that Spirit was letting the rest of this little boy's family know that their father/husband was near them and was doing just fine.

It is amazing to me how connected to the spirit world children can be. And we must never underestimate or belittle this possibility. I encourage us to stay open to all possibilities, and to take seriously whatever our children bring to our attention. They often have powerful messages for us, for they can sometimes see and feel things that are more difficult for adults to experience.

Dreams are another way through which the spirit world connects with us. I often recommend that dreams be recorded in a notebook or journal so that deeper understanding and further clarity can be found by interacting with them. Over time and through writing about dreams, helpful insights and messages can emerge.

One widower hospice patient I worked with had a granddaughter who was having some interesting dreams. Shortly before the gentleman died, the granddaughter had a dream that her grandmother was getting ready for a wedding, on the other side. She was all decked out in her wedding gown, "waiting for the groom." It seems that this was the way she was letting her husband and family know that she was waiting for him to return to her, in heaven!

At a workshop I led, I met Josefina Monroy. During the workshop she shared this wonderful story about her mother's spirit coming to her in a dream shortly after her death. She then wrote about it and gave me permission to share her story.

I was blessed with a mother whose name should have been Star, for she brought light and hope to many. After she died from cancer in 1979, grief was like a black girdle around my heart and I could hardly sleep. On the fourth night after her funeral, however, I had a short dream in which my mother appeared, which I shall treasure forever.

I saw my mother sitting up on a hospital gurney, dressed in a freshly-laundered white dress with pretty flowers. She looked well, serene, and she smiled at me. I was filled with great joy and relief at seeing her and explained, "Ay, mama, I thought you were dead! ... It must have been a dream, then!" She looked at me intently and answered, "Si, mijita (yes, my little daughter), I am alive and you are in the dream."

I woke up then, and was flooded with a sweet-sad feeling, sweet because I knew my mother was safe and well, sad because I was back "in the dream" without her.

~ Josefina Monroy B.

Some books I would recommend if you would like to read more about after-death communications include: *Hello from Heaven*, by Bill and Judy Guggenheim; *After Death Communication: Final Farewells*, by Louis E. LaGrand; *Visitations from the Afterlife* (or *Love Letters from the Infinite*) by Lee Lawson; and *Talking to Heaven*, by James Van Praagh. These writers have shared some moving stories of their own, as well as collected many from others who tell of some fascinating experiences with the other side.

From all the reading I have done on this topic, it would seem that our pets also move on to the other side after they die. In the book *The Other Side of Death*, author Jan Price relates that the very first one to greet her from the other side was her pet dog Maggie, her "beloved springer." Maggie had died less than one month before Jan's experience, and she and her husband were still deeply grieving their dog's loss at the time. (page 38)

Know, therefore, that from the greater silence I shall return. ...
Forget not that I shall come back to you. ...
A little while, a moment of rest upon the wind, and another woman shall bear me.

~ Kahlil Gibran, The Prophet

127

The Interconnectedness of All Things

When we pay attention to and honor and love Mother Earth, it's amazing how she speaks to us. The "shaman" (an ancient word for "healer" or "medicine man/woman") has always known this. The shaman was the one who lived close to the earth, and learned to recognize the signs the earth revealed. If you are interested in learning more about shamanism, I invite you to read books such as *The Shaman: Voyages of the Soul Trance, Ecstasy, and Healing from Siberia to the Amazon,* by Piers Vitebsky, or *Shamanic Guide to Death and Dying,* by Kristin Madden. (See also "Shamanism" section in Chapter 11.)

In *Living Into Dying: A Journal of Spiritual and Practical Deathcare for Family and Community,* Nancy Poer writes about the powerful and poignant signs we can receive from nature, especially in the few days following a death.

Special Signs in Nature

Some of the most special experiences that can happen around a death are unusual events that occur in nature. These can often be noted especially when the one who has died is an individual who has attended to his or her spiritual growth development and has given love in life. The vitality of the dying can sometimes be sensed in a response from the natural world.

In the three days following death, the life forces of the one who dies expand and dissolve into universal life, while the soul and spirit expand into a new existence as well. This can be a powerful, vital movement of energy from the physical to the spiritual plane, and one can look for reflections in nature. Our awareness of nature phenomena can be enhanced during this time as our sensitivities can be heightened by being so close to the threshold through the loved one's death.

Birds have always been the traditional messengers of the spiritual world. Flying free in heavenly space and back to earth is a picture of their interweaving gesture between this world and the next. In the fairy tale, it is the white dove that leads Snow White through the dark wood. It is the white dove that brings the olive branch to Noah; that descends upon Jesus at the baptism as a sign of the indwelling Christ, accompanied by the voice of God.

It is heart warming to be able to tell people to look for nature signs when a loved one crosses. They are often given a gift. Birds can come uncommonly close or butterflies appear. In Grandma Mary Edna's case a rainbow touched down in the back yard. The northwestern Native Americans have rich lore regarding the appearance of birds at various nodal points in life. They speak of the owl as the bird who calls the spirit back from this world to the next. Often with great historical figures, birds appear at death. When Joan of Arc died, a flock of doves assembled over the burning stake immediately afterward. When Rudolf Steiner, a great humanitarian of the 20th century, made his transition, flocks of doves appeared at his funeral. In 1226, as St. Francis lay unclothed upon the ground, bidding his weeping friars to gird him with a hair shirt and spread ashes over him, he died singing in a gentle voice, "Free my soul from prison, so that I may praise Thy name," and at the instant of his death a flock of skylarks arose above him and flew into the sky.

~ Nancy Poer

The day after my mother died, I remember hearing that one of her good friends and counselors had had a mystical encounter with a deer who showed up in back of his home. He was quite certain that this was a "sign" from my mother's spirit. Many people have told me of beautiful signs they have received through nature, like an eagle flying overhead following their loved one's passing, near or on the day of their funerals and memorial services.

The following Native American prayer has shown up in a variety of forms. It is a rich reminder that we never really lose our loved ones; they simply transform, and now share their energy with us in a new and different way. While flipping through the March/April 1989 *Bereavement* magazine, I came across this "original untitled" version:

Do not stand at my grave and weep;
I am not there, I do not sleep.

I am a thousand winds that blow,
I am the softly falling snow.
I am the gentle showers of rain,
I am the fields of ripening grain.
I am in the morning hush,
I am in the graceful rush
Of beautiful birds in circling flight.
I am the starshine of the night.
I am in the flowers that bloom,
I am in a quiet room.
I am in the birds that sing,
I am in each lovely thing.

Do not stand at my grave and cry.
I am not there – I do not DIE.

Attributed to Mary E. Frye, 1932

129

The following is another poem written by Niah, the woman I had the privilege of meeting on our hospice in 1998. I have shared it with numerous bereaved persons and at memorial services, for I feel it conveys the JOY and freedom that spirits that have been released to the other side must feel. I believe Niah would be happy for you to share it with others as well. Please do not make any editorial changes if you do choose to share it.

Save Your Tears

Don't shed your tears for me, dear ones,
For I am joyously happy, my cares freed at last…
My past a distant memory.

Don't shed your tears for me, dear ones,
For I am safe, tucked serenely in your hearts…
Continue to think kindly of me.

Don't shed your tears for me, dear ones,
For I am soaring the galaxy with angels at my side…
Having a grand ole time.

Don't shed your tears for me, dear ones,
For I hear the sorrow in your voices,
I feel the sense of loss in your hearts;
Remember 'tis temporary, this empty feeling.
Don't shed your tears for me, dear ones,
Look for me high above upon a passing cloud,
Watch me shine through the beams of a colorful rainbow,
Know I will always love and be with you in these things.

God, in all His infinite wisdom holds me tight,
The Goddess, in all Her majesty, guides my Light.

Don't shed a single tear my way, dear ones,
For I AM claiming myself again.

God be with you each.
God guide you and give you peace.
And if you truly accept the best of yourself in this world,
There shall I also be…bound for Heaven's Glory!

God speed.

~ Niah Kinczewski

And one more poem from Niah:

Remember Me

Dear friend, remember me when times are rough…
There shall I willfully come, to comfort your distress.

Dear friend, remember me when all in your life is joy…
There shall I be in glee, cheering your heavenly triumphs.

Dear friend, remember me in the songs the whales sing…
There shall I also be, in the flight of many a fairy wing.

Dear friend, remember me in the dance of the butterfly in spring…
There shall I also be, cooperating with angels to speak to thee.

Dear friend, remember me ever so gently,
Look upon the morning star and make a wish.

For there shall I also be…
Come to Earth once more in everlasting Peace.

Remember me.

      Amen.
      God speed.

~ Niah Kinczewski

Here is an Easter story, told by Betty Luttio, the wife of the pastor of the Japanese Congregational Church (UCC) in Seattle, who gave me permission to share it.

An Easter Story

My mother was bedridden for three years before she died. As I watched her over those years, she seemed to drop to lower and lower levels. The last year she grew so weak that she couldn't talk or respond except with her eyes. I was thinking, "How can things get any worse?" On that day, my uncle came to visit and said to my mother, "Remember, Kay, the best is yet to come!"

My first reaction was, "Are you crazy?!" But then I realized, he was speaking of the resurrection. Now, she is in heaven, enjoying perfect health.

Connecting is at the Heart of Our Deep Longing

Rev. Rod Romney, an American Baptist minister who served the Seattle Baptist Church for many years, is a prophet who has the knack of being able to speak to the interconnectedness of all things. The following are some extracts from a piece where he speaks of this connection and how it can bring meaning, especially to our lives of suffering.

Connecting, joining our lives to eternity, always lies near the place of our emptiness where we are forced to penetrate the mystery that permeates our existence. We follow many visible and outward forms to establish this connectedness, which is at the heart of our deep soul longing.... We are all searchers, thrusting out our hands for the incomprehensible and the holy, trying to touch the hem of the robe of the Infinite.

Rod then refers to the book *The Lives of a Cell*, by Lewis Thomas, in which he advances the idea that the earth's life was derived from one single cell. If we are all descended from this one single cell, then we must all be held in some kind of amazing "web of life."

Connecting is one of our tasks, he continues. And yet it is not dependent on our strength alone. A Power, not our own, stands waiting for us at the pit of every peril, illuminating and transfiguring our adversity and promising an eventual triumph. This is what religion means by faith in God. God can be trusted. A table has been prepared in the presence of all our enemies.

And Rod concludes this section with the reminder that it is through connecting with one another that we are reminded about and given strength to continue the struggle for peace and justice for all peoples of the world. Without this commitment and perspective, our religion becomes disconnected, like too much religion in the world of today.

Synchronicities

The more we become aware of the "magic" of life, the more we realize how interconnected and even "synchronized" all of life is. It's as if, when we ask for help from the Spirit, She helps orchestrate our lives in such a way that we keep being blessed with interesting and meaning-filled adventures. I have come to see my life as I move through it as a jigsaw puzzle in which the various pieces are fitting together bit by bit, in a beautiful, colorful pattern. The more I experience life, the more of the puzzle I can see fitting together. The following is one small example of how this synchronicity happens for me.

While working on this book, I had the opportunity to return to the Big Island of Hawai'i with my daughter for a week's vacation. I discovered through a massage therapist on this trip that this island is also called "the Healing Island." We stayed in a condo complex on the northwestern part of the island. On our second evening there, as we were soaking in the hot tub, I struck up a conversation with an older woman named Millie. It turned out that she is a devout Christian who works with the dying, on a volunteer basis. She does this in Pennsylvania and Florida, where she and her husband Bud divide their time during the year. She spontaneously volunteered the following story about her mother, and later gave me permission to share the story here.

Her mother, Florrie Futcher, had been hospitalized due to a serious health problem. Florrie's three daughters came to visit her while she was in the hospital. Before they were about to leave, one of her daughters asked Florrie if she was afraid of dying. Florrie responded by sharing this poem right out of her "memory bank":

> I am not afraid of what can be.
> I am not afraid, why should I be,
> When He is here to care for me.
> A might a million worlds uphold
> Does not concern me anymore.
> He is my shepherd;
> He is my guide.
> I am completely satisfied.

Florrie was 101 years old at the time she recited this poem to her daughters, and she lived another year before she made her transition! Her Jewish doctor was deeply impressed, Millie recalled.

There have been many synchronicities while writing this book. Often, these events have inspired me to include material in this compilation. One such serendipitous occurrence happened at a local Barnes and Noble bookstore. While looking for information on some poetry, I found out that the young gentleman helping me at the information desk was a poet himself. When he heard about my writing this book, he introduced me to the following poem by our nation's then poet laureate (Collins 1991). I was inspired to see if I could receive permission to include it here. Permission was granted!

The Dead

The dead are always looking down on us, they say,
while we are putting on our shoes or making a sandwich,
they are looking down through the glass-bottom boats of heaven
as they row themselves slowly through eternity.

They watch the tops of our heads moving below on earth,
and when we lie down in a field or on a couch,
drugged perhaps by the hum of a warm afternoon,
they think we are looking back at them,

which makes them lift their oars and fall silent
and wait, like parents, for us to close our eyes.

~ Billy Collins

Marlene's Wisdom

I find that even when people have dementia and are quite confused, they can behave as if they are quite lucid. They also often do have very clear moments. Sometimes they let you know they understand exactly what's going on.

One delightful woman in her mid-nineties whom I was visiting was suffering from cancer and dementia. Marlene remained quite stable for months, after moving to the home of her son and daughter-in-law. However, one day, she began to have significantly more pain and confusion. We all sensed that this could be the beginning of the end for her. When I went to visit Marlene next, she was in bed, which was unusual for her; but she was her very pleasant, smiling self. She told me that her husband, who is no longer living, had been in and out to visit her. I wondered what exactly she meant by this, but I believed she was actually seeing him, and that he may well have been part of the "welcoming wagon" that was preparing her for her journey to the other side.

After some further conversation, we were both quiet for a couple of minutes. Suddenly, out of the blue, Marlene proclaimed: "It's a great life if you don't weaken; it's a great death if you don't stiffen." I wonder where she came up with this apropos wisdom? Even her family members wasn't sure where this came from.

Creating Your Own Farewell Piece

One family I worked with on hospice was not very religious, but they were deeply spiritual. They particularly loved the natural world – horses, plants, all things pertaining to the earth. The wife shared a piece she had put together for her husband's funeral that I thought was beautiful in its simplicity. She gave me permission to share it with you here.

With Love to Bud

You were born _____.
You left us for your "Trail Ride" _____.

We will miss you in this life, but life is a circle and we will see you again.
Until that time, we are comforted by knowing that you will be forever
watching over us.

The loving gifts you gave us as a father and friend have forever shaped
our lives and made us who we are.

Your strong sense of values, of fairness, of right and wrong, are all a part
of us.

Our outlook on life, our sense of humor, our interests and talents…
We can see you in all of them.
It makes us happy and proud to know that the qualities in you, that we
have loved and admired so much, are all a part of us.
Though you are gone, you will always be with us…
In our thoughts, in our hearts, in the very fabric of our lives.
Goodbye Bud, "Happy Trails"

~ Family & Friends.

It is the secret of the world that all things subsist and do not die,
But only retire a little from sight and afterwards return again.
Nothing is dead; men feign themselves dead, and endure mock
Funerals and mournful obituaries, and there they stand looking
Out of the window, sound and well, in some new strange disguise.

~ Ralph Waldo Emerson

Our confidence in God's hope-filled future reveals itself in tangible acts of faith carried
out in the concrete world of loving and dying. Hope changes our perspective so that
suffering is no longer an irreducible entity wrecking havoc in our lives. Rather…suffering
is subject to God's…future full of grace and beauty.

~ Jennifer E. Copland,
quote found in the worship bulletin for the
Japan Mission Connection on June 5, 2005

The divine Manifestations since the day of Adam have striven to unite humanity so that all may be accounted as one soul. The function and purpose of a shepherd is to gather and not disperse his flock. The prophets of God have been divine shepherds of humanity. They have established a bond of love and unity among mankind, made scattered peoples one nation and wandering tribes a mighty kingdom. They have laid the foundation of the oneness of God and summoned all to universal peace.

~ Baha'i Holy Writings

Chapter 9
Spiritual Path

Receiving Strength from Our Faith Traditions

Faith is the bird that feels the light
And sings when the dawn is still dark.

~ Rabindranath Tagore

Don't die wondering!

~ A bumper sticker

I have just three things to teach: Simplicity, patience, compassion. These three are your
greatest treasures. Simple in actions and in thoughts, you return to the source of being.

~ Lao Tzu

OUR SPIRIT is the most important aspect of us, the engine of our lives; and it is to the
Spirit that we return at the time of our death. The more we develop our spiritual,
inner relationship with God in our lives – and learn to detach from our material things
– the more comfortable we will be with death when it comes. To be in touch with our
spirituality, I believe, has a lot to do with being open, loving, and accepting of all that
comes to us in life. In the First Letter of John in the New Testament we read, "My dear
people, let us love one another, since love comes from God, and everyone who loves

is begotten by God and knows God." (I John 4:7) And later on in the same passage we read, "Love will come to its perfection in us when we can face the Day of Judgment without fear; because even in this world we have become as God is." (I John 4:17) Abiding and trusting in God, and loving and embracing the connection with all people and every experience in life, including our inevitable earthly death, helps us work out our issues and fears around dying.

A Tibetan lama has stated that the two most important things for a person who is preparing to die are these: 1: to feel the strong, abiding, peaceful love of family and friends, and 2: to practice meaningfully and regularly, one's chosen spiritual practice "in preparation for the extraordinary spiritual opportunity dawning at the moment of death." (Sogyal Rimpoche 1993)

Whenever possible, I make it a point to encourage the dying people I work with to consider what their spiritual practice has been, or what they are drawn to spiritually, and to develop and use it all the more at this time. Whether it's praying, meditating, reading scripture, chanting, listening to music, gazing at a picture of a saint or some spiritual person you feel especially close to – anything that brings you closer to Spirit will be helpful to practice regularly and often.

The Power of Dreams

I encourage honoring our dreams. Dreams, I have learned over the years, often carry with them messages for us from Spirit, so it is good to record them, especially when they impact us powerfully. Dreams are not always straightforward in their communication, so it is particularly important to record them and work with them. We are our own best interpreter of our dreams, although we can get hints and help through seeking out what the symbols and archetypes mean. I invite you to keep a dream journal and record every dream you have, especially while going through a major transition in your life. You will be amazed at the wisdom you find.

While moving through a particularly difficult period in my life I received a remarkable dream one night: I was in a small log cabin looking out over the landscape. Suddenly I was gripped with fear, as I saw four trees coming toward the cabin. The trees were leaning on each other in the shape of a teepee. They had been completely uprooted from the earth, but everything else was intact; the roots were hanging out at the bottom, and birds' nests were still in the tops of the trees. I was afraid that this group of trees was going to come right through my little cabin and destroy me along with it. However, miraculously, they gradually moved to the right side of the cabin, and I escaped injury.

A few weeks later I shared this dream with a spiritual guide who told me that those four trees represented the four parts of me. She said that one of the four trees was larger than the others. When she asked me which part, I started to say "the emotional part," but she corrected me by saying, "It was your spiritual body. Your spiritual body is your engine. It's always out there, knows where it's going and is doing just fine. Next comes your emotional body, then your physical body, and finally your mental body. And when you're going through a change, it's your mental body, the caboose, that goes crazy, because it's at the back and can't see where you're headed."

Dying in Remembrance of God

As the time of your or your loved one's death nears, it may be helpful to keep a picture of your beloved spiritual teacher or guide nearby. I sometimes recommend to people who are virtually bedridden that they might place a picture of Jesus, Mother Mary, Buddha, or their favorite spiritual guide on the wall by the end of their bed. This way, whenever their eyes are open, they will see and be reminded of their beloved one, to whom they may well be returning.

I had an interesting experience with a gentleman who was on our hospice over a lengthy period. I actually got to know Jerry's dear wife much better than I did Jerry, because she was very open and curious about spiritual matters. I sensed she wanted to learn and grow through her husband's experience. About a week before Jerry died, she told me he had asked her for a picture of Jesus to place at the foot of his bed. She had found a lovely, rather unusual, framed picture of Jesus that they had in their possession. She believed it gave Jerry much comfort to see Jesus at the end of his bed as he prepared to enter the spiritual realm.

Also, chanting and repeating the name of a spiritual leader or guide is said to be a powerful way to die. The person who is dying can do this, if he or she is conscious and desires to do so. Otherwise, in planning ahead, a loved one who is with the person as death nears might practice this on the loved one's behalf. Anya Foos-Graber, author of *Deathing: An Intelligent Alternative for the Final Moments of Life*, writes about this technique in Chapter 23 of *Experiencing the Soul*, an anthology collected by Eliot Rosen. She says that invoking the name of a spiritual being or master, one who is "one with God," is a meaningful way to approach death.

In response to the question, "Why is the moment of death so important for the progress of the soul?" Foos-Graber responds:

Many spiritual traditions teach that whatever one focuses on at this moment casts the "flavor" and atmosphere of what occurs after physical death. The way we die... has a profound corresponding effect for our state in the afterlife....

She goes on to share that just as first impressions are important when we meet someone for the first time, so are our last impressions. We can leave a good "mark" on the "cosmic memory banks of the Universal Mind" when we focus on God through a divine being who is powerfully connected to All That Is.

> Be greedy that the end may be noble.
> Be lustful to live like God.
> Be angry at your own weakness.
> Be attached to the Divine Path.
> Be proud of God's grace.

~ Yogi Bhajan, quoted in "Meditation as Medicine"
by Dharma Singh Khalsa

The Healing Power of Ritual

Ritual is critically important in dealing with death and grief. All religious traditions offer various rituals to help us cope with end-of-life moments. Whatever your tradition is, or whichever tradition you relate to, I recommend that you look into what these traditions are, tailor them to your needs, and find solace from them. For more information on the rituals of different religions, I invite you to take a look at a children's book called *Journey's End: Death and Mourning*, by Anita Ganeri. Ms. Ganeri takes a look at six different religious traditions in her book: Hinduism, Buddhism, Sikhism, Judaism, Christianity, and Islam. This would be a wonderful book to read to begin learning more about other traditions as well as using your own. There is also an excellent article in the *Journal of Hospice and Palliative Nursing* entitled, "Culture and the End of Life: A Review of Major World Religions" (vol. 4, no. 4, Oct. – Dec. 2002), to which you may refer.

When I think of ritual and the time of death, I am reminded of the way I have heard that Japanese people honor their dead. The close, intimate family members of the deceased gather together and bathe and dress the body before it is taken away to be cremated. My father was invited once to such a ceremony with a young pastor who had died quite prematurely of cancer. I recall him sharing about this and how meaningful it had been for him to be a part of this ritual.

At our hospice, the staff recommends to our families that they spend as much time with their loved one's body as they need. In one instance, while the family was waiting for the rest of the family to gather, a son continued to read to his mother from a book that she had asked him to read to her at the end of her life. (It happened to be a book that she thought her son would benefit from.) This ritual reminded me of the Tibetan Buddhist ritual, in which a person from the temple comes to read to the deceased soul from *The Tibetan Book of the Dead* for as many as 49 days, for they believe that the soul continues to hear for that long, even after death.

More and more hospitals are also recognizing the importance of ritual at the time of death. There is an article in *Spirituality & Health* (December 2004 issue) entitled, "A Hospital Where Last Rites Are Done Right." In this article, Susan Maas writes about a medical center in Minnesota where the staff is making a big effort to personalize the death experience. This seems to be having a positive effect on both the grieving families and the medical staff.

Prayer Giver – One of My Roles as Spiritual Counselor

I was visiting a woman on our hospice at an adult family home one day. One of the women living in the home asked me if I was "the prayer giver." I was pleasantly surprised by what I thought she'd said. After double-checking that I had heard her correctly, I responded that yes, indeed, I was the prayer giver.

Reflecting on what this stranger asked me left me pondering my role of spiritual counselor. Perhaps the most important thing I do with the people I visit is to remind them of their own spiritual power. I help them to connect or reconnect to Spirit. At the end of almost every visit, I ask the person or people I've been speaking with if they'd like to close with a prayer. The response is almost always positive. Once in a while, a person will tell me that they'd rather not pray with me, usually because they feel it's a very private matter. However, rarely have my hospice families turned me down when I offer to keep them in my prayers.

Prayer is our finest and most direct way to be in touch with the Divine. I highly recommend that you make this connection regularly. It is such a simple thing to do, too: Just open your heart and share your thoughts and feelings with the Divine, however you are comfortable doing so. Then, I encourage you to keep your heart open, and listen and pay attention to what the Divine might have to share with you.

If you would like an anonymous person to call and pray with you, I invite you to call Silent Unity at (816) 969-2000, or (800) NOW-PRAY (669-7729). They are connected to the Unity Church headquarters in Unity Village, Missouri, where they have a 24-hour hotline that anyone can call any time. After a gentle soul prays with you over the phone, Unity also keeps praying with you for the next 30 days. I have used them on occasion, when I needed someone to join me in prayer about something close to my heart. I have never been disappointed. If you are not comfortable calling them, please contact a local church, synagogue, mosque, temple, shrine, or religious organization that you do feel comfortable calling. It is good that you are connected to others when you pray, and your prayer will be more powerful, too.

Prayers for Letting Go

The following are some prayers from various traditions that could be used at the bedside of a person who is dying. When you use these prayers, you can paraphrase them to make them meaningful to the one with whom you are praying. You might also intersperse the verses with words like, "We let you go," or "Go to the light. We love you," and "Look for the light and follow it. The light and love of God [Great Spirit, Divine One, God/Goddess/All That Is, etc.] will set you free and guide you home!"

 Lakota Prayer

> O Great Spirit,
> Whose voice I hear in the winds,
> And whose breath gives life to all the world,
> Hear me! I am small and weak.
> I need your strength and wisdom.
>
> Let Me Walk In Beauty, and make my eyes
> ever behold the red and purple sunset.
>
> Make My Hands respect the things you have
> made and my ears sharp to hear your voice.
>
> Make Me Wise so that I may understand
> the things you have taught my people.
>
> Let Me Learn the lessons you have hidden
> in every leaf and rock.
>
> I Seek Strength, not to be greater than my brother,
> but to fight my greatest enemy – myself.
>
> Make Me Always Ready to come to you
> with clean hands and straight eyes.
>
> So When Life Fades, as the fading sunset,
> my spirit may come to you without shame.

~ found in "Footsteps of Wisdom,"
a booklet from the Red Cloud Indian School, Pine Ridge, South Dakota

Prayer from the Rig Veda (Hindu)

God makes the rivers to flow.
They tire not, nor do they cease from flowing.
May the river of my life flow into the sea of love that is the Lord.
May I overcome all the impediments in my course.
May the thread of my song be not cut before my life merges in the sea of love.

May I be filled with Loving Kindness
May I be Safe from Inner and Outer Harm
May I be Well
May I be Peaceful and At Ease
May I be Happy

~ Tibetan Prayer (Buddhist)

Connecting Prayers with People and Circumstances

I will probably never read the Desiderata again without thinking of the lovely woman I met on hospice. Glenda was a courageous, "salt of the earth" kind of woman who had many children and grandchildren surrounding her with love. We shared the Desiderata at Glenda's funeral, because this was one of her favorite pieces of writing.

About a year after Glenda died, I heard from her husband who shared with me that he had met a woman he had fallen in love with and now was ready to marry. "Would you perform the wedding?" he asked. It was a joyful affair, needless to say, and I was delighted to be able to perform this wedding for a beautiful new couple! Yes, life and love do go on, even after tremendous sorrow and grief.

Desiderata

Go placidly amid the noise and haste, and remember what peace there may be in silence. As far as possible without surrender be on good terms with all persons. Speak your truth quietly and clearly; and listen to others, even the dull and ignorant; they too have their story. Avoid loud and aggressive persons, they are vexatious to the spirit. If you compare yourself with others, you may become vain and bitter; for always there will be greater and lesser persons than yourself. Enjoy your achievements as well as your plans.

Keep interested in your own career, however humble; it is a real possession in the changing fortunes of time. Exercise caution in your business affairs; for the world is full of trickery. But let this not blind you to what virtue there is; many persons strive for high ideals; and everywhere life is full of heroism. Be yourself. Especially, do not feign affection. Neither be cynical about love; for in the face of all aridity and disenchantment it is perennial as the grass. Take kindly the counsel of the years, gracefully surrendering the things of youth. Nurture strength of spirit to shield you in sudden misfortune. But do not distress yourself with imaginings. Many fears are born of fatigue and loneliness. Beyond a wholesome discipline, be gentle with yourself. You are a child of the universe, no less than the trees and the stars; you have a right to be here. And whether or not it is clear to you, no doubt the universe is unfolding as it should. Therefore be at peace with God, whatever you conceive Him to be, and whatever your labors and aspirations, in the noisy confusion of life keep peace with your soul. With all its sham, drudgery and broken dreams, it is still a beautiful world. Be careful. Strive to be happy.

~ Found in Old St. Paul's Church, Baltimore, dated 1692

Here is an ancient Egyptian proverb that reveals the Egyptian belief in reincarnation and the afterlife:

Death is but a doorway to a new life.
We live today, we shall live again, in many forms we shall return to this earth.

The following prayer came to my attention through a colleague who also does spiritual counseling. She shared it with us just after 9/11/01, when many of us in the United States were struggling to live our lives centered in love, not fear. I believe it's a beautiful prayer that helps us cope with just about any kind of grief.

A Prayer for Courage and Patience

May our eyes remain open even in the face of tragedy.
May we not become disheartened.
May we find in the dissolution of our apathy and denial,
    the cup of the broken heart.
May we discover the gift of the fire burning
    in the inner chamber of our being –
    burning great and bright enough to transform any poison.
May we offer the power of our sorrow to the service
    of something greater than ourselves.
May our guilt not rise up to form yet another defensive wall.
May the suffering purify and not paralyze us.
May we endure; may sorrow bond us and not separate us.
May we realize the greatness of our sorrow
    and not run from its touch or its flame.
May clarity be our ally and wisdom our support.
May our wrath be cleansing, cutting through
    the confusion of denial and greed.

> May we not be afraid to see or speak our truth.
> May the bleakness of the wasteland be dispelled.
> May the soul's journey be revealed and the true hunger fed.
> May we be forgiven for what we have forgotten
>   and blessed with the remembrance of who we really are.

~ The Terma Collective

A Prayer or Litany for Blessing of Hands

Look at your hands. Notice their power and gentleness. Let us bless these hands together.
I invite you to say each phrase after me.

> Blessed be the works of your hands, O Holy One. (Echo)
> Blessed be these hands that have touched life. (Echo)
> Blessed be these hands that have nurtured creativity. (Echo)
> Blessed be these hands that have held pain. (Echo)
> Blessed be these hands that have embraced with passion. (Echo)
> Blessed be these hands that have tended gardens. (Echo)
> Blessed be these hands that have closed in anger. (Echo)
> Blessed be these hands that have planted new seeds. (Echo)
> Blessed be these hands that have harvested ripe fields. (Echo)
> Blessed be these hands that have cleaned, washed, mopped, scrubbed. (Echo)
> Blessed be these hands that have become knotty with age. (Echo)
> Blessed be these hands that are wrinkled and scarred from doing justice. (Echo)
> Blessed be these hands that have reached out and been received. (Echo)
> Blessed be these hands that hold the promise of the future. (Echo)
>   (Invite people to add others)
> Blessed be the works of your hands, O Holy One. (Echo)

~ by Diann L. Neu, Co-director of WATER,
The Women's Alliance for Theology, Ethics and Ritual

Prayers as Affirmations of What Already Is

In the book *The Healing Path of Prayer,* by Ron Roth, a spiritual healer who works with medical intuitive Caroline Myss, Ron put together a new translation of the beloved prayer that Jesus gave to his disciples. Sometimes I find that a well-known prayer like this can be heard with new ears when we hear it in new form. This particular version is a direct translation from the Aramaic into English. Ron points out that what is helpful about this version is that the phrases are heard as affirmations – things that are already occurring – not petitions, or requests of God. In other words, it is helpful to affirm that

145

God is already taking care of us as God's offspring; we do not need to ask for the assistance, but simply affirm that it is already with us, which allows the abundance, peace, supply, and joy to happen in our lives! Here is a part of that prayer:

The Lord's Prayer

Our Father, who is everywhere in the universe,
Your name is sacred.
Your kingdom is come among us,
Your will is throughout the earth as it is throughout the universe.

~ translated by Ron Roth

Here's another version of The Lord's Prayer that I found in a friend's newsletter. It offers the same spirit of affirming what already is, and resounds with even more universal flavor.

Father/Mother God who art everywhere,
we honor Thy name in our hearts.
Our will be done, our Kingdom come, on earth as it is in all Creation.
We receive this day the Love and the Energy that is ours by Divine Right.
We know that we are always One with Thee and with each other.
We fear nothing. We embrace and forgive all parts of ourselves and all beings.
We are the Kingdom, we are the Power, and we are the Glory that always has
    been and always shall be.
And so it is, in the name of the Universal Christ Consciousness.
Love We Are! Amen.

More Healing Prayers

I have been requested to use the St. Francis prayer at memorials, and I felt it important to include here. It is a powerful and simple prayer.

The Prayer of St. Francis of Assisi

Lord, make me an instrument of your peace.
Where there is hatred, let me sow love.
Where there is injury, pardon.
Where there is doubt, faith.
Where there is despair, hope.
Where there is darkness, light.
Where there is sadness, joy.

146

O Divine Master, grant that I may not so much seek
To be consoled, as to console,
To be understood, as to understand,
To be loved, as to love,
For it is in giving that we receive,
It is in pardoning that we are pardoned,
It is in dying that we are born to eternal life.

The following is a prayer for healing and wholeness that a Jewish colleague of mine shared with me when I asked for a prayer from her tradition.

Mi Sheberach: A Traditional Jewish Prayer for Healing of Body and Spirit

O God, who blessed our ancestors, Abraham, Isaac, and Jacob; Sarah, Rebekah, Rachel and Leah, send Your blessing to _____.

Have mercy on him/her, and graciously restore his/her health and strength. Grant him/her a *refu-a sheleima*, a complete recovery, a healing of spirit, along with all others who are stricken. May healing come speedily, and let us say: Amen.

Here is a prayer for healing that reminds us that healing not only takes place on the physical level, but it happens in many different ways and on various levels, as we become open to these possibilities through our suffering.

Healing Prayer

There are moments when wellness escapes us,
        moments when pain and suffering are not dim possibilities
        but all too agonizing realities.
At such moments we must open ourselves for healing.

Much we can do for ourselves;
        and what we can do we must do –
        healing, no less than illness, is participatory.
But even when we do all we can do, there is, often,
        still much left to be done.
And so we turn to our healers
        seeking their skill to aid in our struggle for wellness.

But even when they do all they can do, there is, often,
        still much left to be done.

And so we turn to Life, to the vast Power of Being that
    animates the
universe as the ocean animates the wave,
    seeking to let go of that which blocks our healing.

May those whose lives are gripped in the palm of suffering
    open even now, to the Wonder of Life.
May they let go of the hurt and Meet the True Self beyond pain,
    the Uncarved Block that is our joyous Unity with Holiness.

May they discover through pain and torment
    the strength to live with grace and humor.
May they discover through doubt and anguish
    the strength to live with dignity and holiness.
May they discover through suffering and fear
    the strength to move toward healing.

~ Rabbi Rami M. Shapiro

Hymns Revisited as Prayers

I found the following verses to the hymn "Amazing Grace" in a little booklet of healing prayers that I happened upon in a grocery store, of all places. The middle two verses are ones that we do not hear often, yet they are good reminders when death nears.

Amazing Grace

Amazing grace, how sweet the sound,
That saved a wretch like me.
[I like a newer version: "That opens life to me."]
I once was lost, but now am found,
Was blind but now I see.
Yea, when this flesh and heart shall fail,
And mortal life shall cease,
I shall possess, within the veil,
A life of joy and peace.

The world shall soon dissolve like snow,
The sun refuse to shine;
But God, who called me here below,
Shall be forever mine.

When we've been there ten thousand years,
Bright shining as the sun,
We've no less days to sing God's praise,
Than when we'd first begun.

I discovered the following verse in one version of "Children of the Heavenly Father," a Swedish folk melody that was sung at my great aunt's memorial service:

Neither life nor death shall ever
From the Lord His children sever;
Unto them His grace He showeth,
And their sorrows all He knoweth.

~ Lina Sandell, translated by Ernst W. Olson

And here's another lovely hymn/prayer I found, while going through the hymnal and singing for one of our beautiful hospice women who loved music: the fourth verse and chorus of "He Leadeth Me."

And when my task on earth is done,
When by thy grace the victory's won,
E'en death's cold wave I will not flee,
Since God through Jordan leadeth me.
He leadeth me, he leadeth me;
By his own hand he leadeth me:
His faithful follower I would be,
For by his hand he leadeth me.

~ Joseph Henry Gilmore

There are No Limitations Spiritually Speaking

There is a world peace and prayer organization called the Byakko Shinko Kai. The group has a sanctuary in the foothills of Mount Fuji in Japan. Mr. Masahisa Goi founded this organization in 1955, and his stepdaughter Masami Saionji carries on the work at this time, along with her husband and three grown daughters. This group, along with many others, is quietly growing and influencing world peace upon the earth. One of their mottos is "I am a divine being. You are a divine being. Humanity is divine." The following words, which I had just read and learned about, helped me tremendously on 9/11/01, as I struggled to cope with this challenging earthly situation.

Words of Infinite Light

Have you been looking for a way to brighten your mind and change your way of thinking? Here is a suggestion. When a dark thought crosses your mind, counter it with a bright one like infinite light! When a pessimistic feeling surrounds you, pierce though it with a phrase like infinite improvement! If you do this all the time, day in and day out, your life will change before you know it.

You can try the words below, or create new ones of your own.

May Peace Prevail
on Earth

May Peace Prevail
on Earth

May Peace Prevail
on Earth

Infinite Love
Infinite Harmony
Infinite Peace
Infinite Light
Infinite Power
Infinite Wisdom
Infinite Life

Infinite Happiness
Infinite Radiance
Infinite Talent
Infinite Energy
Infinite Potential
Infinite Ability
Infinite Success

Infinite Health
Infinite Vitality
Infinite Creativity
Infinite Originality
Infinite Development
Infinite Growth
Infinite Gratitude

Infinite Joy
Infinite Beauty
Infinite Youth
Infinite Good
Infinite Sincerity
Infinite Purity
Infinite Brightness

Infinite Dignity
Infinite Courage
Infinite Progress
Infinite Betterment
Infinite Strength
Infinite Intuition
Infinite Innocence

Infinite Hope
Infinite Inspiration
Infinite Clarity
Infinite Tranquility
Infinite Freedom
Infinite Grace
Infinite Stillness

Infinite Gentleness
Infinite Abundance
Infinite Generosity
Infinite Integrity
Infinite Sincerity
Infinite Bliss
Infinite Oneness ...

~ Masami Saionji

The Way of Love

If, indeed, we are here on this earth to "grow our souls" and grow in love, then perhaps there is a reason that the following passage on love is so popular. It is often used at weddings, but I find it well suited for a memorial service, as well. Again, I share this scripture from *The Message* version of the New Testament.

I Corinthians 13

If I speak with human eloquence and angelic ecstasy but don't love, I'm nothing but the creaking of a rusty gate.

If I speak God's Word with power, revealing all God's mysteries and making everything plain as day, and if I have faith that says to a mountain, "Jump," and it jumps, but I don't love, I'm nothing.

If I give everything I own to the poor and even go to the stake to be burned as a martyr, but I don't love, I've gotten nowhere. So, no matter what I say, what I believe, and what I do, I'm bankrupt without love.

> Love never gives up.
> Love cares more for others than for self.
> Love doesn't want what it doesn't have.
> Love doesn't strut,
> Doesn't have a swelled head,
> Doesn't force itself on others,
> Isn't always "me first,"
> Doesn't fly off the handle,
> Doesn't keep score of the sins of others,
> Doesn't revel when others grovel,
> Takes pleasure in the flowering of truth,
> Puts up with anything, Trusts God always,
> Always looks for the best,
> Never looks back,
> But keeps going to the end.

Love never dies. Inspired speech will be over some day; praying in tongues will end; understanding will reach its limit. We know only a portion of the truth, and what we say about God is always incomplete. But when the Complete arrives, our incompletes will be canceled.

When I was an infant at my mother's breast, I gurgled and cooed like any infant. When I grew up, I left those infant ways for good.

We don't yet see things clearly. We're squinting in a fog, peering through a mist. But it won't be long before the weather clears and the sun shines bright! We'll see it all then, see it all as clearly as God sees us, knowing [God] directly just as [God] knows us!

But for right now, until that completeness, we have three things to do to lead us toward that consummation: Trust steadily in God, hope unswervingly, love extravagantly. And the best of the three is love.

Peace Pilgrim is a hero of mine. She began "walking for peace" in 1953, trekking more than 25,000 miles across this country, spreading her message for peace: "Overcome evil with good, falsehood with truth, and hatred with love." She carried in her tunic pockets her only possessions. And she vowed that she would "remain a wanderer until mankind has learned the way of peace, walking until given shelter and fasting until given food." The following are her words as recorded in the booklet, "Steps Toward Inner Peace," published by Friends of Peace Pilgrim.

"Beatitudes" of the Peace Pilgrim

Blessed are they who give without expecting even thanks in return, for they shall be abundantly rewarded.

Blessed are they who translate every good thing they know into action – ever higher truths shall be revealed to them.

Blessed are they who do God's will without asking to see results, for great shall be their recompense.

Blessed are they who love and trust their fellow human beings, for they shall reach the good in people and receive a loving response.

Blessed are they who have seen reality, for they know that not the garment of clay but that which activates the garment of clay is real and indestructible.

Blessed are they who see the change we call death as a liberation from the limitations of their earth-life, for they shall rejoice with their loved ones who make the glorious transition.

Blessed are they who after dedicating their lives and thereby receiving a blessing have the courage and faith to surmount the difficulties of the path ahead, for they shall receive a second blessing.

Blessed are they who advance toward the spiritual path without the selfish motive of seeking inner peace, for they shall find it.

Blessed are those who instead of trying to batter down the gates of the kingdom of heaven approach them humbly and lovingly and purified, for they shall pass right through.

...Do you know what it is to know God – to have God's constant guidance – a constant awareness of God's presence? To know God is to reflect love toward all people and all creations. To know God is to feel peace within – a calmness, a serenity, an unshakeableness which enables you to face any situation. To know God is to be so filled with joy that it bubbles over and goes forth to bless the world.... And knowing God is not reserved for the great ones. It is for little folks like you and me. God is always seeking you – every one of you. You can find God if you will only seek – by obeying divine laws, by loving people, by relinquishing self-will, attachments, negative thoughts and feelings. And when you find God it will be in the stillness. You will find God within.

~ Peace Pilgrim

Being Still and Knowing that God is God (All That Is)

Here's an interesting practice you might try. Use the phrase, "Be still, and know that I am God," from Psalm 46:10. As you repeat this verse, shorten it as you go and make it your mantra for today, or for this period in your life:

> Be still, and know that I am God.
> Be still, and know that I am.
> Be still, and know.
> Be still.
> Be.

BE-ing is perhaps the most important focus we can have as we prepare to die.

Blessings and Prayers for Those Departing

Here's a beautiful blessing from the Irish tradition that speaks not only of blessing the living but also of our last farewell on earth.

The Blessing of Light

May the blessing of light be on you, light without and light within. May the blessed sunshine shine on you and warm your heart till it glows like a great peat fire, so that the stranger may come and warm himself at it, and also a friend.

And may the light shine out of the two eyes of you, like a candle set in the two windows of a house, bidding the wanderer come in out of the storm, and may the blessings of the rain be on you – the soft, sweet rain. May it fall upon your spirit so that all the little flowers may spring up and shed their sweetness on the air. And may the blessings of the Great Rains be on you, may they beat upon your spirit and wash it fair and clean, and leave there many a shining pool where the blue of heaven shines, and sometimes a star.

And may the blessing of the Earth be on you – the great round earth, may you ever have a kindly greeting for those you pass as you're going along the roads. May the earth be soft under you when you rest upon it, tired at the end of a day, and may it rest easy over you when at the last you lay out under it, may it rest so lightly over you that your soul may be off from under it quickly and up and off, and on its way to God. And now may God bless you all and bless you kindly.

There are so many powerful pieces of scripture that can teach us about death. This one comes from the Pali Canon, the earliest collection of authoritative Buddhist texts:

Scripture for the Dying

This eye is not me; I am not caught by these eyes.
I am light without boundaries;
I have never been born;
I will never die.
Look at the stars, the moon, the sun, the blue sky, the oceans.
Everything is a manifestation of our collective consciousness.
Since time immemorial I have been free. Birth and death are only doors through
    which I come in and come out.
Birth and death are only a hide and seek game.
So take my hand, smile to me, say goodbye, so that we'll meet again. We have
    already met at the base, and we'll meet each other in all walks of life.

And after the eye or the nose, the tongue, the body, the mind…

Here's a healing prayer from the Hindu tradition that shares God's perspective with us.

A Hindu Prayer

Give me your whole heart.
Love and adore me,
Worship me always,
Bow to me only,
And you shall surely come to me.
This is my promise
For you are dear to me.

Lay down all your duties
In me, your refuge.
Fear no longer,

For I will save you
From sin and bondage.

~ Bhagavad Gita, Ch. 18, verses 63–66

This next Indian verse, found on the Internet, reminds us to be in the present moment as often as possible.

A Sanskrit Proverb

Look to this day for it is life,
The very life of life,
In its brief course lie all
The realities and verities of existence,
The bliss of growth,
The splendor of action,
The glory of power –

For yesterday is but a dream
And tomorrow is only a vision.
But today, well lived,
Makes every yesterday a dream of happiness
And every tomorrow a vision of hope.

Look well, therefore, to this day.

Mother Earth has so much to teach us about life and living in the midst of suffering and limitation. Here's a Native American prayer that reminds us to tune into different aspects of nature for support as we live out our days on earth.

Ute Prayer

Earth teach me stillness
    as the grasses are stilled with light.
Earth teach me suffering
    as old stones suffer with memory.
Earth teach me humility
    as blossoms are humble with beginning.
Earth teach me caring
    as the mother who secures her young.
Earth teach me courage
    as the tree which stands all alone.

Earth teach me limitation
    as the ant which crawls on the ground.
Earth teach me freedom
    as the eagle which soars in the sky.
Earth teach me resignation
    as the leaves which die in the fall.
Earth teach me regeneration
    as the seed which rises in the spring.
Earth teach me to forget myself
    as melted snow forgets its life.
Earth teach me to remember kindness
    as dry fields weep with rain.

                          ~ Earth Prayers

The following is a prayer of remembrance for one who has departed, that I found in a Jewish prayer book belonging to one of my clients. This prayer book had specific, moving prayers for mothers and fathers who have departed, too.

Memorial Prayer for the Departed

O merciful God, who dwellest on high and yet art full of compassion, keep in Thy divine Presence among the holy and pure, whose light shineth as the brightness of the firmament, the souls of our dear and beloved who have gone to their eternal home with Thee. O may their souls be bound up in the bond of life, so that their memories stir us to serve Thee and our fellowmen in truth, kindness and peace. Amen.

                         ~ High Holiday Prayer Book

The following prayers are from the Baha'i faith. They can be very useful and comforting at the time of death.

O, SON OF THE SUPREME! I have made death a messenger of joy to thee. Wherefore dost thou grieve? I made the light to shed on thee its splendor. Why dost thou veil thyself therefrom?

                    ~ Baha'u'llah in *Arabic Hidden Words*

O My servants! Sorrow not if, in these days and on this earthly plane, things contrary to your wishes have been ordained and manifested by God, for days of blissful joy, of heavenly delight, are assuredly in store for you. Worlds, holy and spiritually glorious, will be unveiled to your eyes. You are destined by Him, in this world and hereafter, to partake of their benefits, to share in their joys, and to obtain a portion of their sustaining grace. To each and every one of them you will, no doubt, attain.

~ Baha'u'llah in *Gleanings*

Be not sorrowful on account of separation; verily, thy Lord is of more good to thee than anything in the material world. He is the best companion and the best friend and will accompany thee under all aspects.

~ Contentment: Jewels from the Words of Abdu'l-baha

This is a Baha'i prayer specifically for one who has departed.

O my God! O Thou forgiver of sins, bestower of gifts, dispeller of afflictions!

Verily, I beseech Thee to forgive the sins of such as have abandoned the physical garment and have ascended to the spiritual world.

O my Lord! Purify them from trespasses, dispel their sorrows, and change their darkness into light. Cause them to enter the garden of happiness, cleanse them with the most pure water, and grant them to behold Thy splendors on the loftiest mount.

~ Abdu'l-baha in Baha'i Prayers (US edition)

The following is a beautiful Jewish prayer that we use at the yearly memorial services held for those who have died on our hospice during the previous year.

We Remember Them

In the rising of the sun and in its going down,
We remember them;
In the blowing of the wind and the chill of winter,
We remember them;
In the opening of the buds and in the warmth of summer,
We remember them;
In the rustling of the leaves and the beauty of autumn,
We remember them;

In the beginning of the year and when it ends,
We remember them;
When we are weary and in the need of strength,
We remember them;
When we are lost and sick at heart,
We remember them;
When we have joys we yearn to share,
We remember them;
So long as we live, they too shall live,
For they are now a part of us as
We remember them.

~ Gates of Prayer (Reform Judaism Prayer Book)

Death is but another form of the mercy of God.
It is the last and the greatest of [God's] gifts.
Have you not seen this? Death is not to be feared:
It is to be welcomed, when it comes, for it is the messenger of God.

~ Father Damien, in Molokai

Chapter 10
Grace

The Transforming Power of Grief

Give sorrow words; the grief that does not speak
Whispers the oe'r fraught heart and bids it break.

~ William Shakespeare

To weep is to make less the depth of grief.

~ William Shakespeare

The Mystery of Grief

GRIEF, ALONG with death, is a mysterious reality in all of our lives. We never know when we will have to lose someone or something that is very dear to us. Then, when that loss happens, we never know when or how the grief will affect us. Sometimes, the grief can even make us feel like we might be going crazy in our lives. The scars of loss can be very deep and penetrating; life is never quite the same after a beloved friend and companion dies. John Eldredge, author of *The Journey of Desire*, describes the heart pain and shock of losing the truest friend he had ever known by sharing his embarrassment upon finding himself turning whenever he sees the same silver gray Jeep that his friend Brent used to drive. He knows that Brent is no longer living, but he can't help himself double-checking when he happens to see this kind of Jeep, because his heart at some level cannot accept that Brent is truly "gone." "Or rather," he writes, "my yearning for things to be right is so strong that it overrides my logic and turns my head, in hope against hope, every time."

When our grief does surface, I am learning how important it is that we don't bury it; we need to find ways to express it and work through these sometimes devastating feelings of loss. For a fuller understanding of the grief cycle, you may want to read some of Dr. Elisabeth Kübler-Ross's work, especially her best-known work, *On Death and Dying*, which introduces the five basic stages of grief: Denial and Isolation, Anger, Bargaining, Depression, Acceptance (and Hope).

Any kind of loss has a way of bringing up previous losses, especially those that have not been completely worked through. This has been described to me as current losses "kicking up the dust of old griefs."

The following piece came to me through a co-worker; it describes the pain and joy of grief in a most poignant way.

Random Thoughts

> There's a grief that can't be spoken
> There's a pain goes on and on
> Empty chairs at empty tables
> Now my friends have come and gone
> ~ Les Miserables

Do you know what you have taught me? Do you know what I have learned? Do you know how you have changed me? Do you know how I go on?

There are incredible voids in life. There comes an overwhelming sadness. There are the tremendous gifts of love and of sharing; there are the deepest pains of loss and suffering.

I have learned that I see more with an open heart than with open eyes, and it is when I feel like I have hit the bottom, that I find the roots and foundations that hold me together. When it looks like I have gone nowhere, I find myself in unknown territory. When I am too tired to go further, somehow I am guided to a new beginning, and the distance between the flames of a bonfire and the stars that dance among the pine trees is nothing.

The God I thought I knew is not the one whom I have come to know. More can be accomplished in remaining still than in all the movement I might try. A moment can seem an eternity, and a lifetime is never long enough.

Love does more than endure, love becomes the strength that keeps me alive. I can love beyond the physical and feel comforted by love that is no longer spoken. I hear clearly words that are unspoken and are guided by wisdom from beyond. When I think I am ready, I find that I have more to learn.

Tears will never stop, and memories are never forgotten; laughter can happen; peace can reign. Darkness provides illumination, and light can be blinding. Passion never leaves us, it merely changes form.

Friends can mean well and hurt deeply, and strangers understand what they don't know. When I open my arms for a hug, and no one steps in, then I must remember how to love myself, and I am capable of doing so.

I cannot take away another's pain, I can only allow myself to be present with the pain. I cannot create the healing, I can only encourage the desire to do so. I cannot convince another that it will be better, only that it will be different. The most difficult thing to do is to do nothing…more is spoken with silence than with words.

I still get angry and annoyed, but I know now the worst that can happen – until the next time – and so I try to let the "little things" slide away. I am more patient and more kind, less tolerant of ignorance, but more willing to understand.

I know that I cannot change the world, but I can change the world of an individual who is lost. What I was so sure of is no longer, and things that I thought I forgot now come back to me as truths. True reality is not tangible and often not logical. When I least want to participate in life, life presents me with the most beautiful gifts. There are gifts that I give that I never knew I possessed, and gifts I receive come unexpectedly and without ribbons or bows.

Sometimes life seems unfair and unjust, yet it is all we have to work with. Sometimes it feels like it is too much effort to go on living, yet to give up is betrayal. Courage takes many forms, and to be "strong" can seem so very weak.

Pain strengthens, love heals, life is, sharing helps, the source of peace is in turmoil, joys surprise us, there is more, there is different, there is the legacy that nurtures, there is hope.

These are the random thoughts of a griever, a lover, a helper, a teacher, a student and a friend.

~ by Cecelia T. Perciballi-Clayton

When my grief cocoon allows me
to spread my wings,
my spirit will soar.

~ Diantha Ain

Here are excerpts from another piece by Niah, this time on the topic of letting go – something we are eventually encouraged toward, whether we like it or not, when we grieve a loss in our lives.

Non-Attachment

Some people think that they need to hang on to what they have, for it may be the best they will ever get. If you are thinking about making a change, imagine yourself having something better than you have now. See yourself going through the process easily and feeling happy with the results. Imagine that this will be the best thing that has ever happened to you, even though you might not see why right now. Decide that you are going to trust in your ability to create your higher good, and look forward to the wonderful surprises that are in store for you. ...

Approach change as a great adventure. Believe that all change is for your higher good or it wouldn't be happening. You can learn to cope with change in joyful, peaceful ways by trusting that the universe is friendly and that your Higher Self loves you and is looking out for you. If your personality isn't willing to make the needed changes, sometimes your Higher Self will set things up so that change is made for you! Act upon the whispers before they become shouts; make changes your inner self suggests to you.

One of the most difficult attachments to let go of might be your attachment to your viewpoint, beliefs, and judgments. You are always being challenged to think in new and expansive ways. The path is easy for those who have no preferences and opinions, for they are attachments that can take a lot of your energy. You can find your preferences in even the smallest things, such as the way your food is prepared or the way you drive to work. It is important to discover which preferences truly serve your higher good and which are simply unexamined habits that keep you from discovering new, higher ways to be.

Start practicing non-attachment by taking one small thing you feel attached to and pretending for one day that you are not attached to it. Become an observer and watch yourself. What habits and routines are you attached to? You don't have to give up these preferences, only your dependence on them. Once you can be happy with or without them you are free; you can have them in your life or not, without being controlled by them. ...

You may have a belief that says, "If I act like myself, if I ask for what I want, I won't be loved." Tell yourself that you can have what you want and that people love you for who you are. You are freer to be creative, grow, and fulfill your potential when you are not bound by what others think of you. Are the people you admire the most the ones who always seek approval before they do things, or those who trust and act on their own inner messages? You are not responsible for making other people's lives work: they are! ...

悲

Before you pour energy into changing or assisting people, let go of the need to have other people grow, appreciate you, or act in any particular way. Sometimes the strong desire to have them change may be the very thing that keeps them from growing. As you detach and stop worrying about them, they will be freer to grow.

As you give freedom to others, you become freer yourself. Over time, people will come and go in your life, and one of the greatest gifts you give others is the freedom to go their own way. To serve others, you will need to learn to let go. Do not worry if some of your friends leave your life, for as you increase your vibration, people will either grow and stay in your life or leave. ...

Developing the quality of non-attachment will give you freedom, expand your world, and give you new opportunities to create and grow. When you aren't attached to what others think of you or to having things be a certain way, you are free. You will have a sense of well-being no matter what the people around you are doing.

Literally you create an energy structure in your cells and body that is called being in "a state of grace" when you can live each moment, full of love and joy, trusting that all in the universe is working in your best and highest interests! (Remember, life is meant to be lived in total freedom, and you do have the power to create a "happy ever after ending" to your new beginnings.) Freedom is then, being your Self and loving it!

~ Niah Kinczewski

Grief can Open Up the Compassionate Heart

It would seem that as we come to know and appreciate and fully express our grief, we tap into a deeper kindness and understanding about life. Opening up our hearts, opening up to our feelings, has a way of touching us so deeply that we are able to touch others more deeply and compassionately. And it seems that after we have experienced a huge loss in our lives, we often encounter someone else who is going through a loss. We learn about how to be compassionate toward others as we experience our own suffering and grief.

As a hospice spiritual and bereavement counselor, I receive mailings from other hospices. The following piece, written by a woman who lost her companion dog in 2000, came to me through a bereavement coordinator of another hospice. It conveyed so much powerful emotion and truth that it is shared here with you. Amber is no longer living, but her partner Leah, the woman whose beautiful artwork inspired the cover of this book, gave me permission to include her inspirational writings.

You are not here any longer and I wonder now, time and time again, how I will ever come to terms with a space that no longer contains you. I cannot yet, for the life of me, imagine.

Perhaps it is true, in a very cosmic sense, that we came here from some other place only on loan to each other, to evolve and discover what words we would come to use about ourselves – the who and what of us – all that we struggled to uncover and become.

Now, strangely, among other truths, I am left with a startling realization: winning is not the opposite of losing. Keeping is. And while I always knew that I could not keep you forever, I couldn't refrain from wanting to.

Still, if the purpose of love is to reveal us to ourselves and others, then I will honor now, all that we achieved and the resultant belief that the expression of love is the most profound and worthwhile expression ever, and that love unspent is not love at all, but fear. There is one more truth that I have discovered over time and it is this: allowed to nurture itself and go on interminably – sadness turns to rust.

I will not entertain the thought that someone else can take your place. Impossible. But I will, when I am more finished mourning you than I am now, remember to open myself again, incrementally if necessary, to any signs of love at all – especially in myself.

~ Amber Watson

Amber also wrote the following for a friend who had gone through a divorce after twenty years of marriage.

You must not forget that you are valuable and loved. The pain will subside and you will endure and continue to manifest your own unique destiny and to impact the lives of others. To fear that the hurt will never end would be to imagine that you are immune to the benevolent powers of nature, the wisdom of time, and your unwritten contract with whatever forces brought you here in the first place. Not to mention the persistence of friends who will not, without a fight, let your courage and your heart fail you entirely.

We must not allow ourselves – any of us – to be done in by all that we discover about our weaknesses and fears – rather to focus, in tiny bits and pieces if necessary, on how much there still is to love.

~ Amber Watson

Face the Dark Night and Know that Day will Come Again

The following two paragraphs are shared with those on our hospice who have lost a loved one. Ms. Yates poignantly expresses the mystery of grief. She also reminds us that we do not know how long the journey of grief will take. Grief is always a most individual and personal matter.

No matter how brave we think we are, or think we can be, we must call sorrow by its right name and see it for what it is. Only then can we avail ourselves of the treasure that is hidden in the folds of its dark cloak. I think that we should not, by any twist of the words we use, minimize what we are going through, when death enters upon life and removes a member of our circle, family-close or friendship-wide. There will be time enough to ponder the event, to philosophize about it, to discover its significance. Now, the bleak fact stands: a light has gone out; wherever it may be shining, it is here no longer.

Face the dark night then, as a night, but with the knowledge that there is no night so long that dawn does not sometime end it. When the day comes we shall face it too, stronger and wiser, and, if our prayers have had any breadth to them, far more compassionately. Only those who have gone through a comparable experience know what struggling, what searching, what grasping goes on in the dark. The slow emergence into day may be something like the emergence of a seed as it pushes up through the earth and responds to the sun. A matter of days it may be for some seeds; for others the time may be measured in weeks, or in years.

~ Elizabeth Yates

Making the Time and Space to Express Grief

We live in a society that basically wants to ignore or deny the grief process. At our work places, we typically are given three or four days of bereavement leave and then are expected to "get back to normal." However, in truth, the grief process usually does not even begin until the shock of the loss has worn off, which can sometimes be weeks or even months after the death of our loved one. Therefore, it is very important that we honor this process of "grief work," especially the first year after losing a friend or family member.

In the book *Finding Your Own North Star: Claiming the Life You Were Meant to Live* (Beck 2002), I came across a beautiful piece on grief in which Martha Beck encourages us to deal creatively with the grief process. First, she invites us to "find a safe place to grieve." In other words, make sure you have private, quiet, safe, and comfortable places to go and honor your feelings. Feelings of grief are all good, and to be allowed. Journaling might be useful. Writing a letter to your loved one may be meaningful. Music can help open the heart and heal. If you're having trouble getting in touch with your grief, you might try viewing a bittersweet movie like "Shadowlands" (the story of C.S. Lewis's love affair with his beloved, late in life) or any movie that will touch your heart.

Second, Ms. Beck suggests that we "reserve time to grieve." Some of you may have plenty of time and space on your hands to grieve, but others of you will be bombarded by the needs and schedules of others. When this happens, make sure that you take time out for yourself. You might go to see a hypnotherapist or mentor who can help you learn to relax and enter into your feelings further. When we are grieving, we go through a kind of transformation that is very much an opportunity for growth. It can be helpful to have a guide to help us through these times. You might join a grief support group, or seek out a class or group that will help you honor your process.

It may also be important to give yourself more time to get things done while you're grieving. It is more difficult to concentrate when you are grieving, so accomplishing things may take more time. It will be easier to go through this period if you love and support yourself through the process, rather than be hard on yourself. Also, seek out any support that you need. Ask for help; there's a lot out there. Interact with the friends who support you, not the ones who are critical of you. You might even want to screen your phone calls. There may be people you'd rather avoid at this time. Also, when the sad feelings come, let them come. Even if you have to go to your room or a bathroom, excuse yourself, and let the tears come. It is so cleansing and healing to have a good cry when your emotional self needs and wants this.

There may come a time when you need to schedule a few hours by yourself to get in touch with your grief. Ms. Beck suggests making an appointment with yourself to feel sad. You don't need to give any details to other people; just know that this is a time for you and your feelings. There is a word of caution that she shares with this: Don't mourn all day, every day. At the end of each grieving session, picture yourself placing your sadness in a secure container, closing the lid, putting it on a shelf in a cupboard, and shutting the cupboard door. It will still be there tomorrow...

Third, it's good to maximize comforting activities around this time. I encourage people to treat themselves at least once a day for a period of time. Whatever feels healing and comforting, do it. Perhaps you love animals, and you feel good about cuddling up with your pet in a beautiful setting. Maybe you enjoy being creative, and it will feel healing to get out a hobby and immerse yourself in it. Perhaps there's a project or new activity you want to try, or you might want to schedule a massage or a time at your favorite spa. Perhaps you just want to be by yourself out in nature, or meditate with a candle, or play a musical instrument. Make sure you take the time to be kind and gentle with yourself, and choose only activities that nurture and comfort you around this time.

Finally, you may need to educate your friends and companions about your journey through grief. Everyone is different, and our needs vary during the grief process. Men and women tend to have different needs and expectations. People of various ages tend to have differing needs. Each personality has differing things that heal and sustain them. So it's okay to let your friends and associates know that you have a need for time alone now, or time and space to do the things that will heal you. Allow them into your life experience as much as you feel comfortable, and let them learn from you through your process, if you're comfortable with this. We can all stand to learn more about grief in our death- and grief-denying culture.

Tears are of Healing

The more I learn about grief, the more I appreciate the power of tears to heal. Here is a story by a young person about letting yourself cry when you need to. It is such an important part of grief to be able to let our emotions flow when they surface. I encourage grieving people I talk with to let their tears flow, whenever they need to flow. Even if it means removing ourselves from a gathering of people and going to a private place, it is crucial that we let tears flow. Sadness is not good or bad; it simply is. It comes to bless us, perhaps, as we acknowledge it.

Cry When You Are Sad

On a sunny Monday in April, I had two loving grandmothers near me, but when Tuesday came, only one was left. One of my grandmothers who was dear to me, had died. I had a feeling that this awful day was going to come soon, but now that it was here, all I wanted to do was cry. But I wasn't brave enough to shed a tear, for I was always taught that boys should never cry. Later, as the time came for the funeral activities, I had the hardest time keeping my sadness inside.

My relatives soon arrived from all over the country. I really had to hold back my tears now that my relatives were here, because I did not want to look like a crybaby in front of them. I figured out that my parents, my sister and myself were the only ones that had lived in the same town as my grandma. That explained why her death was hitting me the hardest, while my cousins seemed as though they were here just to get away from home. They really hadn't known her like I had.

Soon, all of my relatives gathered at the funeral home, waiting for the viewing to begin. What I thought was going to be the easiest part of my grieving turned into the hardest. The moment I walked into the room where my grandma was laying in a coffin, my heart dropped. This was going to be the last time that I would ever see her. At first I was afraid to proceed with the rest of my family up to her coffin, but then I realized that I would have to sooner or later. I grabbed hold of my mother's hand and kept my mind on remembering not to cry.

When I came up to the kneeler, in front of where she was laying, my mother made me do something that almost brought me to tears. She told me to touch Grandma's hand, for that was going to be the last time that I would get a chance to touch her. I reached over to her hand very slowly, afraid of what she might feel like. When my hand touched hers, I was relieved for a moment. She felt the same way she always had, except a little cooler than usual.

When I looked up at my mom, she began crying uncontrollably. I knew this was the time that I really had to be strong. I reached my arms around her and slowly walked with her back to our seats.

During the next few hours, I met many different people. All of them were telling me that they were sorry about my grandma passing away. I just smiled and reminded myself not to cry, because I had so often been told, "Boys should be strong and not cry." I kept reminding myself that soon this night would be over, but the next day would be the actual funeral…the last good-bye.

My mother woke me early the next morning, making sure that I looked my best. I promised myself when I was getting dressed that I would hold back my tears no matter what. I had to be strong and help my grieving parents.

When we arrived at the church, we all waited as they took my grandma's coffin out of the big black hearse. We had to follow it in so everyone knew that we were family. Once inside, we took our seats. My family sat in the very front because we were the closest to my grandma. I was surprised to see that even before the service began, my parents were crying. I was trying to hold back my tears, but as the priest began talking about my grandma, it seemed as though not crying was going to be an impossible task.

About halfway through the mass, he began telling the people about how much my grandma was loved by her family and friends. He then mentioned how every night I stayed with her while my parents were working. That reminded me of all of the good times we had together throughout my life. In the summer, we would glide on her swing. In the winter, we would always ride sleds down the big hill behind her house. There were so many good times that went through my mind that I almost forgot where I was. I began to realize that those good times were gone forever. At this exact thought, I began to cry uncontrollably. I didn't care anymore about what other people thought of me. It was something that I just had to do. I could not hold back my sadness anymore.

When my father noticed me sobbing, he leaned me up next to him and we cried together. My father, my mother, my sister and I sat next to each other, crying as if the world was going to end. At this point I promised to myself that if I ever had a son, I would tell him: "Real boys show emotions. Cry when you are sad, and smile when you are happy." This was the last time I would say good-bye to my grandmother, but I was a better person for letting my tears show everyone just how much I loved her.

~ Jonathan Piccirillo (age 15)

Placing Our Grief in the Bigger Context

Here's one more perspective on grief from the Native American tradition. It is a reminder that we must not wallow in self-pity. In the end, it's all a delicate balancing act!

Do not grieve. Misfortunes will happen to the wisest and best of people. Death will come, always out of season. It is the command of the Great Spirit, and all nations and people must obey. What is past and what cannot be prevented should not be grieved for.... Misfortunes do not flourish particularly in our lives — they grow everywhere.

~ Big Elk, Omaha Chief

In reading the following piece that I found through a colleague, I am reminded of our need to work through our grief as freely as we can so that we truly let go of the one who has died. This way, our loved ones can go on with their lives in the next phase and dimension of life. When we hang on to our grief and continue to wish the loved one back to this earth and life, perhaps we make it harder for our loved one to go on.

Letting Go

There are times when life seems like a series of losses. At times, we remember with love and longing those people, closest to us, who have died. Our sense of loss is enormous and we may be overwhelmed by feelings of emptiness. Times and places that were once filled with day to day living, now point to a harsh reality: the empty place at the table, the empty chair in the living room, the person who was only a phone call away, and the one who was always by our side.

And yet, if we sit quietly and let those feelings of loss wash over us, we find in that quiet place, a deeper reality. We find that we are not alone. The memories fill us up.

We can still hear the voice of the one we love. They continue to be with us in a new way. We may long for their physical presence once again, but it is in the letting go of that dream, that we begin to connect in a different, and yet powerful, way. We begin to connect in a way that can perhaps be described as spiritual. It is in the letting go of what we no longer have that we begin to experience what is also real, and indeed eternal: the words, the heart and soul, and the memories of that special person who has died.

Grief is a journey of letting go. It's the dichotomy that we learn as adults: that it is in the letting go of the very thing that we most want to cling to, that we gain the understanding and the strength to carry on. In our grief, when we hold onto the memories of how things were, desperately refusing to accept our loss, we are unable to move through the pain to recovery and even joy. It is in the letting go of the images of how things were, and how we feel they still should be, that we allow ourselves to feel the pain and devastation, the reality of our loss, that we find the strength and tools to rebuild our lives.

It is in letting go that we remember our loved ones as they really were, fully human; not all good, or all bad. We remember the times that they made us laugh as well as the times they made us cry – the rich weavings of our relationship, not black or white, but the many colors that represent our lives together: the joyful times, the times of anger and frustration, those "we'll laugh about this someday" times, and the holiday miracles and the holiday disasters. These are the things that make life, that make us strong and resilient. We know that we must let go in order to survive, and yet, letting go is often one of the hardest things we have to do.

In the darkest hours, unexpected lights may show us the way. As human beings it is often during the crises that the best of who we are comes out. We find time to say those things that need to be said, to listen carefully to another and to find what has meaning for us in this life. We may cry, "It's too soon. I've just begun to live." And yet, can't we rejoice that we lived, that we found one another, that we laughed and cried together, that we shared love, even for so short a time?

We hold within our hearts and minds all the people we have ever known. We are forever enriched by having loved them. We are not "less than" because someone we love died. We are "more than" for having known them.

~Kathleen M. Garner

> Never apologize for showing feelings. Remember that
> when you do, you apologize for the truth.
>
> ~ Benjamin Disraeli

The Rev. Anne Marie Evers shares in the following piece how she found herself going back to read her own words in her book, *Affirmations: Your Passport to Happiness*, after her husband died and she was challenged by her own grief.

Affirmations and the Final Destination

I was reminded that we never die; we merely change form. It is like going from one room to another. When we leave the planet we graduate to a new level, and are then enrolled in the heavenly university.

I read my own words:

悲

"To grieve excessively weakens the mind and body. It does not help the person for whom you are grieving and can actually hinder his or her advancement on the other side. Sad thought-forms that reach the deceased can impede his or her spiritual development and growth.

"Although grief is a real experience, it may also be an adjustment, a major change, or transition from what life once was to a new life that is just beginning. Grieving is work, and to work through what you are feeling and thinking takes time, energy, and a conscious, directed effort. When you experience too much sadness and constantly dwell on it, you begin a process that corrodes your body's cells.

"When you grieve for loved ones who have passed on, you are grieving for yourself, for your own loss, for not being able to see that loved one again in this lifetime. Though you may miss them terribly, it is important to release them so that they may get on with their new spiritual life.

"Everyone who loses someone they love experiences the pain of grief and loss. This is a normal, healthy fact of life. The timeframe involved is different for every individual. We all react to a loved one's death in a personal way. The grieving process could take six to eight months, or two, five, ten years or more. My own experience of grief – with the death of my precious spouses, mother, father, sister, and brother – taught me that the pain does lessen as time goes by. Time is a great healer.

"When you lose that loved one, you lose their physical presence, but the relationship still exists. The loved one is still in your heart, mind, and consciousness."

I realized that I was not helping my husband by holding him here. As my friend suggested, I did the following exercise to let him go, from page 182 of my book:

"I, Anne Marie Evers, deserve to be able to, and now do quickly and easily, adapt to life's changes. I know I will miss Roy. I let him go with love and allow him to grow in his new life experience. I make the appropriate and right decisions and I think clearly. Every day I am filled with the healing and loving energy of God. I have great inner peace and strength. I give thanks to God for the happy memories of my life with Roy. I release Roy and let him go in peace and love to his highest good. I am free; he is free and released. I give myself permission to live and find happiness. I am peaceful and healed to the good of all parties concerned. Thank you, thank you, thank you." …

I found a grief therapist to help me deal with my feelings of loss. I am now coping, one day at a time, one hour at a time, and even one minute at a time. But the important thing is that I am making it, one baby step at a time. I am still teaching affirmations; praying with and counseling people; and speaking at events on the power of God, prayer, and affirmations. Most importantly, I have a renewed, closer relationship with God. I receive God's strength and love on a daily, hourly basis, for which I am truly grateful. This, to me, is proof positive that prayers and affirmations really do work, even at the most difficult times in life. It is my hope to be an inspiration to others who are facing a loss.…

I am not ashamed if I burst out in tears when I hear a favorite song that was special to Roy and me. I am not afraid to show my emotions, even in public, and I am striving to be as patient with myself as I would be with one of my children. With the love and help of God, my strong belief system, my family, and many friends, I am coping one day at a time, one hour at a time, one minute at a time.

~ Rev. Anne Marie Evers

What soap is for the body, tears are for the soul.

~ Jewish Proverb

Working Creatively with Grief

Most hospices and many funeral homes now have bereavement programs that will help you find resources to assist you through your grief. Before closing this chapter, however, I want to share the following ten tips on dealing with grief:

1. Take one day at a time, doing one thing at a time.

2. It's good to let the tears flow. If you need to excuse yourself and find privacy, do so. Please do not "stuff" your feelings.

3. Let go of the idea of "normalcy." When you're in grief, normal time goes out the window. Since it's a crazy time, strive to see the adventure and opportunities in it. See if you can enjoy doing things and "being" in new and creative ways.

4. Prepare yourself for other losses. Everything is undergoing a change in your life.

5. Ask for what you need. Remember to process your grief with friends, counselors, and whoever will listen.

6. Exercise as much as possible. It's good to keep the emotions and energy moving.

7. Sleep when you can or need to. You may become exhausted at times.

8. Don't forget to eat! Easily done, but your body and stamina will pay a price.

9. Reconnect with Spirit; and seek out new ways to develop your spirituality.

10. Honor your memories and your intuition.

Even if death were to fall upon you today like lightning, you must be ready to die without sadness and regret, without any residue of clinging for what is left behind. Remaining in the recognition of the absolute view, you should leave this life like an eagle soaring up into the blue sky.

~ Dilgo Khyentse Rinpoche

For you shall go out in joy,
    and be led forth in peace;
the mountains and the hills before you
    shall break forth into singing,
    and all the trees of the field shall clap their hands.
Instead of the thorn shall come up the cypress;
    instead of the brier shall come up the myrtle;
and it shall be to the Lord for a memorial,
    for an everlasting sign which shall not be cut off.

~ Isaiah 55:12–13 (RSV)

Chapter 11
Resources

Resources for Healing

There is a Law higher than the laws of this world. It is a Law of total love, forgiveness, and healing. ... You do not deserve to be ill. You deserve only to be totally at peace and completely happy. You are a child of a Loving God, and your Father wants only perfect joy for you.

~ Alan Cohen

Introduction

EVEN THOUGH death will come for all of us, sooner or later, most of us usually have the desire to live as long a life as possible, especially if we can do so in relative health. Many people I talk with who are on hospice express an interest in being healed. In fact, when I typically pose the question at the end of a visit, "What shall we pray for today?" it is not unusual to have the person say they would like to pray for their (physical) healing.

The following information on various forms of healing came to me in different ways over the course of my work with hospice in the last ten years. I want to share these healing modalities and tools for relaxation because they may help you or a loved one deal with change, transformation, grief, and death.

Please have an open mind as you explore this information. The more curious you are, the better. Many of these tools are connected to ancient wisdom related to strengthening the immune system. Others have to do with creating relaxation during a stressful time. Seek out the resources or information that you are drawn to and that can be found in your local area. The Internet may also prove to be a very useful resource.

Practicing positive affirmations and visualizations for healing while utilizing these healing modalities will very possibly enhance them. And remember: Healing can come on a variety of levels – spiritually, emotionally, physically, mentally. Sometimes, the greatest healing a person can receive is the ultimate healing that comes through letting go into death and the next life.

This chapter includes the following resources:

Acupuncture	John of God
Aromatherapy	Kangen Water
Art (Mandala)	Labyrinth, The
Breema Center	L.E.A.P.
Chiropractic	Massage
Dan's Enhancer	Medical Intuitives
Diet and Cancer	Reiki
Dr. Lorraine Day	Retreats & Services for Cancer
Dr. Robert Jangaard	Shamanism
Essiac Tea	Soul Support Systems
Guided Imagery	Therapeutic Music
Healing Codes, The	Theta Healing
Home-based Funerals	Transformative Health Studies
Hypnotherapy	Watsu Massage
Jin Shin Jyutsu	Yoga

I had the privilege of meeting Dr. Kayo King, a Licensed Acupuncturist, through the World Peace Prayer Society, or Byakko Shinko Kai. Dr. King has been my personal acupuncturist since I received my first acupuncture treatment a couple of years ago. I have found deep relaxation and help with pain and other issues in my body through this form of treatment. It has been a pleasant surprise to experience how helpful, not to mention how painless, this modality of treatment has been for me.

As a way of introducing acupuncture to you, I would like to share some information from Dr. King's brochure that she shares with her new clients, and that she has given me permission to reprint here:

What is Oriental medicine?

Traditional Oriental medicine is a comprehensive system of health care with a continuous clinical tradition of over 3,000 years. It includes acupuncture and herbal treatment as well as massage, dietary therapy, meditation, and exercise. These therapies work with the natural vital energies inherent within all living things to promote the body's ability to heal itself. This system of health care is used extensively by one-quarter of the world's population who reside in the Orient and is rapidly growing in popularity in the West.

How does it work?

Oriental medicine is based on an energetic model rather than the biochemical model of Western medicine. The ancient Chinese recognized the vital energy behind all life forms and life processes. They called this energy Qi (pronounced "chee"). In developing an understanding of the prevention and cure of disease, the ancient physicians discovered a system of cyclic energy flowing in the human body along specific pathways. Each pathway is associated with a particular physiological system, internal organ, and one of the five elements: 1. Water, 2. Fire, 3. Wood, 4. Metal, and 5. Earth.

Disease is considered to arise because of deficiency or imbalance of vital energy in the energetic pathways and their associated physiological systems.

The pathways or meridians of energy communicate with the surface of the body at specific locations called acupuncture points. Each point has a predictable effect upon the vital energy passing through it. Modern science has been able to measure the electrical charge at these points, thus corroborating the locations of the meridians mapped by the ancients.

Traditional Oriental medicine has also developed methods of determining the flow in the meridian system, using an intricate system of pulse and tongue diagnosis.

Findings from these modalities are combined with other signs and symptoms to create a composite diagnosis. A treatment plan is then formulated to induce the body to a balanced state of health.

What can I expect if treated?

Many conditions may be alleviated rapidly by acupuncture and herbs. However, some conditions that have arisen over a course of years will be relieved only with slow, steady progress. As in any form of healing, the patient's attitude, diet, determination, and lifestyle will affect the outcome of a course of treatment. Traditional Oriental medicine is also an educational process in which the patient becomes more aware of his or her own body, thus increasing its ability to maintain well-being.

Although there are techniques in traditional Oriental medicine for healing most conditions, there are medical circumstances that can be dealt with more effectively by Western medicine. In such cases, your acupuncturist will recommend that you contact a physician. As is the case in China, acupuncture should be seen as complementary to Western medicine.

Is acupuncture safe?

In the hands of a Licensed Acupuncturist, your safety is assured. The needles are in a sterilized, disposable form.

Is acupuncture painful?

Acupuncture bears no resemblance to the feeling of receiving an injection, since the main source of pain from injections is the larger diameter, hollow needle, and the medication being forced into the tissue by pressure. Acupuncture needles are very fine and flexible, about the diameter of a thick hair. In most cases, insertion by a skilled practitioner is performed with a minimum of discomfort. Most patients find the treatments very relaxing and many fall asleep during the treatments. In some cases, it is not necessary to use needles at all.

What can acupuncture treat?

The World Health Organization recognizes acupuncture and traditional Oriental medicine's ability to treat over 200 commonly encountered clinical disorders, among them: gastrointestinal disorders, urogenital disorders, disorders of the bones, muscles, joints and nervous system, emotional and psychological disorders, and chronic and painful debilitating disorders. Acupuncture is especially known in this culture for its treatment of chronic pain.

Some of the reasons it is becoming so well known in the U.S.:

1. It puts people back in control of their own bodies and health care.
2. It works on many health problems for which Western medicine is less effective.
3. It is safe, effective, and has virtually no side effects.
4. It treats the whole person and not just the disease.
5. It uses the body's natural healing processes to effect relief.
6. It feels so good and relaxing to have a treatment!

~ Kayo King, L.AC.
Gentle Acupuncture, 12717 Fourth Avenue West,
Suite C-3, Everett, WA 98204

Recommended reading:

Beinfield, Harriet, L.Ac., and Efrem Korngold, L.Ac., O.M.D. *Between Heaven and Earth: A Guide to Chinese Medicine.* Ballantine Books, 1992.

Chaitow, Leon. *The Acupuncture Treatment of Pain.* Rochester, VT: Healing Arts Press, 1976.

Connelly, Dianne M., Ph.D. *Traditional Acupuncture: The Law of the Five Elements.* Traditional Acupuncture Institute, Inc., 1994.

Hicks, Angela. *Principles of Acupuncture.* Thorsons Publishers, 1998.

Kaptchuk, Ted J. *The Web that Has No Weaver.* New York: Contemporary Books, 2000.

Lawson-wood, Denis & Joyce. *The Five Elements of Acupuncture and Chinese Massage.* Health Science P., 1973.

Aromatherapy: Activating the Power of Essential Oils in Our Lives

I began hearing about essential oils several years ago. However, it wasn't until early last year, after a healing, that I actually began using them. My life has been forever changed. I find that most of my perfumes pale in comparison now. These natural, beautiful oils, with their healing qualities, are taking precedence over all the products I used to use on my body. The company Young Living, started by Gary Young after his discovery of the healing powers of these precious oils in the late 1980s, has taught me a great deal about essential oils already. They can enhance your life, no matter what changes and challenges you are going through.

The Magical Essence of Frankincense

Douglas, my hospice patient, had been struggling to breathe all night long. In fact, breathing had become the major issue in his life during the last week. He was now wearing an oxygen mask. His daughter Marcia was on one side of his hospital bed, his granddaughter Jessica on the other. They had just tucked him back into bed after a sleepless night on the Hospice Unit. Later I found out they'd both been giving him permission to let go all night long, for they felt he was suffering too much.

It was a Monday morning, and I had just listened to my voice mails. One of our palliative care specialist nurses had left me a message saying that Douglas wanted me to come and anoint him with the essential oils as I had done for him last week. As I drove toward the hospice house on the east side of Puget Sound, I had no idea that I was about to witness one of the most profound experiences I've ever had as a spiritual counselor with essential oils.

Having revamped my schedule for the day, I entered Douglas's room with my essential oils and a favorite CD of East/West chants in hand. I felt some power beyond my own guiding me. Upon entering Douglas's room, I knew what needed to be done. First, I anointed him with some oils. Marcia and Jessica made room for me to bless their father and grandfather with the oils. I got out Myrtle, the Believe blend, and Frankincense. I lifted the oxygen mask and let Douglas smell the Believe blend. After anointing the area around his nose and lungs with the Believe oil, I rubbed some Myrtle on his right ribcage and some on his feet. Then I anointed his forehead with Frankincense, my favorite oil. Frankincense, meaning "real incense," I've discovered is also considered the incense of the spirit realm.

The oils almost immediately had an effect. Douglas's breathing slowed and his whole body began to relax. Next, I went over to the CD player and got the beautiful chants by Cynthia Snodgrass filling the room with their special harmony (*Ubi caritas et amor* – "Where charity and love are, God is there"). Douglas's oxygen mask had been removed, and it was Marcia who noticed that Douglas had opened his eyes to look straight up, above his bed.

"He's going, he's going," she exclaimed.

"Well, maybe," I thought to myself, as one never really knows when and how the dying process will happen. I also found myself praying hard at this point. I recall offering a prayer out loud, too, around Douglas's bed with his two beloved ones. Before long, Douglas's breathing had slowed down even more, and it became clear that he was in the final stages of letting go. The three of us witnessing this turn of events were so amazed, it did not even occur to us to leave the room. Within 20 minutes of my entering his room and administering the oils, Douglas had taken his last breath.

After a few minutes of experiencing this sacred time together, one of us left the room to go find a nurse. Two hospice staff came into Douglas's room to help us begin to digest what had just happened. After confirming that Douglas had died, they checked his limbs, noting that there had been none of the mottling that usually happens before a person dies. In hindsight, I believe Douglas realized that the relaxation offered him by the essential oils gave him an opportunity to let go and make his way over to the next realm. This meant that he could forego the usual process of the body's slowing down gradually.

Needless to say, this experience with essential oils opened me up to the subtle yet tremendous power that they can have in the end-of-life and dying process. On some level I have known that the oils possess this kind of magic, since I've heard about how they were used in ancient times around death and burial. However, one doesn't have to be dying or experiencing a transition to enjoy the benefits of these oils. I use them on a regular basis, to lift my mood and raise my vibration. Frankincense is known for its anti-depressant quality and for its ability to connect a person with the spiritual realm; it is also a wonderful tonic for the skin and has anti-tumoral qualities, as well. I heard about a mother who had a son with a brain tumor. She kept her son's head wet with Frankincense. Over time, the son was healed by the power of this oil that was once considered more valuable than gold. Frankincense has also been known to work its magic with people suffering from Alzheimer's. If ever you happen to be with an obstinate person who suffers from Alzheimer's, simply apply some of this wonderful oil to your own hands and then run your hands through their aura (energy field) in some way. This process will very soon have a calming effect on the headstrong individual.

Of course there are many other essential oils with all kinds of qualities. To name just a few, Lavender is a beautiful relaxant and tonic for the skin, Peppermint and Patchouli can help improve your digestion. For more information about these miracle oils, see my web pages at www.youngliving.org/adventure or www.thelastadventure oflife.com (click on the "Essential (YL) Oils" button). My R.N. friend Pam Fry has put together the following from her experience with essential oils.

Aromatherapy includes the use of essential oils to enhance mental, emotional, and physical well being; it is complementary to many other healing modalities, as well as traditional medicine. Essential oils have been used by various cultures for thousands of years in China, India, Egypt, and all over Europe, especially France and England. More recently, essential oils are being used in the U.S. as their value has become apparent. Aromatherapy has stood the test of time because they are a natural and powerful form of strengthening and healing the body holistically.

In the Bible it is common to read of various plant oils used in healing, and especially in the anointing of the dead. The healing properties of these oils, the "life blood" of plants, were understood, even in ancient days, and they were valued, in a spiritual sense, too, even after death. Frankincense, myrrh, angelica, and hyssop are oils frequently mentioned in the Bible.

The essential oils are to the plant what blood is to the human body; the oil is the fluid in the plant that transports oxygen and nutrients and other chemical constituents throughout the plant. When we use these oils, the oxygen and chemical constituents are easily absorbed into the bloodstream through inhalation, or thru the skin, then distributed throughout the body. When the oils and aroma are inhaled these chemicals enter the brain and balance brain chemistry, therefore altering mood and feelings. For example, when one is stressed and inhales a blend of lavender and chamomile, the chemicals in those oils create a calming effect. When oils of basil, peppermint, cardamom, rosemary, or lemon are used, they have a stimulating effect on the brain that improves the level of one's alertness, memory function, and clarity.

For the chemicals in the plant oils to be therapeutic, it is very important how the oils are extracted; very specific steam distillation under tight parameters will ensure the delicate chemicals stay intact and remain therapeutic. What tends to happen, at least in our culture, is that due to the interest and popularity of aromatherapy, cost-saving measures are being used. For example, adulteration of the oils through the use of synthetic chemicals and dilution of oils can occur, not rendering the desired effect beyond a nice fragrance when the oils are used. It is very important to do a bit of research or ask practitioners for the sources of pure essential oils. Many companies profess to have pure essential oils, but they are not truly pure. It is similar to the debate regarding how organic does a product need to be to be called "organic." If you buy oils in a store where the price is $5 to $15 for the whole range of oils, these cannot be pure. The range of prices of individual plant material is great; and pure oils cannot be sold in an inexpensive range without adulteration.

As a nurse for twenty-five years, I have worked intimately with this aspect and can say any hands-on healing, including use of essential oils, can greatly enhance relaxation of the family as well as the individual patient. Essential oils can be used to ease stress, anxiety, worry, fear, grief, sleeplessness, pain, mental clarity, fatigue, as well as on a deeper level, soothing the spirit in the process of letting go. The Egyptians specifically used oils for the process of crossing over to the other side, and often in ancient tombs opened vials of pure essential oils have been found near the body of the deceased. The aroma that permeates the room where they are used will help anyone in the room, as all one needs to do to be benefited is inhale!

The easiest way to use the oils is in dilution with massage oil or even olive oil. Try massaging an essential oil, or a blend of oils, gently into the bottoms of the feet, the neck, or back, and even over the forehead and chest. This can feel wonderful, as the oils will be absorbed through the skin, as well as inhaled into the body. Often, depending on the situation, the feet, belly, or head may be the only accessible places to massage without disturbing the person. When a person is getting close to death, use the oils on the head, not the feet. By massaging oils on the feet, you will tend to keep the person on this earth, rather than encourage them on to the next realm. The belly is a very good place for oils to be absorbed. For the purpose of diluting, usually 10 to 20 drops of essential oils per 1/2 ounce of carrier oil is plenty. Pick some oils or a blend that seems to meet what you want to achieve in using them, or oils that you or your loved one are drawn to.

Frankincense is a holy anointing oil in the Middle East that has been used in religious ceremonies for thousands of years. It elevates the mind, helps in overcoming stress and despair, and helps one to "connect" spiritually. It can be particularly helpful while meditating and as the time of death approaches. Sandalwood is an earthy, woodsy oil that brings a deep calming and contemplative mood. Along with frankincense, it is considered one of the more "spiritual" oils that helps in elevating the consciousness to a broader perspective. It is known in Europe for its ability to oxygenate the pineal gland, the seat of our emotions. The pineal gland is also responsible for releasing melatonin, so sandalwood can also enhance deep sleep, as does lavender with its quality to relax and calm. Chamomile, which is also calming and pleasantly floral without a sweetness that can be overwhelming in some oils, helps with relaxation, stress, rest, and anxiety. Citrus oils such as lemon, orange, and mandarin are uplifting, refreshing, and bring a sense of "sunshine" and joy to the being and the environment. Bergamot specifically is the Prozac of oils, as it has antidepressant properties to it that balance brain chemistry. Lemon, basil, or peppermint can be used for inhalation or massaged into the neck to stimulate alertness and mental clarity when needed. This can be especially helpful when a dying person is distressed by being too sleepy or groggy to interact with loved ones as they would like, or for family and caregivers on long shifts that allow for less sleep.

Besides massage, direct inhalation is another use of the oils that can be effective. You can rub a few drops of oil in the palm of a person's hand, place over the face, and take five or six deep breaths. You can also place a few drops of oil on bed linen or on a cotton ball near the person. Diffusers are available that dispense an aerosol type mist of the oil into the room; this is a nice option for more long-term use and for overall benefit.

All the essential oils, when properly prepared and distilled, have antiviral, antibacterial properties, and can be very beneficial in that way as well. Essential oils also have been found, through gas chromatography, to have vibrational frequencies that are measurable. Since we are alive and are thus "energetic" beings, when we use these oils, on ourselves or around us, that vibrational frequency is added to our energy fields. In this way, we are energetically enhanced by that. An increase in energetic frequency strengthens the immune system, supports healing, and balances emotions, attitudes, and outlook. I have found this to be very apparent when I work at the hospital and "spritz" the halls and rooms where I work with a blend of essential oils in a spritzer bottle of water. Just doing this, I have seen a calming and ease to the day as the day progresses. It has proven to be true without fail, and so much so that other nurses now insist on spritzing when they come to work! This is a good thing for everyone involved. There seems to be an order and ease to the flow of things, more laughing and playfulness, and more energy to get done what needs to be done.

I feel aromatherapy is a very easy, accessible gift we can use to ease a loved one's passage, and to help ourselves through that difficult time as well. I recently had a profound experience of this with a friend who was dying from liver cancer. Over several months he became much more ill, until it was clear he was dying. During the last week of his life, his partner and friends spent time with him, singing, playing music, massaging him, and using essential oils on his abdomen and feet. He had become rather confused and restless the last few days and these oils seemed to be the only thing that calmed him; the blend we used included geranium, lavender, rosewood, bergamot, melissa, and angelica. He had a truly dramatic response by becoming very relaxed and at peace, and sleeping deeply. This was a great relief to his caregivers; when he did become restless, applying more oils was helpful. Toward the last hours, his partner bathed him and then lathered his whole body with the oils, feeling instinctively this was the thing to do. Something about that ritual felt really right, and in the flow of an old tradition. He died that night and his partner called me and talked about how beautiful his passing was, that he had a smile on his face. This was actually hard to believe, and when I went to see him for myself in the morning, he did not look dead; he looked asleep. Indeed, he had a big smile of absolute bliss on his face. I have never seen anything like it! It was as if he was seeing heaven, and got the "joke" that life is, perhaps. I believe the oils facilitated that opening and allowed him to move into such a blissful passage.

I know the oils can cause no harm if used conservatively, and of pure form, diluted with massage oil. Start with what appeals to you and your beloved, for scents are very particular, especially when one is ill. Always test the scent with your beloved, and make sure that they find it pleasing. Only use those oils they enjoy. You can start with single oils and work up to making or buying blends that sound like what you intend. For example, Young Living sells blends called Peace and Calming, Harmony, and Trauma Life, which helps to release emotional trauma resulting from accidents, the death of a loved one, and assault or abuse. I recommend the following sources of oils, although of course there are others. Just be very careful regarding purity. Many books are available for more information on aromatherapy in bookstores and libraries. May you find peace and joy in using the gifts of the plant kingdom to make a difficult time easier.

~ Pam Fry, R.N.
(See also the section in this chapter on High Touch Jin Shin.)

Go to www.youngliving.com or www.quintessencearomatics.com for more information on the oils. Go to Aromatherapeutix: 1-800-308-6284 for catalog; the oils are very reasonably priced.

These oils also can be very helpful when a person is going through the journey of grief, depression, or transformation of any kind. You might experiment with bergamot, myrtle, Roman chamomile, clary sage, eucalyptus globules, juniper, and lavender. For Young Living blends, you might want to try Valor, Release, Joy, Inspiration, Inner Child, Gathering, Harmony, Release, Transformation, Believe, Forgiveness, Present Time, Peace & Calming, or Magnify Your Purpose. Frankincense is one of my favorites to use on any occasion. Anointing the head with it helps to open up the crown and connect with Spirit if one is depressed; it is also anti-tumoral, and generally speaking, a most healing oil. Another favorite healing blend of mine is to mix frankincense with lavender, then add the same amount of jojoba oil to the mixture.

Please refer to my website: www.youngliving.org/adventure. Or you may contact me if you would like to learn more about how to purchase these oils. As a distributor for Young Living, I would be delighted to help you experience the oils firsthand.

Art as a Spiritual Path: Mandalas

My friend Jane Hendrickson is a teacher and artist, one of the most unique individuals I know. She recently let me know that she had had some experience using her interest in art, mandalas in particular, around her mother-in-law's final transition on a hospice in Arizona. I deeply appreciate Jane's taking the time to put together the following material to share with all of us another healing tool that can be used in the completion process at the end of life – and during any time when healing is desired.

Carl Jung, in his practice of Depth Psychology, believed it was important to establish and preserve in the client relationship a protected space, a psychological sense of privacy, *temenos*. He also believed that *tenemos* was often indicated in drawings or dream images of a quaternary nature (four parts), such as mandalas.

The Sanskrit word *mandala* derives from the root *manda*, which means "essence," to which the suffix la, ("container") has been added. In the literary works of Indo-European religion, *mandala* is the term for a chapter, a collection of mantras or verses chanted in sacred ceremonies. In these sacred sounds were patterns of beings and things, therefore the patterns of the Universe. This concept is compatible with Jung's most famous idea, that we are all subject to the "collective unconscious," an aspect of the psyche that finds meaning in archetypal images.

The symbol of the mandala has become widely accepted as a representation of "sacred space." In Jungian terms, it is an expression of unconscious images, and also "a means of protecting the centre of the personality from being drawn out and from being influenced from outside" ("The Tavistock Lectures," *Collected Works* 18, par. 410).

Jung spent six years (1913–1919) in a "self-experiment" of meditation to understand the images that surfaced from his unconscious in dreams and fantasies. None of them came from his remembered experience. The contents seemed to be mythical, the result of his having been in direct confrontation with God *(Imago Dei),* or the collective unconscious. His personal diary of the details has been called "The Red Book" because it was bound in red leather. It contains beautiful drawings, including mandalas. (Portions are included in C. G. *Jung: Word and Image*, Aniela Jaffe, ed., Princeton University Press, 1979.)

Creation of a Mandala

The drawn mandala begins with the center, a dot, the "seed" around which the outside energies are gathered. As the artist incorporates these energies, his or her own energies unfold and are also incorporated. The circular form of a mandala represents dynamic consciousness. Inside, patterns are created from lines drawn until they intersect forming geometrical patterns. A square around these patterns symbolizes the physical world bound in four directions, represented by four gates. The central area of the design is the residence of the deity, or "the essence." The completed mandala contains both outer and inner spaces in one symbol representing wholeness, perfection, such as Heaven, the sun, and God.

The Healing Power of Mandala

Judith Cornell, Ph.D., MFA, a classically trained Western artist, began painting luminous circles filled with "healing light," not knowing that these were traditionally called "mandalas." In 2003, 2004, and 2005, Dr. Cornell applied for and was awarded grants enabling her to offer "Mandala: Circles for Healing" programs free of charge to cancer patients at Mercy Regional Cancer Center in Mount Shasta, CA and at the Community Hospital of Monterey in Monterey, CA. In *Mandala Luminous Symbols for Healing* (Quest Books, Wheaton, 2006) she answers the skeptic's question, "Why Create a Mandala?" She says: It is a meditation process "that focuses and open the heart to the healing power of unconditional love" and "has a calming and relaxing effect on the mind and body, thus focusing and strengthening the will to heal." She says the healing of a sense of psychological fragmentation brings joy, and the process allows expression "of ultimate reality that can be expressed in no other way." It opens perspective to a unity between human existence and cosmos and gives form to spiritual insights. (Contact Dr. Cornell for further information-www.mandala-universe.com/events or call 1-800-833-4668.)

The Mandala and End of Life

Creating art through the use of symbolic images is a spiritual path. Making the mandala penetrates into the space of the personal sacred. The drawing is a re-enactment of the cosmic drama and a pilgrimage of the soul. The form is the visible rendering of that which is invisible. It combines personal experience with archetypal images in the collective unconscious.

Several years ago I began to experiment with the mandala and found that it is not only a great tool for general heath and introspection but also an excellent form for combining symbols and colors to activate untapped energies. It is a means to express latent emotions. Knowing this, and having read Judith Cornell's observations and experiences, I introduced the mandala process to my family over several months during my mother-in-law's final illness in a care home and hospice. Subsequently, I have introduced the mandala to others who are in their last journeys of life, and seeking wholeness.

~ Jane Hendrickson, Ph.D.
janeangel@att.net or 520-825-1188

The Breema Center's Nine Principles

Sometime after 9/11, I received a note from a massage therapist that included "The Nine Principles of Harmony" from The BREEMA Center in Oakland, California, a unique organization that teaches a combination of bodywork and breathing. I loved their principles and was able to get permission to share them with you here.

The Nine Principles of Harmony

Body comfortable: When we look at the body, not as something separate, but as an aspect of a unified whole, there is no place for discomfort.

No extra: To express our true nature, nothing extra is needed.

Firmness and gentleness: Real firmness is always gentle. Real gentleness is always firm. When we are present, we naturally manifest firmness and gentleness.

Full participation: The most natural way of moving and living is with full participation. Full participation is possible when body, mind, and feelings are united.

Mutual support: The more our Being participates, the more we are able to support life and recognize that Existence supports us. Giving and receiving support take place simultaneously.

No judgment: The atmosphere of nonjudgment gives us a taste of acceptance of ourselves as we are in the moment. When we come to the present, we are free from judgment.

Single moment/Single activity: Each moment is new, fresh, totally alive. Each moment, when it's an expression of our true nature, is complete by itself.

No hurry/No pause: In the natural rhythm of life energy, there is no hurry and no pause.

No force: When we let go of assumptions of separation, we let go of force.

Website: www.breema.com; e-mail: center@breema.com.

Chiropractic

I have benefited greatly from chiropractic adjustments over the years, to relieve stress in my back. My chiropractor, Dr. Zografos, agreed to put together the following piece to help us understand the value of chiropractic treatments particularly at the end of life.

Since its inception, the foundation of chiropractic has been that of a health care system that relies on the natural recuperative functions of the body to bring about healing without the use of drugs or surgery. Chiropractic literally translates from Greek as "done by hand" and the laying on of hands remains a fundamental part of the chiropractic treatment even today. There comes a time with the seriously ill or dying patient when the awesome power of traditional medicine is ultimately humbled by disease. There are no more pills to try or heroic surgeries to perform. Yet, often it is the simple laying on of hands, the very foundation of chiropractic treatment, that provides a strong healing comfort. The gentle adjustment of the spine by a chiropractor facilitates the optimal functioning of our bodies. This becomes of critical importance to the chronic pain or seriously ill patient: To renew an appreciation for what one is capable of doing rather than focusing on the limits placed on us by pain or disability or even the finite nature of life.

I am reminded of a long time patient of mine who recently passed away. She had always been fiercely independent, but as her physical condition deteriorated, she became afraid and alone. She was constantly told by others that she shouldn't do this and she couldn't do that. She was treated like a child by her children and lectured to by her medical doctor. I honestly believe that her chiropractic visits were the highlight of her life. She traveled twenty miles each way to come and see me. Certainly my treatments could not restore her posture that had been destroyed by the relentless cruelness of osteoporosis. I could not erase the pain of her spinal compression fractures. But we laughed, we cried, we touched, we hugged, we planned for the future, and we kept focused on what she still could do. I adjusted her neck and massaged her back and her legs. She always stood tall after the treatments, just to show me. She remained active until the last.

~ Gregory Zografos, DC, DABCO
Olympic View Chiropractic
626 128th St., SW Suite 103B, Everett, WA 98204

Dan's Enhancer

In the process of my own healing, thanks to one of my massage therapists, I came across this healing device. It is a Molecular Enhancer, or "full body resonator." By holding it, a person is able to increase the proper functioning of his or her body. In other words, this device speeds up the body's ability to heal itself.

I came to truly appreciate this device on the day that I was feeling nauseous due to some medication I was taking that day – a bit of an overdose for my healing process. I was scheduled to be holding the M.E. about 45 minutes after the nausea came on. The nausea had been coming in waves, and I was still feeling somewhat nauseous when I got to my therapist's home and began holding Dan's Enhancer. However, within three to four minutes of holding the device, I was feeling 100 percent better. I don't understand how it works, but this experience has made a believer out of me. I now have one of these devices so I can use it whenever I feel the need for strengthening my health.

For more information on the M.E. go to: www.dansenhancer.com.

Diet (Acid, Yeast, Fungus) and Cancer

I have personally dealt with the ravages of systemic candida (yeast/fungus overgrowth). In the end, after nearly five years of struggle with my health, it was a medical intuitive who was able to give me a clear diagnosis. Through this process, I have come to learn a lot about the connection between what we eat, our digestive tract, and the link between fungus and cancer. If you are interested in learning more about the connection between fungus and cancer, and how changing your diet can change the way you feel, I would recommend you read any of the following books, or go to the websites for further information:

Cantwell, Alan R., M.D. and Suzanne Henig (ed.). *The Cancer Microbe.* Aries Rising Press, 1997.

Hunt, Beverly T. and Virginia O'Brien. *LifeChange Cookbook: Low-Carbohydrate Essentials for Conquering Fungal Infection.* Dallas, TX: Thornhill Hunt Publications, 2004.

Kaufmann, Doug A. *The Germ that Causes Cancer.* Media Trition, 2002.

Young, Robert O. and Shelley Redford Young. *Sick and Tired? Reclaim Your Inner Terrain.* Woodland Publishing, Inc., 2000.

www.cancertutor@yahoo.com ; www.cancertutor.com/other/currentstudy.html
www.cancertutor.com/AltTreatments/Alt_Diet.html
www.TheWolfeClinic.com/newsletter/reclaim.pdf

Dr. Lorraine Day's Ten Natural Laws for Health

I learned about Dr. Day's material through a gentleman I worked with who was learning to live with cancer. He had come across her work in his own search for wholeness and health. Dr. Lorraine is a remarkable doctor, who finally quit her practice of medicine in order to find the time and energy to heal from breast cancer.

The following is a list of the ten principles she has come up with through her own search and process toward healing. They are a "back to the basics" approach. They worked for her.

1. Proper Nutrition Diet of fresh fruits, vegetables, and grains. *No* animal fat and NO processed foods.
2. Exercise – 4 hours per week.
3. Drink plenty of water. The body uses 10 cups of water a day. Drink *at least* 8 cups of water a day.
4. Sunlight boosts the immune system! Get as much as you can, though perhaps best to avoid the hottest hours of the day (10 AM to 2 PM).
5. Temperance. No tobacco, alcohol, caffeine, drugs (including prescription drugs).
6. Plenty of fresh air.
7. Proper rest at proper time. At least eight hours, beginning around 9:30 PM (when healing hormones start producing).
8. Stress relief – faith/trust in God. "Don't worry; be happy (be in joy)!"
9. Attitude of gratitude.
10. Spirit of benevolence. Even when we are sick, we can pray for others, for the world.

For more info: "You Can't Improve On God!" (video), by Lorraine Day, M.D.

For videos and other materials by Dr. Day, call: (800) 574-2437 or write: Rockford Press, P.O. Box 8, Thousand Palms, CA 92276. Website: www.drday.com/index2.htm.

Dr. Robert Jangaard, ND, and the SEG and VEGA Equipment from Germany

I heard about Dr. Jangaard from many people on Whidbey Island before I finally went to see him. My visit with him was the culmination of my healing process because he was able to go deeper and see what was actually going on in my body. He did this with electro-dermal screening (EDS), or Vega Technology. EDS devices use high technology and ancient medicine in order to help recognize a body's organ dysfunctions even before symptoms begin to manifest. It identifies pathogens and toxins that are making a person ill (unbalanced), and it helps ascertain what supplements and remedies are helpful or harmful to the person. It even determines the dosage that needs to be administered. It does this all very quickly, inexpensively, and noninvasively. Although this technology has been developed in Germany for 30 years, there is still resistance to it here in the U.S. because it is based on principles of

THE LAST ADVENTURE OF LIFE

quantum physics and traditions of energy medicine, which are not taught or understood in our medical schools.

Dr. Jangaard can be reached at his clinic in Freeland, WA: 1657 E. Layton Road.

Scott Moyer, who has been teaching biological medicine and EDS to practitioners in the U.S. for more than ten years, can be reached at (800) 888-9789.

Essiac Tea

There is a powerful detoxifying tea whose ingredients were given by an elderly patient to Canadian nurse Rene M. Caisse in 1922. It is known as Essiac tea (Caisse spelled backward).

An Ojebwa Indian medicine man first gave this herbal tea to a woman who happened to be prospecting in the wilds of Northern Ontario with her husband. At the time, she had a breast that was sore and very painful. Before she left camp, the medicine man told her she had cancer. He said he could heal it with this remedy, known as "a holy drink that purifies the body and places it back in balance with the Great Spirit."

After learning about this tea from the elderly patient, nurse Caisse decided to use it with some of the people she knew. Her mother's sister had developed stomach cancer, along with liver problems. Her aunt had been given six months to live, but after using Essiac tea, she was healed and lived for another 21 years! Later, Dr. Charles A Brusch, JFK's family doctor, learned about it and used it in helping one of the Kennedy sons recover from cancer. Later, a woman named Elaine Alexander developed a similar healing tea called Flor.Essence, which is available at most local natural food stores. There are other forms of Essiac tea available through mail order: Herbal Healer Academy, Inc. Website: www.herbalhealer.com. Order line: (870) 269-4177. You can also brew your own, if you have access to a good herb store. My only cautionary note would be that, due to the toxicity of most of us living in our culture, when you first begin drinking this tea, you are likely to experience some diarrhea and stomach upset for a number of days.

There are also books available on this tea. One is *Canada's Remarkable Unknown Cancer Remedy: The Essiac Report,* by Richard Thomas. It was printed by the Alternative Treatment Information Network in L.A., in 1993. Their telephone number is (310) 278-6611. Another booklet on the tea and about Rene Caisse is called *Rene Caisse's Story Continues in China.* Website: http://www.ralphmoss.com/essiac.html.

You need not be ill to take Essiac tea. In fact, after I learned about this tea more than ten years ago, I decided to try it. The first morning I drank a small amount, I felt a kind of "high." In fact, I meditated after drinking it and had an unusually deep and memorable meditation. Since that time, I've heard a shaman talk about how powerful this tea is from a spiritual point of view, as well. Essiac's key ingredients are burdock root, Turkey rhubarb root, sheep sorrel, and slippery elm bark. Some diseases besides cancer that this "ultimate detoxifier" helps to heal (or minimize symptoms of) include hypoglycemia, MS and Parkinson's, arthritis, chronic fatigue syndrome, ulcers, thyroid problems, fibroids, hemorrhoids, prostate and urinary problems, circulation, diabetes, sleeping disorders, warts, psoriasis, impotence, Alzheimer's, asthma, and allergies.

When I feel a cold coming on or feel a little under the weather, I brew up the Flor.essence version of this tea and take it for two weeks or so. It always makes me feel better, and it allows me to get over the "bug" very quickly. Thanks to this tea and the Young Living essential oils, I have not suffered from a full-blown cold in several years now.

Guided Imagery

Jayne Peterson, a hospice nurse, works at a different branch of the hospice where I worked for many years. Jayne caught my attention because she was offering retreats for her colleagues in hospice work, using her passion for guided imagery as the core piece. I remember that when my mom was dealing with cancer, she found Shakti Gawain's Creative Visualization material a most helpful tool in her process. I've also been aware for a long time of the work that Dr. Carl and Stephanie Simonton have done around healing from cancer through visualization (see *Getting Well Again* in my bibliography). I am most grateful to Jayne for putting together the following piece to help us understand some of the basics of using guided imagery and visualization – for healing, wholeness and personal growth.

Guided Imagery, a form of directed meditation, is a therapeutic tool that allows individuals to interact with the body's natural healing capacity. Imagination is one of our most powerful inner resources, yet few of us are educated in its skillful use. Every image we hold in our minds stimulates a cascade of chemical reactions within our bodies. Fearful images stimulate our body's stress response, compromising health; relaxed, peaceful or loving images activate our body's relaxation response, enhancing health. Anyone can learn to release stress, slow the racing mind and shift the body to a peaceful state of consciousness. On a deeper level, guided imagery is a magical, healing tool that allows us to communicate with the sacred, loving and wise part of ourselves that knows just what we need in every situation.

As individuals experience the end stages of life, guided imagery can be an effective and comforting tool for decreasing fear, anxiety, and pain. There are available truly beautiful guided imagery CDs that address the needs of those in the final stages of life's journey. These guided imagery meditations offer relaxation and facilitate an inner journey, taking a person from a place of love to a place of even deeper love while allowing for emotions of sadness, loss, and grief. Individuals who listen to Health Journeys CDs – *Ease Pain,*

Relieve Stress, Ease Grief, or *Peaceful Dying* – frequently describe increased feelings of peace and comfort.

Working with a certified guided imagery practitioner can further deepen one's experience of inner wisdom, that divine source that is part of each and every one of us. Working with trained practitioners can help to strengthen one's ability to utilize his/her natural inner resources to ease suffering. Here are a few stories of how individuals have used imagery on their end-of-life journey.

Jan, a deeply religious woman with end-stage breast cancer would frequently go to her special place during her imagery sessions, a beautiful and peaceful garden. On one journey in her imagination to this special place, Jesus appeared and walked with her. Three times Jesus asked Jan during this session, "Do you know how much I love you?" His responses to her brought great peace and comfort to Jan on a daily basis as she recalled her imagery experiences and felt comforted by the love Jesus held for her.

Bill, an artist now homebound with end-stage respiratory disease, would go to a park, near a lake, active with people, in his imagination. There he would frequently experience the presence of his inner advisor, a nun/monk-like presence who would take Bill by the hand and show him in pictures and metaphors information that guided him day to day as he struggled with decisions about his treatment needs. These imagery experiences left Bill feeling less conflicted and more at peace.

Kate, suffering from significant shortness of breath related to end-stage asthma, was able to learn a technique, guided by her inner healer during an imagery session, which eased her shortness of breath and decreased her need to use anti-anxiety medication that made her very sleepy. At the onset of the breathing distress Kate would place her hand over her diaphragm, close her eyes and repeat the word "calm" while gently patting her diaphragm. This technique increased Kate's ability to participate in her daily activities, feeling less short of breath and less sedated from medication.

Just sitting with a loved one recalling a pleasant memory can also bring great comfort. Try this exercise with your loved one:

> *Have your loved one think of a memory from a time when he/she felt loved, comforted, and peaceful – the kind of memory that brings on a warm smile and a warm feeling in your chest.*
>
> *Guide your loved one to take a few deep, comfortable, relaxing breaths…deep into the belly…breathing in all that you need as you inhale and releasing all that you don't need as you exhale.*
>
> *Now have your loved one begin to describe their memory, encouraging them to just take themselves back to that time in their mind. Ask questions invoking the use of the senses as you hear this memory. What is the temperature like?*

Let yourself feel that warm sunny day on your skin... or the light breeze. Are there any sounds in the background? Hear the birds... or the leaves rustling in the wind. Are there any smells? Breathe in the fragrance of the garden, the aroma the forest. And ask, "How do you feel as you recall....?

We have all that we need within us and imagery is a tool that can help connect us to this sacred knowledge. Each and every one of us has the capacity to use imagery. In fact, when we worry about what might go wrong, we are using imagery. Unfortunately, this worrying creates states of stress or tension in our bodies rather than relaxation and peace. Directing our thoughts to those of love, peace, and joy brings great comfort to the body – physically, emotionally, and spiritually. Where the mind goes the body follows.

Guided Imagery CDs:
Belleruth Naparstek, www.healthjourneys.com (800) 800-8661
Dr Marty Rossman, www.thehealingmind.org (866) 879-2231

To find a guided imagery practitioner near you:
Beyond Ordinary Nursing, www.imagine@integrativeimagery.com
(650) 570-6157
Imagery International, www.imageryinternational.org

Jayne Peterson, RN, BSN, is a Certified Integrative Imagery Practitioner. She has a private practice in Kingston, WA at the Harbor Healing Center where she uses imagery techniques for relaxation and stress management, accessing inner wisdom and resources, coping with chronic illness, pain and symptom relief, and preparation for surgical or medical procedures. Jayne also works as a home health and hospice nurse, incorporating relaxation and guided imagery techniques into her daily nursing practice and teaching other health care providers these techniques. Jayne can be reached by phone at (360) 620-4460 or by email at jaynepeterson@prodigy.net.

The Healing Codes

Almost two years after publishing the first edition of this book, I discovered The Healing Codes. They are very easy-to-use "finger holds" on the facial area that help release old patterns of belief that no longer serve us. They are helping me to put the finishing touches on my physical, mental, and emotional healing.

I highly recommend that no matter what your life challenges are right now – whether they be mental, emotional, spiritual, or physical – you go to the link for The Healing Codes on my website (under "Tools for Healing") or www.thehealing codes.com and see if this site speaks to you. My belief is that, no matter what, we could all benefit from doing The Healing Codes in these times. And they are so simple to do. They involve placing one's hands on or near parts of one's face and head, and releasing negative thought patterns and energy by doing so. The Healing Codes are likely to bring you more health, wealth and happiness – most of all, increased joy and well-being, almost as soon as you start using them. I would be delighted to hear how your life changes as you work with these Codes. For me, they have been just like magic!

Home-based, Natural Funeral Services

In keeping with the philosophy of the hospice movement, there is now a movement afoot to help people create more natural, environmentally friendly, personalized, "home-made" after-death care and funerals. Some of the people and organizations that I have come into contact with are these:

Natural Transitions Funeral Guidance
P.O. Box 17848, Boulder, CO 80308. (303) 443-3418. www.naturaltransitions.org.
This organization helps families to "direct their own funerals." The mission is to reclaim after-death care for families and communities, empowering them to make choices that are more meaningful, affordable, and environmentally conscious. Their team includes a former hospice worker, an end-of-life caregiver, and a healer and energy worker.

JerriGrace Lyons, Final Passages
P.O. Box 1721, Sebastopol, CA 95473. (707) 824-0268. www.finalpassages.org .
The founder of this company is a minister, Reiki master, and death midwife who has pioneered in the field of "home funeral guidance." In the past ten years JerriGrace has assisted more than 250 families in Sonoma and other counties in California with home or family-directed funeral arrangements. She has appeared in USA Today, was interviewed on FOX and CNN Headline News, and is featured in a new PBS documentary called, "A Family Undertaking" (see below). JerriGrace is available for workshops and speaking/teaching engagements.

Nancy Jewel Poer
5595 White Feather Way, Placerville, CA 95667. www.nancyjewelpoer.com or
www.whitefeatherpublishing.com.
This author of Living into Dying: A Journal of Spiritual and Practical Deathcare for Family and Community is the co-founder of Rudolf Steiner College, a Waldorf teachers' college near Sacramento, where she has taught for twenty-six years. She lives with her husband of 48 years in the Sierra foothills on White Feather Ranch.
PBS Documentary

Recently, PBS aired a documentary called "A Family Undertaking" on the program P.O.V. ("point of view"). This documentary shares information on how families can forego a more "typical" American funeral to care personally for their loved ones at home. To order a copy of this video, call (800) 937-4113.

Hypnotherapy

Darlene Harris is a hypnotherapist who works in North Seattle. She agreed to share the following material to help us better understand how hypnotherapy can be used when serious illness occurs or when death nears.

Contributions of Hypnotherapy for Dying Persons, Care Givers and Their Loved Ones

Hypnotherapy processes can address needs of dying patients and family members for sleep issues, releasing anxiety, pain management, and dealing with impending separation, loss and grief.

For some patients, pain management strategies can provide alternatives to morphine and drugs to allow at least short periods of time for communication between the dying person, spouse and relatives. This can be useful for creating quality family time and saying goodbye.

The natural trance state commonly referred to as hypnosis accesses the benefits of the theta brain wave state, measurable by EKG, which enables those with ability to focus and willingness to follow suggestions, to achieve a level of relaxation. In a state of trance the power of the imagination can be tapped for a variety of benefits, including comfort and peace, calming anxiety, releasing worries and concerns, gaining clarity in decision making, inducing sleep, Soul level communication for resolving trauma, abuse and old issues, and generally enhancing quality of life.

Albert Einstein has said, "Imagination is more powerful than knowledge.... Everything has changed with the splitting of the atom, except one thing – the way we think. We must change the way we think."

Persons with capability to focus and willingness to learn can be taught to access or create a special place in their imagination, or a favorite place in nature, for relaxation, comfort, and temporary relief from anxiety. For patients who have varied ability to focus, there are guided imagery scripts that can be read aloud. This process has the quality of accessing infinite possibilities as the nature of the imagination is expansive. It can be playful and fun.

When ability to focus is lost, music can be useful. If sound/music has been incorporated into the imagery process of the favorite place in nature, that type of music can be played to associate the person to the comfort of their favorite place when they can no longer maintain cognitive focus. Those who are nature lovers may like recordings that combine nature sounds with music. Of the five senses, it has been suggested that the sense of hearing may be maintained the longest.

Since the capability to hear is often maintained by persons in coma, hypnotherapists who are specifically trained can sometimes establish a level of communication with persons in a coma.

When a person has learned to access the memory of a favorite place in imagination, this can be a rich source of comfort, tranquility and serenity. Once this resource is established and experienced as pleasant, caregivers and loved ones can suggest or remind the patient to use the resource. It can be particularly helpful at the end of a care-giving or visiting session to make the suggestion, "In a few moments I will be leaving. Would you like to focus on your favorite place in nature for a time?" Or, "Would you like me to turn on music for you before I leave?" Being able to offer an alternative to occupy the mind may ease the pain of parting with a loved one, particularly when the realization is present that this may be the "last time" of being together.

A caregiver or loved one can create quality time with a dying/transitioning person by guiding them into a light state of trance, then speaking of favorite memories of the past, reading passages requested from their chosen spiritual tradition, or guided imagery scripts with inspiring and uplifting thoughts for nurturing the soul. Some possibilities could be to suggest to the patient being held in the tender, loving arms of God or the deity of their spiritual tradition; being lulled to sleep with soft, tender phrases of love and compassion; suggestions for going on an imaginary trip to meet loved ones who have gone before; or an adventure in a time machine exploring the infinite creations and galaxies of space.

It is important to understand and keep in mind that suggestions given during a natural state of trance, when the conscious mind is set aside, are more easily accepted as the unconscious mind is open and receptive to imagination and fantasy. This is a wonderful way to relate to a child, who retains a strong inclination toward imagination, as well as an elderly person who may be reverting to a state of dependency in the dying/transition process.

There is a wealth of books and cassette tapes available on guided imagery, and guided meditation that is similar to prayer. If family members would like to use some of these ideas but are feeling the press of responsibilities at a time of need which prohibits the leisure of becoming self-taught, you may wish to consult a hypnotherapist for ideas to fit your particular situation. With this large reservoir of resources, along with the hope and comfort of your own spiritual tradition, you can create quality of life in the midst of adversity and grief.

~ Darlene Harris, M.A.
www.allianceoflightcenters.com

Jin Shin Jyutsu, The Power of Touch

I met Pam Fry, an R.N. who teaches Jin Shin Jyutsu, through my interest in learning more about Jin Shin Jyutsu. Pam has a wealth of knowledge and many years of experience with this healing art. She is also familiar with the Young Living essential oils, and she graciously agreed to write a couple of pieces for this chapter, based on her expertise in these areas. Thank you, Pam.

High Touch Jin Shin

Jin Shin Jyutsu is an ancient Japanese healing art that dates back at least 5,000 years. In ancient times it was a system of hands-on healing for restoring health, harmony, and balance. Jin translates to mean "Man, compassionate Spirit"; Shin means "God, Spirit"; and Jyutsu, "Art." Loosely translated it means "The art of God coming into man of compassion and knowing." My teacher, Mary Iino Burmeister, calls it the art of knowing and helping myself; a gift from the Creator, meant to be shared for the health and well being of everyone.

Human Energy

The human energies are a network of functions that govern every aspect of being alive, from the thoughts we think, to the food we digest, to making our heartbeat. They follow very specific pathways, just like our circulation and nervous system does. These lines of energy are traceable with radio-isotopic dyes injected into acupuncture points. Consider the electromagnetic energy of the body like the wiring of a house; you can't see it but when you turn on a light, it is working. If a circuit blows, the light, or whatever is governed by that circuit, no longer functions properly. It is very much the same in our bodies. When a pressure point that governs the circulation of this electrical energy through the body becomes congested with tension, stress or toxins, it ceases to function properly and some areas become congested and overloaded, while others are now deficient of vital energy. The symptoms arise first as mental/emotional attitudes of stress, and progress to many of the physical distress symptoms of which we become aware.

These energies flow freely within the body, like rivers, feeding and cleaning every cell. With stress of any kind (mental, emotional, physical, traumatic), a block in the flow of energy can occur and the healing potential of the body is diminished. Over time, more and more of these circuits become blocked and inefficient, thereby diminishing one's health.

This vital, life-sustaining energy comes to us through the air we breathe (prana), the live food we eat (the integration of the action of the sun, earth, and water), and through the sun which is absorbed by the skin and integrated into these pathways. It is the energy reflected by EEG, EKG (electrical energy of vitality). We all have had experiences of having more or less of this vital, life-giving energy; it's called "VITALITY!" Health is not just the absence of disease, but a vital, energetic, healthy, happy countenance, an

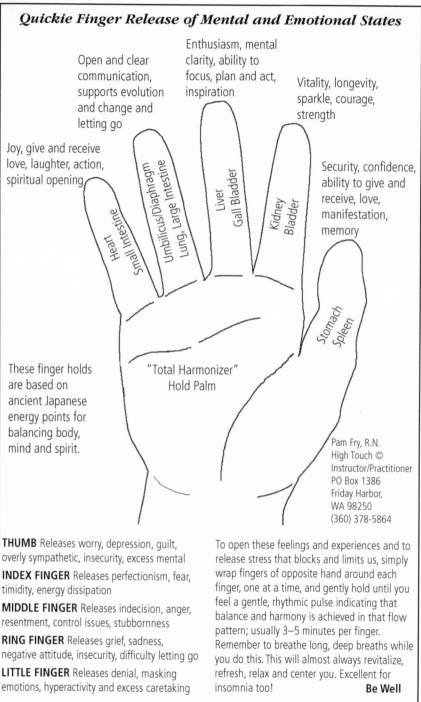

Quickie Finger Release of Mental and Emotional States

Open and clear communication, supports evolution and change and letting go

Enthusiasm, mental clarity, ability to focus, plan and act, inspiration

Vitality, longevity, sparkle, courage, strength

Joy, give and receive love, laughter, action, spiritual opening

Heart
Small Intestine

Umbilicus/Diaphragm
Lung, Large Intestine

Liver
Gall Bladder

Kidney
Bladder

Security, confidence, ability to give and receive, love, manifestation, memory

Stomach
Spleen

These finger holds are based on ancient Japanese energy points for balancing body, mind and spirit.

"Total Harmonizer" Hold Palm

Pam Fry, R.N.
High Touch ©
Instructor/Practitioner
PO Box 1386
Friday Harbor,
WA 98250
(360) 378-5864

THUMB Releases worry, depression, guilt, overly sympathetic, insecurity, excess mental

INDEX FINGER Releases perfectionism, fear, timidity, energy dissipation

MIDDLE FINGER Releases indecision, anger, resentment, control issues, stubbornness

RING FINGER Releases grief, sadness, negative attitude, insecurity, difficulty letting go

LITTLE FINGER Releases denial, masking emotions, hyperactivity and excess caretaking

To open these feelings and experiences and to release stress that blocks and limits us, simply wrap fingers of opposite hand around each finger, one at a time, and gently hold until you feel a gentle, rhythmic pulse indicating that balance and harmony is achieved in that flow pattern; usually 3–5 minutes per finger. Remember to breathe long, deep breaths while you do this. This will almost always revitalize, refresh, relax and center you. Excellent for insomnia too! **Be Well** enthusiasm for life and the energy to fulfill our dreams. Acupuncture, shiatsu, acupressure, and many other systems of healing acknowledge and utilize the principles of these energy flows.

Jin Shin Treatment

Jin Shin is truly a holistic therapy. It does heal at the level of body, mind, and spirit, seeking the source of the imbalance and restoring harmony.

A treatment can be done on oneself, or on another. The client lies on a table, fully clothed, face up, while the therapist uses LIGHT touch over acu-points on the body. Two points are held simultaneously until the tension is cleared, signaled by the synchronous pulsation felt at the point(s); then the hand is moved to another point, and so on along the areas of tension, much like re-mapping out the flow pattern and checking the circuitry along the way. It is very much like placing a jumper cable on a battery and adding just a boost to the person's system to clear the congestion and stress out of the blocked point. When the circulation pattern is restored, the body knows where the energy is needed, and goes about the job of healing.

Each point can take seconds to minutes to release and re-energize. Treatments generally take 45–90 minutes with a short period of rest and teaching of self-help. Aromatherapy essential oils are often used to enhance relaxation and pain relief. Stress management and lifestyle are discussed to the degree that they apply to the circumstance presented. Repeated treatments depend on the individual and the particular situation. For some chronic situations, a period of regular treatments may be needed; often there is great improvement with just a few sessions. Many people have come for relief of back/neck pain, asthma, insomnia, digestive problems, PMS, chronic fatigue, and general stress-related problems. Some people are aware that they have been over-doing and just need a "tune-up." It is always up to the individual, and I will offer recommendations. Many people use Jin Shin as a preventive therapy to maintain optimal health and vitality.

Jin Shin is a special gift to give yourself. It is deeply relaxing and pleasurable. After a treatment, symptoms may or may not be relieved. Often they are improved within 8 - 24 hours. People often feel invigorated and sleep better. Early release of tension is good preventive care. When stress is held and repressed in the body over a period of time, disease can result. It is called DIS-EASE – not at ease! Experience this for yourself!

~ Pam Fry, R.N. pam@rockisland.com.

Websites with more information:
www.hightouchnet.com and www.jinshinjutsu.com

Recommended reading:

Bach, Edward, M.D. *Bach Flower Remedies.* Keats Publishing, Inc. 1983.
Brennan, Barbara Ann. *Hands of Light.* New York: A Bantam Book, 1987.

Burmeister, Alice. *The Touch of Healing: Guide to Jin Shin Jyutsu.* New York: A Bantam Book, 1997.

Cameron, Julia. *The Artists' Way: A Spiritual Path to Higher Creativity.* Penguin Group (USA), 1992.

Gerber, Richard, M.D. *Vibrational Medicine.* Inner Traditions International, Ltd., 1988.

Haas, Elson. *Staying Healthy with the Seasons.* Ten Speed Press, 1982.

Hay, Louise. *You Can Heal Your Life.* Carson, CA: Hay House, Inc., 1995.

Myss, Carolyn. *Anatomy of the Spirit.* New York: Harmony Books, 1996.

John of God

I have been hearing about "John of God" for some time now. His real name is Joao Teixeira da Faria, and he is a medium of extraordinary healing capabilities who resides in Abadiania, Brazil. People visit John of God from all over the world and receive incredible healing in some astonishing ways. He is able to incorporate 33 entities in his mediumship, all of whom were remarkable individuals during their own physical lives. These entities are spirits of doctors, surgeons, healers, psychologists, and theologians who have died. They are of such high soul vibration that they no longer need to reincarnate into this physical place. They do continue to elevate in the spirit plane through their benevolence and charitable works.

Joao is able to incorporate only one entity at a time, though he can change entity as the need arises. Any number of entities can perform operations at the same time outside his body, however. The first incorporation by Joao happened when he was only 16 years old, and the spirit was that of King Solomon. Joao is still working with King Solomon today – a reminder to us that spirit is immortal.

For more information on John of God, or if you are interested in receiving a healing through him or one of his coworkers, see www.johnofgod.com. You can send a recent photo and a few pieces of information of yourself and the entities will work with you long distance. For a payment of $60, you will also receive some herbs to take during the next month and a half to help you with your healing.

Kangen Water

In my journey of exploration into health and wellness, I have come across Kangen water, or "antioxidant water," also known as ERW, electrolyzed reduced water. Kangen water is made by a machine that typically sits on a kitchen counter. The water undergoes electrolysis, and two types of water are produced at the same time: Kangen water which has a high alkali content, and acidic water, at a 3:1 ratio. Kangen water shows a minus ORP, or oxidation reduction potential, which means its "reduction potential" is increased, to neutralize active oxygen, or free radicals. (Kangen water contains a higher percentage of active hydrogen than tap or bottled water.) Aging is largely caused by oxidation and free radicals, which attack our body cells, tissues, and DNA, and cause over 90 percent of diseases. Therefore, drinking Kangen water helps keep us healthy by neutralizing free radicals in the body.

This technology was developed in Japan in the 1950s, and the first machine came out in 1955 for agricultural use. Today, many hospitals, hotels, and restaurants in Japan use this machine, especially for sterilization, using strong acidic water. There are also many clinical studies and experimental treatments being conducted to treat diseases, both by drinking Kangen water and by topically applying acidic water. I observed one man on video who arrived in a clinic in Japan, having been told he would likely need to have his foot amputated due to the ravages of diabetes. About a month and a half later, after drinking lots of Kangen water and using the acid water externally on his foot at a hospital, he was shown walking out the door of the clinic with both feet intact!

Below are some practical uses for Kangen and acid water.

1. Drinking Kangen water after exercising: This will replenish the electrolyte balance three times faster than other waters do. This is because the body more easily absorbs the smaller water clusters of Kangen water. Therefore, recuperation is also faster. Animals also find this water enjoyable; it can help keep your pets happy and healthy.
2. Cooking with Kangen water: Foods cook faster and water heats up more quickly because of the smaller water clusters in antioxidant water. Many restaurants use Kangen water because it draws out the flavors and foods become more flavorful.
3. Tea, coffee and other beverages: Antioxidant water adds flavor to and brings out the best in beverages.
4. Vegetables: Wash vegetables with Kangen water and get the maximum taste and flavors from them in salads. Vegetables are crisper and last longer after being soaked in Kangen water. Cut flowers also last longer when they are placed in Kangen water instead of tap water.
5. Acid water for beautiful skin, for cleaning, and as a substitute for pesticides: The acidic water that is created through the electrolysis can be used as a beauty and cleaning aid. Use it to help clean mirrors, windows, bathtubs, and to disinfect cutting boards. It can also be used when washing clothes, as a fabric softener. Acidic water is also used for firming up and toning your skin, especially for your face and scalp; and it can be used for organic farming purposes, too – in lieu of pesticides.

For more information on Kangen water, see www.enagic.co.jp/english. I am a distributor of these machines, so please contact me (the author) by email if you are interested in purchasing a Kangen water machine.

The Labyrinth

The labyrinth, an ancient spiritual tool for transformation, is being rediscovered. Labyrinths are usually constructed from patterns using circles and spirals, based on principles of sacred geometry. They have been found around the world and are known as sacred patterns or "divine imprints." These sacred symbols have been passed down through the ages; they are in churches of medieval Europe, on the walls of caves, on coins, and in natural settings. They are usually constructed directly on the ground and have been used for "walking meditation" and rituals. They can also be drawn on paper or carved into wood. In this case they are traced, using the fingers (known as "finger labyrinths").

The labyrinth has been used as a spiritual tool for at least 4,000 years. It is a physical metaphor for life's journey – the journey of healing. Labyrinths have been utilized in a variety of ways: as a tool for initiation, such as for warriors before they entered into battle; for psychological and spiritual growth and transformation; for enhancing right-brain activity; and for restoring faith and healing to troubled or stressed souls.

The labyrinth teaches trust and can be used as a tool for spiritual practice. It is different from a maze in that it is not a puzzle: as long as you follow the path step by step, you end up at the center; when you leave the center, you follow the same path back to the beginning. The labyrinth is a good place to work with questions that need to be addressed in your life. You can take the question with you as you walk the labyrinth; after reaching the center, you can pause, meditate, reflect. You might receive added inspiration and guidance. The "return" walk can be a time of preparing to move out into the world again, having received the gifts that were needed.

In our times, labyrinths are being constructed on school grounds and in parks, churches, universities, businesses, community centers, and even private homes and gardens. As their benefits are being recognized, their use and popularity are growing.

I invite you to look into the labyrinth for yourself and use it in your own creative ways. There is much yet to be explored with it, especially in the areas of grief, death, and transformation.

Here are a few websites you might begin with: www.labyrinthsociety.org, www.ispiritual.com, www.gracecathedral.org/labyrinth/.

LEAP: Life Essence Awakening Process

Both the medical intuitive and the theta healer who worked with me identified some inner child work that I needed to do. There were some lingering "abandonment issues" from when I was four or five years old, I was told. My massage therapist had just finished learning the LEAP healing modality, so I asked her if she might work with me using this method to help heal my inner child. I had most remarkable healing and breakthrough with Laurie through a one-hour session using LEAP.

LEAP was developed by Jaya Sarada, the Director of Wellbeing Foundation, a non-profit organization "devoted to the sacred essence of the heart and spirit." LEAP uses soul kinesiology (muscle testing) and energy field kinesiology to locate disturbed energy patterns in the etheric, emotional mental, and spiritual energy fields. Then, using techniques such as meridian healing, affirmations, and "the forgiveness process," these disturbances are worked with (released) and balance is brought back to the whole human being.

You can find out more about LEAP by going to: www.wellbeinginstitute.org or call (800) 282-5292.

Email: info@wellbeinginstitute.org. You can also contact Laurie Keith, massage therapist and LEAP practitioner, at (360) 221-4010.

Massage

The power of massage in my own health and well-being as a hospice worker has worked wonders. I find it most helpful in reducing my stress. Similar to meditation, it helps "refill my cup." Massage helps me continue to give and share the best of myself. As a single woman today, it has been even more important to experience the power and healing of touch from another human being. I make it a point to get a massage at least once a month.

I met a massage therapist while attending a one-of-a-kind workshop on becoming an expert in one's particular field of work. Carolyn told me of the healing between herself and her mother at the end of her mother's life. I felt that it was something worth sharing.

Massage – a Journey into Healing

"Carolyn, don't forget your jacket." That was Mom, always reminding me of things that I, at age forty-one, should be very able to remember to do myself. But for this moment, I did need the reminder. I had become increasingly weary and worn-out beyond exhaustion, due to my daily visits to Mom at the hospital a few weeks prior to this day. Now, at this hospice, it was one of Mom's final days on "God's beautiful world," as she always would say. As feeble as she was, Mom was still sharp enough to notice my jacket draped over the couch, which indeed I would have forgotten.

Leaving (with jacket in hand), I kissed Mom, stroked her hair and reminded her I loved her. I drove home, thinking how my life's activities had come to a halt since we learned that a cancer had been thriving in Mom's stomach and spread to her pancreas and liver. Before this discovery, I was driving my efforts and time into restarting a business in massage, work that I'd enjoyed since my mid-twenties. Moving to Washington set my work back by a decade since my prior education and experience didn't equal this state's qualifications of needing to attend one of their approved schools and passing the licensing exam. Strapped for money and time, I took odd jobs along the way, weaving this into the time I'd invested in being at home for my family. As quickly as children grow and time passes, I soon met and welcomed the opportunity to attend school again, pass the exams, and once again share my work with others. Throughout, Mom never understood why I didn't choose more conventional work, and would say, in her Chinese-flecked, broken English – "Many jobs you can choosing, but you only become a massage terrapeest."

"Yes, Mom," I would reply, resigned and hoping that she would simply one day accept my vocation and be happy for me. "I really love this work. It helps people feel…." I stopped as she would take up another topic to discuss. There were always wedges between our understandings of each other. Whether they were due to our age gap, our relationship as mother and daughter, our philosophies and points of view, or our different upbringings in two different cultures, I always felt I had to explain myself to her--only to be cut off and told how I should be according to her standards. Although I was her daughter, I felt completely unknown, unseen by her. She didn't seem to mind an occasional shoulder or neck rub I would give her, yet she couldn't comprehend how I could enjoy this as a way to make my living, even after I'd shared with her some of the good I'd seen emerge from this tactile profession: stiff joints gradually becoming more mobile, aches and pains subsiding, if not altogether ending. But by this time, Mom would interject her thoughts with the merits of other vocations related to banks, offices, and hospitals. In all fairness, I couldn't understand how she could see me content at a desk job. Granted, I'd had my share of some very good experiences working in offices, and had attained great skills for such work; yet my varied interests led me to this arena of holistic health, where the whole person counts in all the ways we know: body, mind and soul. This was a place I could see expansion, improvement – a right livelihood for me.

During Mom's last weeks of life, she looked forward to her daily massages. I noticed in other hospice rooms that touching a loved one who was dying was a rare event. Families and friends would come to visit, stay for a while to talk, watch TV, sing or sit quietly, usually all done without the presence of touch. Perhaps a hand was held. Maybe a forehead was kissed or patted. I didn't see much touch, certainly not as much as I was increasingly growing to hope the dying would receive. Just holding Mom's hand kept her settled; she didn't need to keep looking around for me to see if I'd gone for the evening. It provided a genuine comfort for me as well, as we diverted from words to a dual solace.

Over the next couple of days, Mom became so physically weak, it was a difficult balance to lift her without hurting some part of her now delicate and bedsore body, while applying gentle strokes to soothe her arms, legs, or back, and help with whatever circulation remained. She released a vocal sign of contentment as I worked on her face and scalp – "Remember, behind my ears." Mom's belabored breathing did not keep her from making sure her favorite spots were given proper attention. Working on and around her ears, Mom took in a long, deep, slower-than-ever breath, saying, "Now I understand what you do. Even though I am dying, you massage, making me feel light and alive...and ...soooo good."

My eyes began to heat and a balloon seemed to be expanding itself in my throat. These physical sensations did not match my thoughts: "Why could you not see this sooner? Why couldn't we have had more connections like this well before this day? Why...." The questions softened as I came back to the present. Those years of explaining, convincing, defending, resisting, had culminated into this moment: our last genuine connection, in a most rare meeting of minds. "Thanks, Mom — I'm glad you know," was all I could quietly utter.

Mom passed away, in the middle of the week, in the near middle of the month. As I am now also in the middle of my life, I hope that I am doing my share of understanding, or at least accepting, of my children and their decisions as they come into their own. I also hope more people come to understand the unspoken language a caring touch carries with it, and share it with those you love. I will continue to move forward, onward, and upward as I live my time here in "God's beautiful world."

~ Carolyn Mateos, Licensed Massage Practitioner, carolynlmp@yahoo.com

Medical Intuitives

When many people hear the term "medical intuitive" they think of a leading persona of this versatile field, Caroline Myss. A medical intuitive has the ability to "see" what is not usually visible and can access information from a person's bio-energy fields and body systems. Each medical intuitive is blessed with a different skill. Some see pictures, some see events like a motion picture, some see or hear messages from the body. Some, like Patricia Zapatka, whom I worked with, "know" things that lead to the flushing of emotional or mental blocks that then seem to dissolve the problem area. In addition, they might use an EAV/EDS device called a Bio-Tracker as a feedback mechanism to verify their way through a session. Patricia uses this. It is designed to identify and remedy in a detailed way what's going on inside the body on many levels.

I first met Patricia by phone when my cat had developed a growth on her backside. I talked with a friend of mine whose dogs had been healed with Patricia's help. When I called Patricia by phone, she was able to "see" Midnight's tumor and that it was already beginning to heal. She gave me some suggestions on how to continue to help her heal up. Another time Patricia assisted in healing a deep gash Midnight had sustained at the base of her tail. I had wondered if she might need stitches, but Patricia assured me that she did not, and Midnight did heal up over time, without a visit to the vet. However, if your intuition tells you to see a medical doctor or a vet, do so; I'm learning that our intuition usually gives us the most helpful information.

When I met Patricia for the first time in person, she detected the systemic candida that had invaded my body, probably for several years. I had developed digestive problems and thought that I had food allergies for the first time in my life. No medical doctor had been able to detect the candida in me. She also helped detect and heal some giardia that my daughter was dealing with.

See Patricia's website: www.energyworks-healthcoach.net. (See also John of God.)

Reiki and Other Forms of Healing using Light and Energy

There are many healing modalities surfacing and resurfacing on the planet today. Many of these use light and universal energy. Reiki is a form of "laying on of hands" healing based on the idea that everyone carries within them the positive life force, or "universal life force energy." This technique was rediscovered by a Japanese man, a devout Buddhist by the name of Mikao Usui. Dr. Usui was questioned about the doctrine of "faith healing" by one of his Bible students in the late 1800s. He was so intrigued by his student's question that he spent the next seven years of his life searching for the healing described in the Bible. He ultimately found his answer in Sanskrit, through a description of the Buddha's method of healing.

In 1935, Hawayo Takata was healed from her cancer through a series of Reiki treatments at the Chujiro Hayashi's Reiki Clinic in Tokyo. Ms. Takata was from Hawaii, but she sold everything to go to Japan with her two daughters and be taught Reiki. In 1938 Mr. Hayashi initiated her as a master in Reiki healing. Since 1980, her granddaughter, Phyllis Furumoto, has been teaching in the United States the Usui system of Reiki healing that was passed on to her.

Reiki is taught in three steps. A Reiki master is one who has gone through all three "degrees" of this training. Reiki is spiritual, not tied to any particular religion. The practitioner balances your vital energy by placing her hands over your major organs and chakras, considered to be energy centers. It is believed that the harmonious balance that comes as a result assists the body in healing itself. Both the recipient and the practitioner feel the energy flow as warmth during a Reiki session, and both receive the healing energy.

Recommended reading:

Honervogt, Tanmaya. *The Power of Reiki: An Ancient Hands-on Healing Technique.* New York: Henry Holt and Co., 1998.

Stein, Diane. *All Women Are Healers: A Comprehensive Guide to Natural Healing.* Freedom, CA: The Crossing Press, 1990.

See also: www.Reiki.7gen.com.

Recommended reading in related areas of healing:

Brennan, Barbara Ann. *Hands of Light.* New York: A Bantam Book, 1987.

Eden, Donna, with David Feinstein. *Energy Medicine.* New York: Jeremy P. Tarcher/Putnam, 1998.

Gerber, Richard, M.D. *Vibrational Medicine.* Inner Traditions International, Ltd., 1988.

Gordon, Richard. *Quantum-Touch: The Power to Heal.* Berkeley, CA: North Atlantic Books, 1999.

Hover-Kramer, Dorothea. *Healing Touch: Guidebook for Practitioners.* Taos, NM: Redwing Book Co., 2002.

Radha, Swami Sivananda. *The Divine Light Invocation.* Palo Alto, CA: Timeless Books, 1990.

Sanford, Agnes. *The Healing Light.* New York: Ballantine Books, 1972 (Revised ed.).

Retreat Centers and Services for Cancer Patients and Survivors

I have come across a number of retreat centers and organizations that work with people who are survivors of cancer or who are living with cancer. Some of these organizations are listed below.

American Cancer Society: (800) ACS-2345; www.cancer.org. Information on local treatment options.

Cancer Treatment Centers of America: (800) FOR-HELP; www.cancercenter.com. CTCA is the home of integrative and compassionate cancer care. "We never stop searching for and providing powerful and innovative therapies to heal the whole person, improve quality of life and restore hope."

Harmony Hill: (360) 898-2363; www.harmonyhill.org. Gretchen Schodde had the vision for this beautiful retreat setting located on the Olympic Peninsula. There are four labyrinths on the grounds of this center that you can walk as part of your spiritual practice. Various healers and professionals come to this center to help facilitate retreats like "Spa for the Soul" and "Living with Cancer: Tools for the Journey."

Make-A-Wish Foundation: (800) 304-9474. This foundation makes wishes come true for children who are battling life-threatening medical conditions. For adults, see www.dreamfoundation.com.

National Cancer Institute: (800) 4cancer; www.nci.nih.gov. Contact for information on clinical trials.

Sacred Art of Living Center: (541) 383-4179; www.sacredartofliving.org. You can now purchase Richard Groves' and Henriette Klauser's book, *The American Book of Dying,* through this website. The Center is an education and retreat center in Bend, Oregon, which encourages people to trust and deepen their spiritual experiences. It also challenges people to transform their life's priorities. Founders

Mary and Richard Groves brought their extensive experience in hospice ministry to create the "Sacred Art of Dying," one of the nation's first comprehensive educational programs for spirituality in end-of-life care. Over time, the Center has evolved to include other programs and retreats related to spirituality, such as the enneagram, men's and women's rites of passage, the world's great spiritual traditions, and spiritual direction.

The Hospice Education Institute: Three Unity Square, P.O. Box 98, Machiasport, Maine 04655-0098. (207) 255-8800 and (800) 331-1620. Website: www.hospiceworld.org. Hospice Education Institute is a non-profit national organization that provides advice, referrals, and support to friends and families who are seeking information regarding the last adventure of life. They have a toll-free HOSPICELINK telephone (800) 331-1620 that provides free information. The staff who answer these phones are good listeners who have unhurried time and space for people to share their experiences and stories. HEI also provides support and education to those who work with hospice. They publish a book on symptom control in hospice care. They also have a Small Gift Fund to offer immediate assistance to hospice patients in need. They support individuals and groups of citizens who work in their communities to improve care for the dying and the bereaved. Please utilize this resource if you or someone you know could use their support or information.

Shamanism

Shamanism has taught me a great deal about many things, particularly the interconnectedness of all things. I have been blessed to experience several soul retrievals while going through some huge changes in my own life. I have also been a part of shamanic experiences with those desiring healing. These experiences have always served a purpose and have brought deeper meaning to the situation.

In one situation, I took a woman on our hospice who desired to be healed, to see a shaman. Laurie had a second visit with the shaman, unbeknownst to me. After her death, I was glad to find out through the shaman that Laurie had been able to talk to her about her death on that second visit. (Until that time, Laurie had not spoken of her death to anyone, as she was so totally focused on healing.) Laurie also had made a "journey" with the shaman, in which an eagle came to take her Home. Laurie suddenly took a turn for the worse the week before she died, so we had not been able to talk about these things. Needless to say, it was especially meaningful to me to find out that Laurie had had a "practice session," if you will, of leaving her body, thanks to the help of a shaman and an eagle.

In another situation, I worked with a dying man who loved horses. He was particularly attached to one of his horses who had died; in talking together, we came up with the idea that he could visualize riding off on this horse through a particular window of his room to the other side, when the time was right for him. I strongly believe that our beloved pets and (power) animals are ready to help us in these ways.

The following is a brief introduction to shamanism and how it relates to end-of-life issues. It was written by Janine Ellison, a shamanic practitioner whom I have had the privilege of meeting on Whidbey Island. I hope you will be in touch with someone like her in your area, if you desire further knowledge regarding shamanism and how it can help with the process of letting go.

Traditionally, one of the roles of the shaman was to offer healing to both the living and the dead. In current times also, the shaman is trained in administering healing to those who are living, and in the grieving processes over the loss of a deceased loved one. He/she is also skilled in offering assistance to people in the dying process, to help alleviate the fears and uncertainties that arise during this passage. The shaman is also knowledgeable in offering assistance to souls who have already crossed over, and who are in need of shamanic help and healing in order to move forward in their evolution.

To be effective in this work, the shaman needs to be very familiar with the territories and evolutionary processes of the soul…before, during, and after death. Through extensive training, involving explorations into these vast terrains, the shaman acquires great knowledge and skill in assisting the dying, as well as in offering help to the deceased. Oftentimes, the shaman would also gain wisdom and knowledge from personal initiatory experiences, such as in the case of a serious illness, or a near-death experience, which adds to the genuine compassion and empathy that he/she brings to the work.

Recommended reading:

Cowan, Tom. *Shamanism as a Spiritual Practice for Daily Life.* The Crossing Press Inc., 1996.

Harner, Michael. *The Way of the Shaman.* New York: HarperCollins Publishers, 1980.

Ingerman, Sandra. *Soul Retrieval: Mending the Fragmented Self.* New York: HarperCollins Publishers, 1991.

Ingerman, Sandra. *Welcome Home: Following Your Soul's Journey Home.* New York: HarperCollins Publishers, 1993.

Vitebsky, Piers. *The Shaman: Voyages of the Soul; Trance, Ecstasy, and Healing from Siberia to the Amazon.* London: Duncan Baird Publishers, 1995.

Wolfe, Amber and Victoria Pierro, ed. *The Truth About Shamanism.* Llewellyn Worldwide Ltd., 1997.

Recommended websites:

The Foundation for Shamanic Studies: www.shamanicstudies.org

Tom Cowan: www.riverdrum.com

Sandra Ingerman: www.shamanicvisions.com/ingerman.html or
www.shamanicteachers.com

Soul Support Systems

I learned about Soul Support Systems through reading Flo Magdalena's book, *I Remember Union: The Story of Mary Magdalena*. Flo wrote the book based on her visions of Jesus Christ and Mary Magdalena. I invite you to read the book; it has the potential to change your consciousness, as it reminds us that we are one with all things, especially when we live and see from the heart.

Soul Support Systems is dedicated to bringing the essence of the soul into everyday life. It is our premise that as the individual and collective memory of the soul emerges and the divinity of all life is recognized, societal structures and current systems will evolve naturally and merge into a new theory of systems that are interwoven and intrinsically linked to a greater design of inherent order and union.

Using a technique called Soul Recognition, we assist each person to ride the wave of the soul by going through layers of memory, conditioning or holding that have become "normal" for them and go deeper into the causation of the patterning of the body. It has been our experience that during the process of transition (dying), the riding of the soul wave allows the person to move gracefully from the physical plane to that of the afterlife.

Our facilitators have used this technique to assist friends and family members to easily shift from the physical body to that of the spirit. Since the soul is the individuation point of the original point of light from which the human journey begins, it is natural to reconnect with this point to complete the human journey.

For more information regarding Soul Recognition in all of its aspects, please visit www.soulrecognition.com, or call Flo Aeveia Magdalena at (800) 542-7685 or Toni Elizabeth at (360) 293-2853.

Therapeutic Music

> And the more souls who resonate together, the greater the intensity of their love and, mirror-like, each soul reflects the other.
>
> ~ Dante

Attending a conference on music therapy, I was reminded how music has the power to open our hearts. I have also learned recently that it is the heart within the heart, the "sacred heart," if you will, where we connect with everything. No wonder music is such a powerful, healing blessing to us. The following is by Jeri Howe, a Seattle musician who offers her healing, magical harp melodies to the dying, through an organization called Sacred Harmonies.

At the Root of All Caring Is Touch

Sacred Harmonies, using harp and voice, offers music at the bedside of the ill or dying to ease physical, spiritual, and emotional pain, and to create an atmosphere of loving kindness that supports the soul in transition. Often we forget that the dying are losing their whole world: their body, their relationships, their identity. These are overwhelming losses to face. A music "vigil" at the bedside is very beneficial for both the patient and loved ones. The musical medicine that is offered is prescriptive to the patient and conveys a sense of serenity and consolation that can be profoundly soothing. Deeply spiritual in intention, the musical vigils are very practical; often the music aids in helping people sleep, or find deep rest and peace.

We play our harps for the dying because of our love and appreciation for life. The music provides a voice for this love. We play our harps so the music can accompany and journey with the person who is dying – to ease their fears and surround them with a sense of beauty and blessing. We play our harps for those suffering with pain, anxiety, and dementia, to bring them comfort. Music is a living language that communicates without words. The music carries and accompanies us into the unknown and helps release our fears and attachments. It provides us with beauty, warmth, light, and hints that we are not alone.

Music-Thanatology

The work of Sacred Harmonies is part of a contemporary field called Music-Thanatology. Music-Thanatology, developed by Therese Schroeder-Sheker over the last three decades, is a contemplative and spiritual practice but is not confined to a particular religion. Its historical inspiration comes from the Medieval Christian monks and the Gregorian chants they sang. Central to their spirituality was the understanding of the human need for beauty as one way to encounter the face of the divine. These medieval monks kept constant vigil with the dying with oration and singing of the psalms and prayers. The soothing melodies of the Gregorian chants sustained a sacred space around the dying one, a space of protection and love.

Why do we recommend live music?

Our human bodies are like musical instruments. Our heart beating within provides a steady rhythm. How fast we breathe is a rhythm that is in relation to our heartbeat. Our human voices arise from within us and we give birth to sound. Through the sound of our voices we can bring comfort and joy to one another. The vibrating strings of the harp offer soothing sound in a noninvasive way that is gentle yet penetrating. We are trained as music-thanatologists to be responsive to the changing states of the patient. No two musical deliveries are ever the same. Sometimes a patient might need pure melody with major tonalities. Recorded music from a CD or tape can be helpful, but lacks the overtones of live music and does not have the same presence or healing effect. Patients respond more directly and deeply (even when unconscious) to the tones of harp and voice played at the bedside. Our goal is to lovingly serve the physical and spiritual needs of the dying through the delivery of prescriptive music.

"It was a miracle! The minute the harp started my mother began to relax and sleep. It was the greatest blessing to us ever."

Why do we use harps?

The harp is an ancient instrument made from the wood of certain trees. Many, many stories and myths from various cultures are told about the harp and its magical qualities. Just as a tree stretches from earth to heaven, as if holding the two together, so the strings of the harp stretch up and down and symbolically represent a connection between this life on earth and whatever might come before or after this life. It is also important that the folk harp is a polyphonic instrument that is portable enough to be easily transported, and its pure tones are among the most beautiful of any musical instrument.

Description of service

Using harp and voice, music is shared at the bedside to create an atmosphere of reverence and loving kindness. This musical medicine can stimulate or soothe processes in the physical body; these processes, in turn, affect emotional, spiritual, and psychic levels, as evidenced by decreased pain, reduced physical and emotional anxiety, and deep sleep. Through observations of vital signs and the focus on breathing patterns of the individual, the music is synchronized to resonate with the person's individualized needs, making each session a unique and sacred one.

Death bed vigils

Musical medicine addresses anxiety, spiritual and physical pain, and issues of grief and letting go. It can support the unbinding process, inviting in sacred grace, which can facilitate a peaceful death. It is contemplative, sacred music that seeks to transcend diverse affiliations of faith and culture. Vigil music is prescriptive music because it is played to assist the patient's specific condition and situation, and the music changes as the patient's respiration, pulse, physical, and emotional states change. Alternating sound and silence allows for a sense of expansion and contemplation. A vigil, which lasts about an hour, is recommended when a patient has a prognosis of six months or less, has a Do Not Resuscitate (DNR) order, and is receiving palliative care (treatment for the relief of pain and promotion of quality of life). The music is also beneficial when a patient is being removed from artificial life support systems. It helps bridge the gap between the sounds of the machines and the silence that follows. In the months before an inevitable death, it is often helpful to the patient to schedule vigils at regular intervals, which brings an element of beauty and blessing into their lives. This offers patients and loved ones something meaningful and specific when medical technology is no longer beneficial.

The music can help the patient and their family and friends process the reality of an approaching death, and help them to find peace in the midst of loss.

"To say thank you is not enough for what a wonderful gift you gave my mom, and my family and friends. The music inspired us, gave us strength, and got us through. How beautiful!"

Support of grieving processes

Sacred music can help free emotions locked within the body, allowing the work of grieving to take place. Music in the room can help people access a whole range of feelings that most of us don't know how to articulate in words; and yet it is gentle, safe, and comforting.

~ Jeri Howe

When music is desired at the bedside, hospice staff can sometimes arrange for it. Some hospices have music volunteers whose visits are free. Other music is often available on a sliding scale. You might check with your medical institution to see if funding might be provided for this service or suggest to friends that musical medicine could be a gift in lieu of flowers or candy.

Sacred Harmonies is based in Seattle, Washington.
P.O. Box 60213, Shoreline, WA 98160-0213. sacredharmony@earthlink.net
For a national website, see http://www.music-thanatologyassociation.com.

Shakuhachi Flute Healing Music and the Dying Process

I have heard that the *shakuhachi* flute is considered not unlike the harp in our culture, as it is an instrument that carries people into the next realm. So I was delighted to learn about a Canadian artist named Debbie Danbrook who plays the shakuhachi; I learned about her through another Canadian woman who was visiting my neighbor thanks to an international organization called Women Welcome Women World Wide.

At the age of 97 my dad was more than ready to die. He had been gradually letting go over the five years since my mom and his wife of 57 years had died. Dad was a great father; loving, fun, supportive and calmly content with his lot in life. We had had a wonderful relationship and the love I felt for him was simple and clear. As his health deteriorated and he had to give up the little pleasures in life I felt my heart aching more and more for him. The last year became increasingly sad. I would talk to dad each night and he often sounded like his self of old when we spoke on the phone but each visit showed him weakened and more distant, so frail.

Often family and friends feel helpless around a dying loved one. I am very lucky to have the gift of music in my life and I was able to play my *shakuhachi* flute each time I visited with my dad. I could see how he enjoyed my playing and how he would relax and often drift off into a light sleep as the music wrapped itself around him. At night, the wonderful staff at his retirement home would put one of my CDs on for him to go to sleep by. It was such a comfort to me to know that I was in some small way helping him during this last process--the dying process--that he was going through.

I needed and wanted to give dad a final, parting gift. I felt compelled to record a CD of music for him. While recording the songs, all improvised, I felt a channel of light, clear and strong, opening as a gateway for my dad. I felt that I was here but not here as this music flowed through me. It was the music of my heart connecting for the last time on this earth with the heart of my dad through our guides, our angels. I was able to play this recording one time for my dad. I sat there holding his hand, knowing that this would be the only time that he would hear this Sacred Sounds for the Soul while in his earthly body.

Dad was asleep most of the time now. On my last visit I played my flute for him and he awoke and beckoned me over. In a clear and surprisingly loud voice he said his last words to me. "You are a good flute player."

Thank you, dad, for being my greatest fan. I love you.

~ Debbie Danbrook

The "Sacred Sounds for the Soul" CD has been embraced by the palliative care community. For more information on the music of Debbie Danbrook, please go to her website: www.healingmusic.com.

There are now a number of organizations which prepare musicians to be at the bedside with those who are dying. The following are some of the better-known training organizations:

Music for Healing and Transition Program, Inc. www.MHTP.org
American Music Therapy Association www.musictherapy.org
Chalice of Repose Project www.chaliceofrepose.org
International Harp Therapy Program www.harprealm.com
The Clinical Musician's Home Study Course www.laurieriley.com
International Healing Musician's Program www.healingmusician.com
Bedside Harp www.bedsideharp.com

資

Theta Healing

Theta healing was introduced to me through a friend of a friend who did a healing with me as I was writing this book. He worked with my belief systems, helping me let go of beliefs that no longer served me and bring in new beliefs that could help me in the present.

Theta healing was developed by Vianna Stibal, herself a medical intuitive, who had developed leukemia in 1995. She was determined to heal, and through a fortuitous sequence of events, found this technique that allowed her to work directly with God and heal herself. She has written two books, *Go Up and Seek God* and *Go Up and Work with God.* You can learn more about her and theta healing at www.thetahealing.com.

Donna Baverman and Asara Lovejoy are theta healers in the Puget Sound Area. Donna can be reached at (360) 929-8458 or (360) 222-3134. Asara can be reached through www.asara.com.

Transformative Health Studies

Maggie Seymour is a friend and healer on Whidbey Island who is sharing her own style of healing work with the world at this time. The following is a short description of what she does.

A terminal cancer diagnosis is not the end of your life. The Transformative Health Studies [THS] cancer treatment program brings stage IV cancer patients into remission without surgery, chemotherapy, or radiation. Using the inherent capacity of the mind-body connection, individuals meet with me one on one for a series of psycho-social-spiritual interventions. During these sessions I assist you in both identifying the underlying cause of the disease and in developing your program of treatment that results in personal transformation. Personal transformation usually coincides with the onset of remission.

Alternative therapies for cancer treatment have been researched by leading oncologists for years. Individual stories have been published documenting case after case of seemingly spontaneous remission achieved by men and women given cancer diagnoses. I assist you to achieve this same result. To begin, we talk on the phone and then meet for an evaluation session prior to initiating the treatment program. Upon completion of our treatment sessions, an exam by your oncologist will confirm the results of our work.

The treatment fee is established by a sliding scale based upon family income. Post treatment sessions and ongoing participation in a group are recommended, but optional. Fees for these sessions are in addition to the treatment fee. If you have questions or want more information, please visit my website or request a brochure. Maggie@transformhealth.org; www.transformhealth.org.

~ Maggie Seymour

Watsu Massage

Watsu is an increasingly popular form of bodywork/therapy. It involves being cradled in a warm body of water by a Watsu-certified therapist who gently stretches and guides your body through a series of flowing movements. My first and only time to experience Watsu so far was in Hawai'i, and it felt like my practitioner was guiding us as we danced in the water. We were preparing to swim with the dolphins in a bay where the water becomes very deep very quickly, and our facilitator wanted us to have a "safe and secure" frame of reference that we could return to in the water, when necessary. I remember it as a most delightful and relaxing experience.

Watsu was developed in California in the 1980s. It has now become a popular stress reduction method used at health spas in many parts of the United States. It is also used in some rehabilitation centers to treat people with problems ranging from muscle and joint injuries to stroke and cerebral palsy. To find a practitioner, go to www.waba.edu (Worldwide Aquatic Bodywork Association).

Yoga and the Power of Physical Relaxation

I remember when my mother learned to live with lung cancer toward the end of her life. One of the things that helped her a great deal was yoga. She had lived as a fairly traditional Christian, but being a missionary in Japan had opened her eyes. She came to understand that she had things to learn from "other traditions" as well. She also became a fan of Joseph Campbell in those days, and together we watched the mythology series for which Bill Moyers had interviewed him.

Yoga classes opened Mom up to receive strength and renewed energy from her own body. I watched her find comfort in breathing more deeply as she stretched and learned to nourish her lungs, not to mention the rest of her body.

The practice of yoga, which is is more than 6,000 years old, has its roots in ancient East Indian philosophies. It is a spiritual tradition whose purpose is to lead us to discover our true nature. It deeply honors the union of body, mind, and spirit, and in its pure form it can alter consciousness. It literally means "the science of union with the Divine," and its original goals were the liberation of the body from earthly desires and the quieting of the mind. It helps one develop "breath awareness" and can bring a person to their natural state of equilibrium.

Today, Hatha Yoga ("Yoga for strength") is the yoga most commonly practiced here in the West. Yoga body postures, stretching, and breathing exercises have both preventative and curative value, and they help to fortify a person against stress. Therefore, practicing yoga can be especially helpful for people dealing with most illnesses as well as stress-related disorders, such as hypertension, diabetes, asthma, and obesity.

It is interesting to note that a posture that is often practiced at the end of a yoga class (sometimes along with a guided meditation by the instructor) is called the Savasana, or Corpse Pose. In this posture, the body is lying on the floor as motionless as a corpse, in total relaxation. This pose allows one's organs of perception (eyes, ears, tongue) to withdraw from the outer world. The body and mind merge into one, and an inner silence can be experienced. This is the beginning step for the practice of meditation. As my current yoga teacher suggests, this is a pose in which one can "practice death."

For more information online, go to: http://www.yogainternational.com.

Recommended reading:

Iyengar, B.K.S. *Yoga: The Path to Holistic Health.* New York: Dorling Kindersley Publishing, 2001. (This large book has lots of pictures and descriptions of the postures, also their correlation to your body health.)

Lad, Vasant, M.A.Sc., Dr. *Ayurveda: The Science of Self-Healing.* WI: Lotus Press, 1990.

Lidell, Lucy. *The Sivananda Companion to Yoga.* Simon & Schuster Adult Publishing Group, 2000.

Radha, Swami Sivananda. *Hatha Yoga: The Hidden Language.* Timeless Books, 1996.

Satchidananda, Sri Swami (trans. and commentary). *The Yoga Sutras of Patanjali.* Las Vegas, NV: Brotherhood of Life, Inc., 1993.

At the hour of death, when the body is disintegrating, we only have
our inner resources to fall back on.
All of yoga…is preparation for our final hour on earth.
It matters how we exit from life, because death is only a doorway
to another state of existence.

~ Georg Feuerstein

All shall be well,
and all shall be well,
and all manner of thing shall be well.

~ Julian of Norwich

Afterword

READERS OF the first edition of my book have asked for two explanations. In response, I'd like first to explain how the name "Dancing Heart" came to bless my life, and then to share some of my reflections on the divine mystery of life and death.

My daughter Heather has never particularly liked going to church. During the last months of 1999, a healer and ceremonialist friend of ours named Starfeather began a light-worker's circle for the healing of Mother Earth. It was kind of an "experiment" to help us all support the Earth through the end of the millennium. The gatherings were held once a month, on the evening of every first Friday. Heather and I began attending, and I recall Heather specifically letting me know that she enjoyed attending these gatherings more than she liked going to church.

I've always sensed my daughter's wisdom and I like to support and honor what works spiritually for her as much as possible. We continued to attend the light-worker circles, and they continued to take place well into the new millennium. We would always begin the circle by going around the circle, introducing ourselves by name and adding a piece to the opening prayer, if we so desired. One Friday night when we were just beginning the circle, I remember thinking to myself, "I'd like to have a Native American name, just like many here in our circle have." Almost immediately after having that thought, the name "Dancing Heart" popped into my head. As I recall, I heard the name just in time to share it as we went around the room.

I began using it regularly in circle, adopting it as my new "circle name." And what a perfect name it turned out to be for me, as I've been working on healing from a series of betrayals in the first half of my life; the name helps me open the heart that's been closed. Spirit certainly has a way of knowing exactly what we need… I'm finding myself living into my "dancing heart" as I midwife deeper and deeper healing in my midlife years.

Some years later, as I was preparing to put this book together, it occurred to me that I already had the perfect pen name for myself. What a delight to have this joy-filled name, and to be living into it more fully as I move forward in my life; thank you, Dear Spirit!

God/Goddess/All That Is has unconditional, unlimited love for all human life on earth, that which is born and that which is unborn. God fully accepts each one of us exactly as we are and where we are; we have been given the gift of free will. During the course of history, humanity has been sent many prophets and visionaries who have shown us "the way" to live on earth. For me, Jesus the Christ stands out as the most sterling example – the one I know best and choose to follow – the one with whom I have developed the strongest personal relationship. There are also universal laws that are in operation on the planet. The Law of Attraction is one example; therefore, "what goes around comes around!" We can be sure that we will reap what we sow on this earth, sooner or later. (I have found the book *The Light Shall Set you Free* [Milanovich and McCune 1996] most helpful in this regard.)

When we leave our bodies and this earthly life, we are joyously welcomed home, back to the other side, in God's all-encompassing arms. However, for those who have things to hide and who are not ready to "move into the light," it's likely that they will remain in the darkness for some time – perhaps until they are ready to return to God and the Light. Our life will go on in spirit form, although we cannot see exactly how while we are on the earth. As we leave this earth behind, those who are "left behind" may feel a tremendous sense of loss. But in some incredible way, we are all connected, and we will in time "see" and be with one another again. As we trust in the interconnectedness of all, and in God's care for each and every one of us, we will continue to remain safe and secure. There is absolutely nothing to fear. Only love is real, true, and lasting.

In closing, I would like to share with you my all-time favorite hymn. It is a 19th-century Christian hymn that always reminds me of the joy of life, and of the hope of the better place we are moving toward as humanity!

How Can I Keep from Singing

My life goes on in endless song;
Above earth's lamentation,
I hear the real though far-off hymn
That hails a new creation.
Above the tumult and the strife
I hear the music ringing;
It sounds an echo in my soul--
How can I keep from singing?
What though the tempest loudly roars;
I hear the truth, it liveth.
What though the darkness round me close;
Songs in the night, it giveth.
No storm can shake my inmost calm,
While to that rock I'm clinging.

219

Since Love is lord of heaven and earth,
How can I keep from singing?

I lift my eyes; the clouds grow thin.
I see the blue above it.
And day by day, the pathway clears,
Since first I learned to love it.
The peace of God restores my soul,
A fountain ever springing;
All things are mine, since I am loved –
How can I keep from singing?

This hymn can be found in various forms in songbooks and hymnals, including *The New Century Hymnal* published by Pilgrim Press. The music is credited to Baptist minister Robert Lowry; words are by Anne Warner and Doris Plenn.

It just may occur that, as you learn to handle death and rebirth,
you might learn to handle life in the process. This is unavoidable,
and if by chance you do happen to handle life better because of it,
don't despair; you'll never get out of it alive.

~ E. J. Gold, *American Book of the Dead*

Annotated Bibliography

• Articles • Books • Books for Caregivers • Magazines and Journals • Music •
Tapes • Videos and DVDs • Websites •

Articles

"A Triumph Over Cancer: Facing a Terminal Diagnosis, One Woman Beat the Odds with a Deceptively Simple Eating Plan," Portland Halmich. *Alternative Medicine,* Sept. 2004 (61–64).

"Culture and the End of Life: A Review of Major World Religions," Charles Kemp, CRNH, FNP-C; Sonal Bhungalia, BSN, RN. *Journal of Hospice and Palliative Nursing,* Vol. 4, No. 4, Oct.–Dec. 2002.

Books

Albom, Mitch. *Tuesdays with Morrie: An Old Man, a Young Man, and Life's Greatest Lesson.* New York: Doubleday, 1997. This work was televised and has become quite well known. It is the story of a professor and his student who decide to meet regularly on Tuesdays, after the professor, Morrie, discovers he has ALS, or Lou Gehrig's disease. Bernie Siegel writes: "This book is an incredible treasure. One's sense of mortality is a great teacher and source of enlightenment. To have a teacher share this experience provides us with profound wisdom and insight. I laughed, cried, and ordered five copies for our children." Albom has published additional excellent books, including *The Five People You Meet in Heaven* and *For One More Day.*

Altea, Rosemary. *The Eagle and the Rose: A Remarkable True Story.* New York: Warner Books, 1995. This is a autobiography of a woman with psychic gifts who was at first very skeptical about them. In her mid-thirties she was introduced to some people who gradually helped her develop her gifts, and she has now become a world-renowned psychic. Altea also shares case studies of some of the many people she has helped to heal through her ability to connect the spirits of this world with those on the other side.

Anam Aire, Phyllida. *A Celtic Book of Dying: Watching with the Dying, Traveling with the Dead.* Scotland, UK: Findhorn Press, 2005. I am indebted to Phyllida for helping me find Findhorn Press who is now helping publish the 2nd edition of my book. I happened upon this transformative work online one day, and thought that if Findhorn was interested in publishing this kind of book, they might be interested in my work as well.

Phyllida Anam-Aire is a former nun and mother of two, a singer, bridge-builder between life and death, and "carer of the soul." Through her own experiences of grief, she has touched the depths of sorrow and release. Through her Irish background she learned earth wisdom and the gifts the Celtic Goddess Brigit offers to all who stand at and work in the Threshold. I highly recommend this practical work full of Celtic tools and understanding of how death connects us to life. (See pp. 113–115 for a magnificent Incantation for the Dead Person.)

Andrews, Ted. *Animal-Speak: The Spiritual & Magical Powers of Creatures Great and Small*. St. Paul, MN: Llewellyn Publications, 1993. Andrews, a volunteer and worker in animal rehabilitation, shares his expertise on the animal kingdom in this resource book. This book will help you meet and understand 45 animals, 60 birds, eight insects, and six reptiles as possible totems in your life. By learning their behaviors and symbolism in the physical world, you will be able to come to appreciate the signs and meanings they bring to you when they show up in your life.

Arnold, Johann Christoph. *I Tell You a Mystery: Life, Death, and Eternity*. Farmington, PA: The Plough Publishing House, 1996. Arnold has taken his title from I Corinthians 15:51: "Lo! I tell you a mystery. We shall not all sleep, but we shall all be changed." He draws from stories of the people he has known as pastor and elder in the Bruderhof communities, sharing how suffering can be worked through and meaning found, even in the most challenging of situations. This book has beautiful pictures and vignettes taken directly from communities of people who live out their faith in a unique and thoughtful manner in the U.S. and in England. In 2002 Christoph published another thoughtful book on death called *Be Not Afraid: Overcoming the Fear of Death* (also Plough Publishing).

Babbitt, Natalie. *Tuck Everlasting*. New York: Mirasol, 1993. This is a thought-provoking fantasy intended for young people, but it's really a good read for adults as well. When Winnie, an overly-protected child, meets the Tuck family and falls in love with one of their sons, her life is changed forever. The family members have inadvertently drunk from a well that freezes them in time and gives them everlasting life. The plot thickens as a malicious character learns about their secret. This book can help us view death from a different vantage point, allowing us to open up to the gift that it really is. (This is also out in a film by the same name.)

Beck, Martha. *Finding Your Own North Star: Claiming the Life You Were Meant to Live*. New York: Three Rivers Press, 2002. A monthly columnist for *O: The Oprah Magazine*, Dr. Beck has been a teacher of career development. In this book she shares a practical program that can help you take the journey to your ideal life. She incorporates case studies, questionnaires and exercises to guide you to read your internal compass, nurture your intuition, cultivate your dreams, and much more.

Bennett, Rita. *To Heaven and Back: True Stories of Those Who Have Made the Journey*. Grand Rapids, MI: Zondervan Publishing House, 1997. Bennett is an Episcopalian laywoman who has been active in "spiritual renewal" since 1960. In this book she approaches the near-death experience from a biblical perspective. She tells stories of Christians whose NDEs deepened their faith, and of non-Christians who were converted through such an experience. Bennett also explores the scriptures and shares a biblical view of heaven and the afterlife.

Benson, Herbert, M.D., with Marg Stark. *Timeless Healing: The Power and Biology of Belief*. New York: Scribner, 1996. Benson shows his readers that science and faith share a powerful path to wellness. No matter what our spiritual path or who the deity, belief helps us to transcend and heal our human struggles. This book synthesizes and expands on Benson's earlier works on the power of meditation, such as The Relaxation Response and The Mind/Body Effect.

Bernard, Jan Selliken, R.N., and Miriam Schneider, R.N., CRNH. *The True Work of Dying: A Practical and Compassionate Guide to Easing the Dying Process*. New York: Avon Books, 1996. A book by two hospice nurses in Portland, Oregon, who call their business Angels Work. They look at death in light of the birthing experience and see their hospice work as synonymous with being midwives in the "deathing" experience. They share cases from their firsthand experiences, reflecting on the physical, emotional, and spiritual aspects of care and healing. They include topics such as spirituality and death, ritual, and pain management.

Borysenko, Joan, Ph.D. *Guilt Is the Teacher, Love Is the Lesson.* **New York: Warner Books, Inc., 1990.**
In this healing, life-affirming book, Borysenko reaches out to the wounded parts of our souls and offers us new ways to approach and heal guilt and blame. She helps to free our inner child from shame in all its guises: fear of success or failure, alcoholism, workism, bitterness, etc. There is ancient wisdom here that can guide us all in the healing process. This book is highly recommended for anyone who struggles with guilt.

Brinkley, Dannion. *At Peace in the Light: The Further Adventures of a Reluctant Psychic Who Reveals the Secret of Your Spiritual Powers.* **New York: HarperCollins Publishers, Inc., 1995.**
This is Brinkley's second book, in which he writes about how he has been affected by his two near-death experiences. After a great deal of work toward healing, he now believes that his mission is to serve those who are getting ready to die. He goes into some detail about his healing work with hospice patients—e.g., how he helps them share their life reviews, techniques he uses with their energy and breathing, and so forth.

Brown, Erica. *Happier Endings: A Meditation on Life and Death.* **New York: Simon & Schuster, 2013.**
A remarkably practical book covering a wide range of topics related to death and our culture, by a young Jewish religious scholar. See: www.ericabrown.com

Brown, Rebecca. *The Gifts of the Body.* **New York: Harper Collins, 1994.**
Brown is a former home-care worker who writes sensitively and movingly about the details of taking care of people with AIDS. This is a "brave, true story about dying and death, in language so sparse and direct that you don't notice its power until your stomach knots and your eyes fill with tears."

Browne, Sylvia. *Mother God: The Feminine Principle to Our Creator.* **Carlsbad, CA: Hay House, Inc., 2004.**
Renowned psychic Sylvia Browne, who is also the founder of the Society of Novus Spiritus, explores the divine feminine in this book that is so needed in our time. She begins by examining the evidence of the feminine principle in the major religions. Then she moves into describing who exactly "Mother God" is, and the experiences many are having as a result of petitioning her. She closes the book with answers to frequently-asked questions, letters and stories from her readers, and prayers and meditations.

Browne, Sylvia. *The Other Side and Back: A Psychic's Guide to Our World and Beyond.* **New York: Penguin Putnam Inc., 1999.**
Having worked as a psychic and spiritual teacher for 47 years, Browne has convinced many of the existence of the other side. In this book she shows how psychic energy works and how it can be used as a tool for deepening our spirituality and our faith, not to mention creating more joy in our lives. Her first chapter describes the kind of help we have from the other side from our angels and spirit guides.

Brussat, Frederic and Mary Ann. *Spiritual Literacy: Reading the Sacred in Everyday Life.* **New York: Scribner, 1996.**
This book provided me with the inspiration to write my book. The Brussats have compiled quite a collection of material from all walks of spiritual life and put it together in chapters representing aspects of life—things, places, nature, animals, creativity, relationships, and so on. They have also put together an "alphabet of spiritual literacy" that they develop throughout the book. I appreciate their universal and unifying perspective that is so needed in our world today. The Brussats are also the media and web editors for Spirituality and Health magazine. See www.spiritualityhealth.com

Buechner, Frederick. *Listening to Your Life: Daily Meditations with Frederick Buechner,* compiled by George Connor. New York: HarperSanFrancisco, 1992. This is a collection of 366 inspirational quotations, one for every day of the year, from the writings of novelist and preacher Frederick Buechner. Buechner's friend, George Connor, Professor Emeritus of the University of Tennessee, culled the pieces for this gem of a devotional book.

Buechner, Frederick. *Whistling in the Dark: A Doubter's Dictionary (or, Whistling in the Dark: An ABC Theologized).* New York: HarperCollins, 1998/1993. One of the more than 20 novels and nonfiction works that Presbyterian minister and storyteller Buechner has authored, this work is a dictionary of terms. In Buechner's own words, his idea was "to take a series of just ordinary words…and to try to listen to them in some of the same ways that I am suggesting one listens to one's own life to hear what lies beneath the surface of perfectly everyday words standing for perfectly everyday experiences."

Bunick, Nick. *Transitions of the Soul: True Stories from Ordinary People.* Charlottesville, VA: Hampton Roads Publishing Company, Inc., 2001. This collection comes through Bunick, the subject of a book called The Messengers, a true story about an international businessman who discovered his spiritual purpose on earth and changed his life dramatically. Here, Nick has collected mystical and miraculous stories of ordinary people who have had their loved ones come from the other side to let them know they are still with them. It is reminiscent of the book Hello from Heaven, by Bill and Judy Guggenheim.

Byock, Ira, M.D. *Dying Well: The Prospect for Growth at the End of Life.* New York: Riverhead Books, 1997. Byock is president of the American Academy of Hospice and Palliative Medicine. He shares numerous stories throughout the book from his own professional and personal experience, including being a part of his own father's dying process. He believes that the possibility for us all to "die well" is just around the corner: "The day is at hand when no pain among the dying will be considered unmanageable." (See also Byock's newer book, *The Four Things that Matter Most.*)

Caine, Kenneth Winston and Brian Paul Kaufman. *Prayer, Faith, and Healing: Cure Your Body, Heal Your Mind, and Restore Your Soul.* New York: Rodale, Inc., 1999. This is a book I found in the home of one of our hospice patients. I like the openness with which it introduces a variety of prayer methods and spiritual practices that express the Christian faith. It includes advice from many religious leaders, counselors, doctors, and scientists in the United States. Dr. Bernie Siegel shares his thoughts on prayer and love in the foreword.

Callanan, Maggie and Patricia Kelley. *Final Gifts: Understanding the Special Awareness, Needs, and Communications of the Dying.* New York: Poseidon Press, 1992. This a mystical, astonishing book, which will bring tears to your eyes. It is by two hospice nurses, about their experiences with the dying and their loved ones. It will help you understand why hospice workers consider ourselves so fortunate. This is really a "must read" for anyone who is works with hospice.

Chödrön, Pema. *The Places That Scare You: A Guide to Fearlessness in Difficult Times.* Boston: Shambhala Publications, Inc., 2001. Chödrön, an American Buddhist nun, encourages us to move toward the places that scare us. Her message is that we always have a choice about how we handle the challenging circumstances of our lives, and that we can use our challenges to open us up to become more loving, courageous, flexible people. She has a whole chapter dedicated to the meditation practice of Tonglen, a practice for activating loving-kindness and compassion for those who are suffering.

Clark, Dawn E. *Gifts for the Soul: A Guided Journey of Discovery, Transformation and Infinite Possibilities.* **Houston, TX: Aarron Publishing, 1999-2001.**
> This beautiful story is by the founder of the Center for New Beginnings, a healer who uses many modalities of healing in her work. Along the way, she was shown a new way using symbols (pictures) that would empower people to heal themselves. I invite you to read for yourself some of the simple ways in which people are learning to heal and move forward in constructive ways.

Cohen, Kenneth. *Honoring the Medicine: The Essential Guide to Native American Healing.* **New York: Random House, Inc. (A One World Book), 2003.**
> Kenneth "Bear Hawk" Cohen, an internationally-renowned health educator dedicated to the Community of All Relations, has compiled this magnificent work to help us reconnect with traditional ways for healing the earth and ourselves. I am especially drawn to Chapters One (The Power of Silence) and Nine (Cultivating the Good Mind). He includes material on the vision quest, moontime rituals, energy therapies and the need for touch, the benefits of ancient purification ceremonies such as the Sweat Lodge, the purpose of smudging, fasting, and chanting, and many other modes of healing connected to Native American traditions.

Cope, Denys, RN, BSN. *Dying: A Natural Passage.* **Santa Fe, NM: Three Whales Publishing, LLC, 2008.** (www.beyondcoping.com)

Dalai Lama, His Holiness the. Translated and edited by Jeffrey Hopkins, Ph.D. *Advice on Dying: And Living a Better Life.* **New York: Atria Books (Simon & Schuster, Inc.), 2002.**
> The Tibetans have a saying, "Everyone dies, but no one is dead." His Holiness the Dalai Lama fully embraces it in this little book that bases an exploration of the stages of death on a 17th-century poem. These are the same stages we experience when we go to sleep, faint, or even when we reach orgasm. By helping to prepare us for a death without fear or upset, the Dalai Lama also teaches us how to enrich our time here on earth.

Dass, Ram. *Still Here: Embracing Aging, Changing, and Dying.* **New York: Riverhead Books, 2000.**
> Ram Dass, a visionary and spiritual teacher who has been through and amazing life of twists and turns, published this collection after his own close encounter with death. He was woven together material from his personal experiences and talks he's given on conscious aging. In this gem of a book, he has included chapters on, for example, "Old Mind, New Mind," "The Body in Question," and "Learning to Die."

Davis, Lance L., M.D., MPH, and Albert H. Keller, D.Min. *At the Close of Day: A Person-Centered Guidebook on End-of-Life Care.* **Mt. Pleasant, SC: 2004.**
> This book has a practical "how to" approach to end-of-life care. Lance and Keller share stories and highlights regarding medical and legal concerns to hospice and comfort care concerns from both their medical and spiritual perspectives respectively. They share specific planning aids which help one take proactive steps to minimize fear, pain, and wasted time.

Destefano, Anthony. *Travel Guide to Heaven.* **New York: Doubleday, 2003.**
> This is an interesting and entertaining book, intended for Christian readers. Destefano has put together an idea of what heaven might look like, using the Bible as his guide. He also uses his practical sense of logic, adventure, and fun to help us imagine that this highly spiritual place might actually be quite "physical." He writes in great detail about the kind of place we will find, the kind of people who will be there, what we might do when we get there. In essence, he likens going to heaven to going on a trip and having an "eternal vacation." He shares some of his own physical journeys along the way to describe what the adventure of getting to our "final destination" might be like.

Didion, Joan. *The Year of Magical Thinking.* **New York: Knopf Publishing, 2005.**
> My stepmother called my attention to this book which is receiving rave reviews. Joan shares her deep grief after losing her husband in late 2003, having spent months at the side of her hospitalized

daughter. She not only shares the story of her personal grief, but the struggle our entire culture has with being up-close with death and mourning.

Dyer, Wayne W. Dr. *Your Sacred Self: Making the Decision to Be Free.* New York: HarperCollins Publishers, 1995. "Wayne Dyer takes us on a sacred journey where the spirit triumphs over the ego. This book will serve as an extremely valuable guide to all those who seek the exultation of the spiritual experience and who value total freedom as the ultimate goal of life." (Deepak Chopra).

Eadie, Betty Jean. *Embraced by the Light.* Placerville, CA: Gold Leaf Press, 1992. Eadie, daughter of a Sioux mother, raised Mormon, shares her near-death experience that happened after a hysterectomy she had when she was 31 years old. This is one of the most detailed accounts of an NDE anyone has recorded in recent history. I was deeply comforted by reading this book after it was published, a few years after my mother's death. Although I knew my mother's spirit was fine, it was meaningful to get a fuller picture of where she is now, and how she is, and what she might be doing. I frequently recommend this book to our hospice patients. Many have said that it's a book that has changed their lives. Its message is that we are here on earth to "grow in love."

Eldredge, John. *The Journey of Desire: Searching for the Life We've Only Dreamed Of.* Nashville, TN: Thomas Nelson Publishers, 2000. This is a reflective book about living a Christian life in the midst of paradox, the contradictions of life. Eldredge shares some deeply personal and painful experiences around loss and death throughout the book. He also challenges us to remember and follow our deep, God-given desire in the journey of life, something Jesus encouraged people to do by taking them "into their hearts."

Elison, Jennifer and Chris McGonigle. *Liberating Losses: When Death Brings Relief.* Cambridge, MA: Perseus Publishing, 2003. This groundbreaking work examines life situations when the one "left behind" is expected to grieve, yet is not sad. Instead, he or she may feel a combination of relief, happiness, and even hope and joy due to the liberation they are experiencing. In a culture that is able to keep people alive much longer than was previously possible, these feelings are becoming more common. Jennifer's husband died in a car accident after she told him that she intended to divorce him; Chris's husband died after living with MS for fifteen years. Their intimate sharing and insights will offer comfort and new understanding to many. Elison serves as a grief and transition counselor. McGonigle is an author who has also written Surviving Your Spouse's Chronic Illness.

Fischer, William L. *How to Fight Cancer & Win.* Baltimore, MD: Agora Health Books, 2000. The subtitle for this book is Scientific guidelines and documented facts for the successful treatment and prevention of cancer and other related health problems. It is a book full of information on cancer and how to work with it using diet, visualization, eminent doctors and alternative cancer treatments, and prevention (including avoidable carcinogens). It is written for the layperson, presented in a practical, easy-to-read manner. Fischer has been involved in medicine, health care, and natural healing for over 30 years. He worked with some large pharmaceutical manufacturers in his native Germany before moving to the U.S., where he has been publishing books on natural healing.

Foos-Graber, Anya. *Deathing: An Intelligent Alternative for the Final Moments of Life.* York Beach, Maine: Nicolas-Hays, Inc., 1989. In this book Foos-Graber compares and contrasts a conscious death with an unconscious death. She also shares techniques for preparing for a conscious death. This is a rather "advanced" book.

Frissell, Bob. *Something in This Book Is True*. Berkeley, CA: Frog, Ltd., 1997, 2003. Frissell has put together a training manual for navigating a future full of danger and hope. This work considers earth changes, pole shifts, Hopi prophecies, the secret government, and more. Bob uses a warm, personal style in this second book (the first is *Nothing in This Book Is True, but It's Exactly How Things Are*). He includes topics such as polarity consciousness, emotional body clearing, and higher selves, and makes it clear to the reader that humans are spiritual beings having a human experience.

Ganeri, Anita. *Journey's End: Death and Mourning*. New York: Peter Bedrick Books, 1998. This is one of a four-book (Life Times) series regarding rites of passage of six major world religions. The book takes a look at how people from the Hindu, Buddhist, Sikh, Jewish, Christian, and Muslim faiths mourn the deaths of their loved ones. It includes rites, rituals, and beliefs surrounding death and dying. The book is written in plain language, using stories and legends, so young people can also read and understand it. It includes beautiful illustrations and photographs.

Gerard, Vicki. *There's No Place Like Hope: A Guide to Beating Cancer in Mind-Sized Bites*. Lynnwood, WA: Compendium, Inc., 2001. Gerard has had quite a journey since 1992 when she was told to get her affairs in order, as she was diagnosed with Stage Four breast cancer. She not only fought her cancer and survived it, but also became a tireless patient advocate, speaker and writer, traveling the nation while working with medical staff and cancer support groups. In her book she shares various practical aspects of what she learned in her own journey, from diagnosis to survivor's guilt.

Ginsburg, Genevieve David, M.S. *Widow to Widow: Thoughtful, Practical Ideas for Rebuilding Your Life*. Cambridge, MA: Fisher Books, 1995. Ginsburg lost her husband suddenly one day as he was playing tennis. She has since founded Widow to Widow Services, located in Tucson, Arizona. She is an author and therapist whose book offers practical and detailed information that could help any widow or family member of a widow.

Gold, E. J. *American Book of the Dead*. Nevada City, CA: Gateway Books and Tapes, 1999 (25th Anniversary Edition). Gold, an author, teacher, and painter, has written a "consciousness classic" to help any "voyager" on earth, not just the dying, wake up from our slumber and live in fuller consciousness. He shares his art as well as instructions and readings that could be used with those who are actually transitioning to the other side (in keeping with The Tibetan Book of the Dead). His editor suggests that "if we are able to make this voyager's book our own, we may be able to bring its trans-dimensional technology… to be of service to other voyagers as well as ourselves."

Goldberg, Bruce. *Peaceful Transition: The Art of Conscious Dying and the Liberation of the Soul*. St. Paul, MN: Llewellyn Publications, 1997. Dr. Goldberg, a clinical hypnotherapist, is a strong proponent of conscious dying. In this book he covers many topics, including near death experiences, the stages of dying, out-of-body experiences, and the moment of death. He also shares some historical approaches to conscious dying, taking a look at the Tibetan and Egyptian Books of the Dead, Greek Mystery Schools, Christian Masses, and Emanuel Swedenborg and Theosophy on the topic of death. (see www.drbrucegoldberg.com)

Gowell, Elaine Childs, A.R.N.P, Ph.D. *Good Grief Rituals: Tools for Healing: A Healing Companion*. Barrytown, NY: Stanton Hill Press, 1992. Most of us need to grieve at various times in our lives, and for a variety of reasons. It takes time and energy to do so. Good rituals can help provide new ways for us to grieve. This little book provides creative ideas for rituals that you can use when you want to honor and express your grief. Gowell is a psychiatric nurse practitioner who has a Ph.D. in anthropology. This study has led her to learn about Shamanic Healing Practices from North and South America. See www.goodgriefrituals.com for more information about the author and her book.

Greene, Phyllis. *It Must Have Been Moonglow: Reflections on the First Years of Widowhood*. New York: Villard Books, a division of Random House, Inc., 2001.

Phyllis Greene, the mother of syndicated columnist and author Bob Greene, shares in this "intimate, candid, and engaging memoir" about her experience of losing her partner after 56 years of marriage. She began keeping a diary soon after her husband's death, thanks to a granddaughter who presented her with a beautiful journal. That became the basis for this book, which is not so much about grief as about inspiration, strength, and a new adventure in life.

Groves, Richard F. and Henriette Anne Klauser, Ph.D. *The American Book of Dying: Lessons in Healing Spiritual Pain*. Berkeley, CA: Celestial Arts, 2005.

This is a recently-published book is intended for a friend or companion (*anam cara*) of a dying individual. The first part of the book is a look at the history and background of hospice, beginning with European and Celtic traditions, and including Eastern (Tibetan) traditions as well. The second part includes nine beautiful and varied stories of deaths in which Groves was personally involved. Enneagram archetypes are utilized in these. The third part is a "tool chest" in which 18 traditional healing tools are shared, including breath work, dream work, healing and assistance from ancestors, journaling, and others.

Guggenheim, Bill and Judy. *Hello from Heaven*. New York: Bantam Books, 1995.

This book began when the Guggenheims watched Elisabeth Kübler-Ross on the Donahue Show during the summer of 1976. The book is a collection of 353 accounts of after-death communications (ADCs) of all kinds, beginning with sensing a presence, hearing a voice, feeling a touch, or even smelling a fragrance. In their last chapter, "Love Is Forever," Bill and Judy reflect on how you, too, can move toward experiencing your own ADC, through prayer, meditation, and the like.

Hanh, Thich Nhat. *No death, No fear: Comforting Wisdom for Life*. New York: Riverhead Books (Penguin Putnam Inc.), 2002.

Using a blend of philosophy, magnificent analogies, and guided meditations, Vietnamese monk Thich Naht Hanh takes us through an examination of death, fear, and the nature of existence similar to what Buddhist monastics have been doing for 2500 years. We can come to understand through his teachings that death does not need to be a terrifying ending to this life. In fact, there is no death; and we can be released from our fears about death, and about living, too, for that matter!

Hanson, Warren. *The Next Place*. Golden Valley, MN: Waldman House Press, 1997.

Warren Hanson, writer, designer, musician, and illustrator, has put together this beautiful children's book to share an inspirational journey of light and hope for those who have lost a loved one. One suicide survivor writes that "this book has given our grief a voice where we were all struggling for words." It has brought comfort and meaningful tears to many readers, young and old alike.

Hayasaki, Erika. *The Death Class: A Story About Life*. New York: Simon & Schuster, 2014.

By following a popular "death class" teacher for over four years, Hayasaki, an award-winning journalist "shows how Norma steers four of her extraordinary students from their tormented families and neighborhoods toward happiness." See www.thedeathclass.com

Hickman, Martha Whitmore. *Healing After Loss: Daily Meditations for Working Through Grief*. New York: Avon Books, Inc., 1994.

This is a wonderful little collection of meditations, quotes, and affirmations—one for every day of the year—for anyone who is grieving. My stepmother used it after my father died and found it most helpful.

Ingerman, Sandra. *Soul Retrieval: Mending the Fragmented Self.* **Harper San Francisco, 1991.**
   In this book Ingerman describes the ancient shamanic healing method of soul retrieval and how she has applied it in our culture today to heal emotional and physical trauma. It is a wonderful introduction for those who wish to learn more about shamanism and soul retrieval. If you wish to read a "second part," see another title by Ingerman: *Welcome Home.*

Jeffers, Susan, Ph.D. *End the Struggle and Dance with Life: How to Build Yourself Up When the World Gets You Down.* **New York: St. Martin's Press, 1996.**
   I was introduced to this book by a family member who is learning to live with cancer. Jeffers outlines in her book ways people can change their attitudes toward the struggles and challenges in their lives. She works with themes such as "rising above the clouds," "releasing," and "embracing," and gives practical, no-nonsense suggestions on how to bring more joy into our daily lives.

Kabat-Zinn, Jon. *Wherever You Go, There You Are: Mindfulness Meditation in Everyday Life.* **New York: Hyperion, 1994.**
   Kabat-Zinn is the founder and director of the Stress Reduction Clinic at the University of Massachusetts Medicine Center. In this book he maps out a simple way to cultivate meditation (mindfulness) in one's life. This book can speak to beginners as well as seasoned practitioners. He uses short chapters with titles such as "You Have to Be Strong Enough to Be Weak," "Getting Your Body Down on the Floor at Least Once a Day," and "Parenting as Practice" to share his wisdom.

Kagan, Annie. *The Afterlife of Billy Fingers: How My Bad-Boy Brother Proved to Me There's Life After Death.* **Charlottesville, VA: Hampton Roads Publishing Company, Inc., 2013.**
   An extraordinary afterlife experience is shared in this book by the actual sister of a "bad boy" who left the earth through an accident at age 60. See **www.afterlifeofbillyfinger.com**

Kessler, David. *The Rights of the Dying: A Companion for Life's Final Moments.* **New York: HarperCollins Publishing, Inc., 1997.**
   Kessler shares insights and stories out of his extensive experience working with end-of-life issues as a lecturer and consultant. He is founder of the Progressive Home Health Care Agency, a pioneer in the contemporary hospice movement.

Klein, Allen. *The Courage to Laugh: Humor, Hope, and Healing in the Face of Death and Dying.* **New York: Jeremy P. Tarcher/Putnam, 1998.**
   Klein wrote his first book, *The Healing Power of Humor*, after his wife died of a rare liver disease. He calls himself a "jollytologist," lecturing and leading seminars on humor. In this work he presents a compilation of many personal stories taken from his research on death and dying, and he shows the important role that laughter and tears play in the grieving process. Klein stresses that humor need not be used to cover up grief, but that for everyone involved appropriate laughter is a significant tonic in the face of illness and loss. He is never glib. His humorous stories allow for a necessary measure of relief for moments of distress and times of loss. His stories shared with seriously ill children are poignant.

Kornfield, Jack. *A Path with Heart: A Guide through the Perils and Promises of Spiritual Life.* **New York: Bantam Books, 1993.**
   Kornfield shares insights from his experience with Buddhism, including helpful ideas for meditation. The book is also "filled with practical techniques, guided meditations, stories, koans, and other gems of wisdom" that can help enrich our journey through this sometimes perilous world.

Kovacs, Betty J., Ph.D. *The Miracle of Death: There is Nothing but Life—To Experience This Essential Truth Is to Experience the Miracle of Death.* **Claremont, CA: The Kamlak Center, 2003.**
   This book was literally placed in my hands by a friend while I was working on my book. It is one of the most powerful books I have read recently, as it weaves a personal story of one woman's sudden and dramatic losses together with her experience of the mystical and symbolic. Dr.

Kovacs, a professor of literature and mythology, lost her mother, her only son of 20 years, to whom she was very close, and her beloved husband, all through fatal car accidents, and all in the space of four years. She chose not to succumb to a sense of desperation or victimization. Instead, through her interest in dreams and mysticism, and her tremendous faith and courage, Betty came to see these experiences as another doorway. From the other side, her son and husband were able to help her see and connect with a deeper understanding of life and the shift in consciousness that is sweeping the globe today. Thanks to Betty and her family members who are alive and well in another dimension of life, we are given renewed evidence that death is not an end but, rather, the beginning of a new chapter of life. We are also given hope that the whole earth is in a process of profound healing and growth. All of us can participate in this exciting process as we wake up to our connectedness to all, through a new appreciation of "the healing circle of infinite possibilities."

Kramer, Herbert and Kay. *Conversations at Midnight: Coming to Terms with Dying and Death.* New York: William Morrow & Co., Inc., 1993. Ten years into his marriage to Kay, Herb Kramer was diagnosed with incurable, metastatic prostate cancer. This book describes this couple's journey through Herb's last two years of life, as they entered into late night conversations, searching for answers to his many questions. Herb was a communications consultant for service organizations; Kay is a clinical social worker with a private practice.

Kübler-Ross, Elisabeth, M.D. *On Death and Dying: What the Dying Have to Teach Doctors, Nurses, Clergy and Their Own Families.* New York: Macmillan Publishing Co., Inc., 1969. This is that classic book which helped our society come to terms with death and dying on a new level. Kübler-Ross, who took her own last breath in August of 2004, shares the stages of dying and grief in six of the 12 chapters. She uses actual conversations between hospice patients and their doctors and chaplains to illustrate her points. She has written numerous other books, but this is the best known. You may wish to go to her website, www.elisabethkublerross.com, to read more about her, her inspirational work, and the ongoing work related to hospice.

Lamm, Maurice. *The Jewish Way in Death and Mourning.* Middle Village, NY: Jonathan David Publishers, Inc., 1969, 2000. This book was introduced to me by a Jewish friend who told me that she wished she had found it before her father died rather than afterward. It brought her great comfort to discover that her tradition embraced life after death, for example. This work is recognized as a classic, as relevant today as it was when it was published 35 years ago. It is well researched, sensitively written, and it addresses a wide range of issues that have taken on greater significance over the years. The paperback edition claims it to be "one of the ten best Jewish religious books of the year."

Lawson, Lee. *Visitations from the Afterlife: True Stories of Love and Healing.* New York: Harper San Francisco, 2000. Lawson is a painter and storyteller who shares many meaningful "soul stories" in this work. "This book is her love letter across the world, the evidence of a sensitive spiritual life, one that presents the case for amor aeternus, eternal love and unbreakable kinship between souls," writes Clarissa Pinkola Estes. I have shared three of the stories from her book in this book (now also published under the title Love Letters from the Infinite).

Leal-Pock, Carmen. *Faces of Huntington's.* Belleville, Ontario, Canada: Essence Publishing, 1998. One of the diseases I have come to learn about through one of our hospice patients is Huntington's disease. This is a devastating illness that slowly takes over a person's body. It is a hereditary disease, so many families have to deal with several family members going through its ravages. The wife of the man with HD whom I came to know is a closet writer; she was the one who introduced me to this book and its author. Leal-Pock draws upon her own and others' experiences with great sensitivity, courage, and humor. For more information on Huntington's disease, contact www.hdsa.org or (800) 345-HDSA.

LeShan, Lawrence. *How to Meditate.* Boston, MA: Bantam Books, 1974. This is a wonderful pocket book for someone who is interested in the basics of meditation. LeShan's practical programs and exercises provide tools for you to begin your own exploration into meditation as a spiritual pactice. He explores the why's and how's and benefits of meditation, answering some commonly-asked questions along the way.

Levine, Stephen. *A Year to Live: How to Live This Year As if It Were Your Last.* New York: Bell Tower, 1997. Levine and his wife Ondrea spent one year "as if" it were their last year of life on earth. This book comes out of their personal experiment with this process. It is full of practical ideas and meditations that can assist us in beginning to think about our own deaths, no matter what our circumstances. We are taught through this book to live each day and each moment mindfully.

Levine, Stephen. *Healing into Life and Death.* Garden City, New York: Anchor Press Doubleday, 1987. This book is a compassionate guide for anyone seeking physical, psychological, emotional, or spiritual healing. Levine shares his vision of healing, which was acquired while working with those who came to him to die. He deals with the choice and application of treatments, and also offers original techniques for working with pain and grief.

Levine, Stephen. *Who Dies? An Investigation of Conscious Living and Conscious Dying.* New York: Anchor Books, Doubleday, 1982. "Today, approximately 200,000 people died." So begins this book by Stephen Levine, a long-time student of Elizabeth Kübler-Ross and a prolific writer on subjects such as meditation, awareness, and death. In this book he examines the various ways and kinds of people who die, and the approaches to death we can take. He includes meditations for working with pain and those to be used around an actual death. He strongly encourages us to develop an "open heart" regarding all matters, while letting go of the mind and the dualistic thinking in which we are prone to live our lives.

Lewis, C. S. *A Grief Observed.* New York: A Bantam Book, The Seabury Press, Inc., 1961. In this short classic, Lewis shares candidly the many aspects of his grief later in life, having lost his wife Joy "after four brief, intensely happy years." The movie that retells this unconventional love story is called Shadowlands. I highly recommend it.

Lindbergh, Reeve. *No More Words: A Journal of My Mother Anne Morrow Lindbergh.* New York, NY: Simon & Schuster, A Touchstone Book, 2001. The youngest child of Charles and Anne Morrow Lindbergh writes this thoughtful and descriptive memoir of the last year and a half of Anne's life. Reeve, also an accomplished author, deeply struggled with her mother's inability to communicate due to a series of small strokes that left her virtually speechless and quite frail. Those who care for an elderly person disabled by speechlessness will find themselves resonating with and comforted by Reeve's moving story.

Longaker, Christine. *Facing Death and Finding Hope: A Guide to the Emotional and Spiritual Care of the Dying.* New York: Doubleday, 1997. Longaker's experiences with death and care of the dying began in 1976 when her husband was diagnosed with acute leukemia at age 24. His illness helped them discover that they were lacking a spiritual path to cope with their situation. She is now a leading spokesperson on death and dying from the Tibetan Buddhist perspective.

This book would serve as a handbook for anyone facing death, helping a loved one face it, or working in the care-giving field.

Lotz, Anne Graham. *Heaven: My Father's House.* Nashville, TN: W Publishing Group, 2001. Anne, the second daughter of the Rev. Billy Graham, writes this book from a Christian point of view. She weaves together biblical scripture and her own thoughts and reflections about death – that it is nothing to fear, especially for Christians. She states, "Heaven is the home of your dreams: a home of lasting value that's fully paid for and filled with family where you will be wanted and welcomed." The book's full title is In Troubled Times, Looking Forward with Hope to Heaven: My Father's House.

Lynes, Barry. *The Rife Report: The Cancer Cure that Worked! Fifty Years of Suppression.* Ontario, Can.: Marcus Books, 1987. Lynes, an investigative health reporter, has written a comprehensive story about scientific genius Royal Raymond Rife, who discovered a cause and a cure for human cancer. He began searching for a cure in 1920 and by 1932 had isolated the cancer virus. He developed a healing technology in which he electronically destroyed the cancer virus in patients and allowed their own immune systems to restore their health. The machine he developed is called the Rife Machine. Unfortunately, Rife's theories and treatment methods conflicted with orthodox views, and he and his colleagues were eventually forced underground. This is the first book of its kind, produced with the assistance of John Crane, a longtime friend and associate of Roy Rife, in which you can read the entire account of what took place in connection with this man and his machine. (www.energetic-medicine.net/Rife.html)

MacGregor, Molly. *The Sky Goes On Forever: A Book about Death for Children.* Kapaa, HI: M.M. Press, 1988. This is a lovely children's book about death. Using the example of Dirtball the Bird, it speaks to the reader in a candid manner about what death is, what happens to us after we die, and how we can let someone go when they are dying. Molly speaks in universal, spiritual terms, rather than using any particular religious perspective, so that families can appreciate reading and sharing this book together. It could serve as a wonderful "conversation starter."

Menten, Ted. *Gentle Closings: How to Say Goodbye to Someone You Love.* Philadelphia, PA: Running Press, 1991. For many years Menten has been visiting children in hospitals, gifting them with teddy bears. This book comes out of his volunteer work to assist terminally ill children, adults, and their families. It is a book "about making memories, having courage, and letting go with honor and emotional honesty." It's also "about joy and jelly donuts and wishes granted and tiny miracles."

Miller, James E. *When You Know You're Dying: 12 Thoughts to Guide You Through the Days Ahead.* Fort Wayne, IN: Willowgreen Publishing, 1997. This is a booklet of sixty-plus pages that gives some practical suggestions on what to do and how to be as death approaches. Miller advises one to "let your feelings out" and "let go of that which blocks your well-being and growth." It will help you reflect, with quotes and simple, clear ideas, on how to face the dying process, from a psycho-spiritual perspective.

Miller, James E. *Winter Grief, Summer Grace: Returning to Life After a Loved One Dies.* Minneapolis, MN: Augsburg, 1995. This book was shared with me by one of our bereaved widows. She had found great comfort by reading it, so I wanted to share it here. It is an inspirational book with pictures and space and is meant to be read slowly and contemplatively. It moves the reader through the four seasons, beginning with autumn, and shares practical suggestions and ideas on coping with grief and sorrow. It is a reminder that "grief is both natural and necessary" and that we are never alone in our grieving.

Moody, Dr. Raymond A., Jr. *Life After Life.* Harrisburg, PA: Stackpole Books, 1976. This book is a classic on the life that may well come for all of us after death. Moody has been studying and researching this topic for many years. It is also "an investigation into the remarkable similarity of experience among those who have returned from the end of this life," those who have had near-death experiences.

Morris, Virginia. *Talking About Death Won't Kill You.* New York: Workman Publishing Co., Inc., 2001. I love the title of this book! Morris is a journalist specializing in health issues. She has also written *How to Care for Aging Parents.* In *Talking About Death Won't Kill You,* Morris makes the distinction between "obsessing blindly about death" and "learning about death." She shows how the latter can be deeply empowering. Virginia skillfully weaves together personal stories, scientific fact, practical advice, and emotional sensitivity that will help us see that at any age we can begin to prepare for a "good death." Emphasizing communication, and sharing information on matters from living wills and medical directives to hospice, Morris gives us a blueprint for finding a more gentle and meaningful way to die.

Morrissey, Dianne, Ph.D. *Anyone Can See the Light: The Seven Keys to a Guided Out-of-Body Experience.* Walpole, NH: Stillpoint Publishing, 1996. Morrissey shares about her near-death experience firsthand. She also shares ways we each can help ourselves learn to have out-of-body experiences.

Morse, Melvin, M.D., with Paul Perry. *Closer to the Light: Learning from the Near-Death Experiences of Children.* New York: Villard Books, 1990. Pediatrician Morse shares many of the rich and varied stories he has heard from the children he has worked with, regarding their near-death experiences. You could be uplifted and taken to new dimensions by reading this book!

Morse, Melvin, M.D. *Parting Visions: Uses and Meanings of Pre-Death, Psychic, and Spiritual Experiences.* New York: Villard Books, 1994. Dr. Morse shares some of the death-related dreams, premonitions, and visitations he has been told about during the course of his practice. He includes his own interpretation of these and shows us that pre-death visions can empower both the dying and the living. Morse has written at least two other books that you may want to look into: *Transformed by the Light: The Powerful Effect of Near-Death Experiences on People's Lives* (Villard Books, 1992) and *Where God Lives: The Science of the Paranormal and How Our Brains Are Linked to the Universe* (HarperCollins, 2000).

Mukai, Linda Pratt, with Janis Fisher Chan. *Living with Dying: A Personal Journey.* San Anselmo, CA: Butterfield Press, 1996. This is a story of one courageous, highly successful woman in her mid-forties who was diagnosed with metastatic colon cancer in 1992. Three weeks later, she asked her friend Janis Chan to help her write this book. Linda Mukai is no longer living, but her story got published, thanks to her husband and Janis, a couple of years after her death. Linda shares some very intimate moments and feelings as she reflects on her journey. She recognizes that every person's experience with cancer is different, but she has shared her story "so that other patients who are living with terminal cancer, and their friends, families, and caregivers, may be better prepared to choose what's right for them." Thank you, Linda!

Munsch, Robert, illustrated by Sheila McGraw. *Love You Forever.* Buffalo, NY: Firefly Books, Ltd., 1986. This is a beloved children's book that shares the story of a newborn son whose mother looks at him lovingly and sings, "I'll love you forever, I'll like you for always, As long as I'm living my baby you'll be." The boy goes through the stages of life and becomes a man. Later, he shares in his mother's end of life. Actually, this is a book that people of all ages can enjoy together, over and over again.

Nouwen, Henri J.M. *Our Greatest Gift: A Meditation on Dying and Caring.* New York: HarperSanFrancisco, A Division of HarperCollins Publishers, 1994. Fr. Nouwen is a beloved spiritual writer of our time who died rather suddenly several years ago. Before his death, challenged to examine and "befriend" his own death, he returned to a community where he had lived to help bury a much loved, differently-abled community member. In Part I he writes on "Dying Well," in Part II on "Caring Well," and he concludes with "The Grace of the Resurrection."

Orloff, Judith. *Intuitive Healing: 5 Steps to Physical, Emotional, and Sexual Wellness.* New York: Random House, Inc., 2000. Orloff shares personal experiences related to "intuitive healing" through her reflection on the body, the emotions and relationships, and sexual wellness. She reminds readers that "we are the keepers of our own healing," and offers practical techniques we can use to develop intuition in order to heal. In Chapter 5 she includes a thoughtful piece on "death as healer and teacher." As a bridge-person between psychic and medical worlds, I find Judith's views most engaging and helpful as we move toward becoming the multi-sensory beings we truly are.

Orloff, Judith, M.D. *Second Sight.* New York: Warner Books, Inc., 1996. Dr. Orloff was born a gifted clairvoyant, who later became a psychiatrist. She recounts her unique and adventurous life story in her autobiography in the first half of this book. In the second half, she shows how each one of us can develop our own psychic powers. She shares practical advice, from how to create an altar in your home to discovering the significance of prayer, meditation, dreams, and synchronicities in our everyday lives. I have had the pleasure of hearing Judith speak, and I found her to be a woman of deep spirituality and integrity.

Poer, Nancy Jewel. *Living into Dying: A Journal of Spiritual and Practical Deathcare for Family and Community.* Placerville, CA: Nancy Poer, 2002. Poer, an author, teacher, and artist, has put together a fascinating book based on her personal experiences of death and dying. Based on her family's experiences with death, she covers topics such as "community threshold work," "spiritual view(s) of dying," and "toward a new community." She is a strong advocate of "home death," and even offers legal and practical considerations on how to deal with the body of your loved one after they die, including specifics on how to build a casket.

Pollock, Constance and Daniel, compilation by. *Visions of the Afterlife.* Nashville, TN: Word Publishing, 1999. This is a collection of quotes, poems, and Christian scripture that share visions of heaven and hell. The work interweaves pieces from literary masters such as Shakespeare, E. Dickinson, C. S. Lewis, J. Donne, J. Joyce, H. B. Stowe, T. S. Eliot, C. Dickens, and many others, with hymns and scripture verses. The Pollocks have put together an interesting compilation of material that reflects on the afterlife in these changing, often confusing times around the millennium. Following the last chapter on the Book of Revelation, they have included short biographies of the writers quoted in their book.

Price, Jan. *The Other Side of Death.* New York: Ballantine Books, 1996. Here is another account of a near-death experience by a woman who almost died of a heart attack. Price recounts some of her spiritual experiences in that "other dimension," as well as the important lessons the experience taught her. She also ruminates on why near-death experiences happen, and why they seem to be so common today. In Chapter Eight she refers to the connection between death and sexual ecstasy that some authors such as Rodney Collin (in The Theory of Celestial Influence) have written about. Inspirational author, John Randolph Price, Jan's husband, also contributes to this book.

Remen, Rachel Naomi, M.D. *Kitchen Table Wisdom: Stories That Heal.* New York, NY: Riverhead Books, 1996. Remen tells many beautiful stories collected over the years from her personal practice of psycho-oncology. She is the cofounder and medical director of the Commonweal Cancer Help Program in Bolinas, California, and she lives with Crohn's Disease. She has another title with similar stories: *My Grandfather's Blessings: Stories of Strength* (Riverhead Books, 2000).

Reoch, Richard. *To Die Well: A Holistic Approach for the Dying and Their Caregivers.* New York: HarperPerennial, 1996. Unfortunately, this book is no longer in print. However, it is important to mention it here, as it is kind of a forerunner of my own book. Although he does not go as deeply into the spiritual aspects as I have, Richard has included a host of practical material and resources in his book that could help anyone coping with end-of-life matters. There are beautiful pictures and illustrations in his book, as well. If you can find a copy of this book of treasures consider yourself lucky!

Rinpoche, Sogyal. *The Tibetan Book of Living and Dying.* New York: HarperCollins Publishers, 1993. This is a "manual for life and death and a magnificent source of sacred inspiration from the heart of the Tibetan [Buddhist] tradition. Sogyal Rinpoche delivers a lucid and inspiring introduction to the practice of meditation, to karma and rebirth, to care and love for the dying, and to the trials and rewards of the spiritual path." This whole book is filled with rich material related to life, death, and change from the Tibetan Buddhist perspective. Chapter Thirteen in particular has a wealth of information on caring spiritually for the dying.

Rogers, Sandra. *Lessons from the Light: Insights from a Journey to the Other Side.* New York, NY: Warner Books, 1995. Rogers, who experienced a near-death experience after trying to commit suicide, shares many of her spiritual learnings, about topics from angels and children to values and wisdom. Very succinct and candid.

Ronan, Margaret and Eve. *Death Around the World: Strange Rites & Weird Customs.* New York: Scholastic Book Services, 1978. This small paperback book includes some interesting facts about customs surrounding death from different cultures around the world. It ponders questions such as, What is death? Where do we go when we die? When is a person really dead?

Rosen, Eliot Jay, ed. *Experiencing the Soul: Before Birth, During Life, After Death.* Carlsbad, CA: Hay House, Inc., 1998. Rosen was the former head of the Social Work Department at Hospice Hawaii and is the current director of For a World We Choose Foundation. His book includes chapters written by well-known authors and spiritual teachers on the topics of death and dying, thanatology, transformation, and the like. Contributors include the Dalai Lama, Jean Houston, Raymond Moody, Marion Woodman, and Betty Eadie.

Rupp, Joyce, OSM. *Praying Our Goodbyes: Understanding the Spirituality of Change in Our Lives.* New York: Ave Maria Press, 1988. Rupp writes a guide "to accepting our inevitable goodbyes [in life], even as it reminds us that when we are suffering most deeply, the seed of hope still lives within us." She includes a variety of specific ideas for prayers and rituals around saying goodbye and letting go.

Schachter-Shalomi, Zalman, and Ronald S. Miller. *From Age-ing to Sage-ing: A Profound New Vision of Growing Older,* New York, Warner Books, Inc., 1995. Rabbi Schachter-Shalomi is the one who taught me that in the last 100 years or so, our culture has "pathologized" death (and birth) by moving it to the hospital. Several generations ago, people died and were born in their own homes. Now, thanks to the hospice movement and midwives, we are gradually reclaiming the natural cycles of life to bring them back into the home! In this compassionate and thoughtful work, Rabbi Zalman takes aging Americans through a powerful transformation: he shows readers how to use their life experience to enrich their elder years, face grief and death, reconcile relationships, develop a regenerative spirit, and share wisdom with future generations. It's a "must read" for anyone desiring to reframe growing old in our culture.

Schuller, Robert H. *Tough Minded Faith for Tender Hearted People.* Boston, MA: G.K. Hall & Co., 1985. This inspirational book by Rev. Schuller will help you begin to see your life in a new way. The devotional pieces in this book are short, mostly one or two pages, and they begin with an opening: "Faith is...." They will help you see your life from a more positive perspective.

Siegel, Bernie S., M.D. *Love, Medicine & Miracles: Lessons Learned About Self-Healing from a Surgeon's Experience with Exceptional Patients.* New York: Harper & Row, Publishers, Inc., 1986. Dr. Siegel shares his dynamic vision for the "exceptional patient" who takes control of his or her own healing. He interweaves stories from his own patients who deal with cancer, and has a powerful message for physicians who care for these patients, too. There is a new paradigm brewing for the patient-doctor relationship, and Dr. Siegel is a leading proponent of this paradigm. (My mother used this as her "Bible" for a time through her experience with cancer. She was blessed with a couple of years of remission, and I am convinced that the ideas set forth in this work along with a workshop led by Dr. Siegel contributed toward these blessed years.)

Simonton, O. Carl, M.D., Stephanie Matthews-Simonton, and James L. Creighton. *Getting Well Again.* New York, New York: Bantam Books, 1978. The Simontons share some significant research and information regarding the scientific basis for the "will to live." They profile the typical "cancer personality" and show how positive expectations, self-awareness, and self-care can contribute to surviving illness. This book offers the self-help techniques their patients have used to successfully reinforce typical medical treatment – techniques for experiencing positive attitudes, relaxation, visualization, goal setting, managing pain, physical exercise, and building a support system for emotional and mental well-being.

Smith, Doug, and Marilu Pittman. *The Tao of Dying: A Guide to Caring.* Vero Beach, FL: Caring Publishing, 1998. This is a beautiful, simple book, full of black-and-white photos of those who are dying, young and old, and including caregivers, as well. Doug Smith has done a lovely job of honoring death and presenting the allowing, accepting perspective that is so needed and appreciated throughout the dying process.

Smith, Rodney. *Lessons from the Dying.* Somerville, MA: Wisdom Publications, 1998. Smith is a teacher of Insight Meditation who has spent over 14 years in hospice work, including social work, bereavement work, and management as a program director and executive director. He shares from a spiritual perspective, with many examples from his personal experience, covering topics such as "delighting in the Mystery," "learning from every experience," and "listening from the dying." Smith also has a "Reflections and Exercises" section at the back of every chapter.

Snow, Lois Wheeler. *A Death with Dignity: When the Chinese Came.* New York: Random House, 1974. Snow, a journalist, shares about her family's experience of working through her husband's dying process while in China. They were privileged to experience the Chinese concept of "total care" – that is, "medical personnel, the patient and patient's family working together, consulting on, and understanding, every step of the integrated treatment, from diet to the relief of pain, to the facing of death and bereavement."

Stern, Ellen Sue. *Living with Loss: Meditations for Grieving Widows.* New York: Dell Publishing, 1995. This small but thick booklet includes daily meditations that can be used over the course of a year. Each day includes a topic, a brief quote, then a meditation, and closes with an affirmation. It could be very useful for any woman suffering the loss of a husband, companion, lover, helpmate, or dear friend. It will help you to move on: "to cope with today, cherish yesterday, and thrive tomorrow."

Stickney, Doris. *Water Bugs and Dragon Flies: Explaining Death to Young Children.* Cleveland, OH: The Pilgrim Press, 1982. This is a wonderful little booklet that tells the story of the water bug who turned into a dragonfly and tried to keep his promise to return with his water bug friends to let them know what had happened to him. He came to discover, however, that since he now had wings, he could not enter the pond where his friends were. After telling the story, Stickney shares a personal experience and reflects on how we might openly talk with our children and grandchildren about death, when the opportunity comes.

Stoddard, Sandol. *The Hospice Movement: A Better Way of Caring for the Dying.* New York: Random House, Inc. First Vintage Books Ed., 1978. Stoddard visited hospices all over the U.S. and also volunteered in the pioneer modern hospice, St. Christopher's in London before writing this classic about the hospice movement. Dr. Cicely Saunders, the director of St. Christopher's, helped edit this book that sensitively and vividly portrays how hospice works. Stoddard helps to make come alive the essence of the hospice concept: "True hospitality."

Stone, Ganga. *Start the Conversation: The Book About Death You Were Hoping to Find.* New York: Warner Books, Inc., 1996. Stone, founder of "God's Love We Deliver," has offered six-week classes entitled "Start the Conversation" since 1989. She shares many practical ideas about how we can begin to think about a conversation on death, which most Americans would like to avoid. She also helps us to let go of our fear around death through allowing us to understand that there actually is no such thing as death.

Tatelbaum, Judy. *The Courage to Grieve: Creative Living, Recovery, and Growth Through Grief.* NY: Lippencott & Crowell, 1984. Tatelbaum's brother died in an automobile accident when she was 17 years old. She was deeply traumatized by the event, and around her 40th birthday began to write this book. She realized that her entire life had been geared to writing this particular book, as she learned to become fearless about loss and death. This book teaches us, through personal experience, how we, too, can choose to live unafraid, among the omnipresent reminders of our inevitable encounter with the reality of death, loss, and grief.

Taylor-Good, Karen. *On Angel's Wings.* Nashville, Tennessee: Insight Publications, Ltd., 2003. I heard about this book through a co-worker who attended a hospice conference where Karen was featured. My friend was deeply impressed by Karen and her music. This CD/ book shares 14 songs written and sung by Karen. They are songs that come out of her own life, or real stories that have touched her. Karen is not afraid to look suffering in the eye and share the truth. She opens our hearts with her inspirational music and writing, and she reminds us that we are never alone.

Terkel, Studs. *Will the Circle Be Unbroken? Reflections on Death, Rebirth, and Hunger for a Faith.* New York: The New Press, 2001. Once again Studs Terkel has interviewed a variety of people, this time about their views on the final experience of life and how it impacts the way they live.

He begins with healthcare workers, includes a Hiroshima A-bomb survivor, a death-row parolee, and a woman who emerged from a two-year coma. His interviews share an element of grace in dealing with a topic that many still have trouble discussing freely and openly. Terkel's interviews address a whole realm of religious beliefs, including expectations of an afterlife and reincarnation, uncovering an amazing range and complexity of experience and belief.

Tipping, Colin. *Radical Forgiveness: Making Room for the Miracle* (Second Ed.). Marietta, GA: Global 13 Publications, Inc., 2002. This book will likely change and heal your life in some way because of what it stirs up inside you as you read it. Tipping updates and makes easy to understand a concept that's been around for a long time, but was until now inaccessible to most people.

Tobin, Daniel R., M.D., with Karen Lindsey. *Peaceful Dying: The Step-by-Step Guide to Preserving Your Dignity, Your Choice, and Your Inner Peace at the End of Life.* New York: Perseus Books, 1999. Dr. Tobin founded the FairCare program for peaceful dying by first piloting it at the V.A. Hospital in Albany, New York. This is a 26-step practical program designed to return control and peace to those who have entered the last stage of earthly life. The book outlines these steps in a down-to-earth, clear, focused manner. Tobin has a vision to expand the hospice perspective to all people who are dying, and to pave the way so that a peaceful death can be within everyone's reach.

Truman, Karol. *Feelings Buried Alive Never Die.* St. George, UT: Olympus Distributing, 1991, 2003. Karol Truman, a practicing therapist and spiritual healer, has put together a practical work on how we can release our old, "buried" emotions through a method called "Scripting." Her own health challenges and curiosity about how to heal led her first to a study of nutrition and weight control: *Looking Good, Feeling Great*, 1983. After that, she came in touch with how deeply physical health is linked to emotional and spiritual health. This book comes out of her awakening around that and her study of the Laws of Cause and Effect. Please see pp. 100–103 for more ideas on forgiveness and letting go of old feelings that are no longer serving you.

Van Praagh, James. *Talking to Heaven: A Medium's Message of Life after Death.* New York: Penguin Group, 1997. Van Praagh, a world-renowned medium, shares in this book his story of growing up Catholic, then attending seminary for a year, only to find God, who "is unlimited," in his heart. He later went back to school hoping to become a screenwriter, but his psychic gifts began to vie for his attention, and he could no longer ignore them. Through his writing, he offers a way of dealing with grief in a positive and healing manner. He also offers us suggestions as to how we can contact the spirit world on our own and become aware of the signs that our loved ones may be sending us. Some of his other titles include: *Healing Grief: Reclaiming Life After Any Loss; Reaching to Heaven; Heaven and Earth: Making the Psychic Connection; Looking Beyond: A Teen's Guide to the Spiritual World;* and *Meditations with James Van Praagh.*

Viorst, Judith. *Necessary Losses: The Loves, Illusions, Dependencies and Impossible Expectations That All of Us Have to Give Up in Order to Grow.* New York: Ballantine Books, 1986. Viorst writes about the growth and change we can experience through the inevitable and necessary losses we each move through during the course of our lives: stages of life, relationships, dreams and expectations, loved ones, and so forth. She believes that as we deal with and work through our grief and loss, we gain deeper perspective, maturity, and true wisdom about life. We learn that meaningful mourning can lead to creative and healthy change. It is a life-affirming and transformative book.

Wainwright, Richard M. *Closer Than We Imagine.* Palm Coast, FL: Family Life Publishing, 2001. I came across this book through the PMA self-publishers magazine. Wainwright chronicles the experience of living with his first wife who contracted uterine cancer and subsequently died (1995). He sought out contact with Spirit, through George Anderson, after D'Ann's loss and he shares openly and generously from these contacts.

Weenolsen, Patricia, Ph.D. *The Art of Dying: How to Leave This World with Dignity and Grace, at Peace with Yourself and Your Loved Ones.* New York: St. Martin's Press, 1996. Weenolsen lends much practical wisdom by going step-by-step through many of the practical issues facing an individual who is preparing to die. Some topics included in her book are coping with pain, coping with emotions, euthanasia, forgiving the unforgivable, and active hope. She is a psychologist specializing in lifespan development and death and dying.

Weiss, Brian, M.D. *Many Lives, Many Masters.* New York: Simon & Schuster, Inc., 1988. When Dr. Brian Weiss, who started out as a traditional psychotherapist, met a new client named "Catherine," they shared a life-altering session together. As Dr. Weiss hypnotized Catherine during their session, she began recalling traumas from a previous life that seemed to hold the key to her recurring nightmares and anxiety issues. Over time, Dr. Weiss's skepticism diminished, especially when Catherine began to channel messages from "the space between lives" that contained remarkable revelations and wise material that would prove helpful to him concerning his family and his dead son. Using past-life therapy, Dr. Weiss was able to successfully assist Catherine with her issues. As a result, he embarked on a new and meaningful phase of his own career. His other books include Through Time Into Healing, Only Love Is Real, Messages From The Masters, and Same Soul, Many Bodies.

Wilber, Ken. *Integral Psychology: Consciousness, Spirit, Psychology, Therapy.* Boston, MA: Shambhala Publications, Inc., 2000. It has been said that Wilber may be the most comprehensive philosophical thinker of our times. He is the author of more than twelve books. Wilber notes that meditation is the one obvious tool that inevitably moves a person into the next stage(s) of his or her development in consciousness. Dr. Larry Dossey says of this book, "(It) is the closest anyone has come to a 'theory of everything' uniting consciousness, spirit, psychology, and therapy."

Wolpe, Rabbi David. *Making Loss Matter.* New York: Riverhead Books, 1999. I first learned of Rabbi Wolpe and his book when I saw him on Bill Moyer's four-part TV special on end-of-life and hospice-related issues, called "On Your Own Terms." David, the son of a rabbi, discovered that his wife Eliana had cancer nine months after their daughter was born, and while he was working on his book. David shares deeply and wisely about grief from his personal experience. He writes of hope, dreams, and love in the midst of grief, and of how to find faith, hope, and purpose in the midst of difficulty. In the first chapter he shares the interesting fact that Eliana's doctor told her that "she had never had a patient who survived cancer for any length of time who did not end up blessing the cancer."

Woodson, Meg. *Making It Through the Toughest Days of Grief.* New York: HarperPaperbacks, 1994. Woodson, a grief counselor who has struggled through her own losses (two children and a mother), shares in candid ways how to deal practically with grief. She suggests ways to work with and through our feelings, and also how to cope on those first holidays after we have lost loved ones. Her pragmatic, no-nonsense approach is refreshing. She includes ideas on how to cry when you can't, how to be angry and not harm others, how to make up with God, how to live with people who grieve differently from you, how to work with your guilt, and how to feel safe as you move into the future.

Zukav, Gary. *The Seat of the Soul.* New York: Simon & Schuster (A Fireside Book), 1990. This is a book which will help you understand the deep change that is going on in the world today from a metaphysical perspective. Zukav talks about how we are moving from being five-sensory to multi-sensory human beings. His other books include: *The Dancing Wu Li Masters* and *Soul Stories.* He has also co-authored with Linda Francis *The Heart of the Soul and The Mind of the Soul.*

Books for Caregivers

Coberly, Margaret, Ph.D., R.N. *Sacred Passage: How to Provide Fearless, Compassionate Care for the Dying.* Boston, MA: Shambhala Publications, Inc., 2002. Sharing from her experience as a nurse in trauma centers and hospice settings, Coberly examines the problem of denying death in our culture. She shares from her practical as well as mystical experiences how she grew and expanded through working with the dying. In her seeking Margaret came to appreciate the Tibetan Buddhist perspective on death; in the second part of the book she goes into detail about the Tibetan Buddhist tradition on facing death not as "the end," but rather as an opportunity for spiritual growth and expansion where we can develop honesty, courage, and compassion.

Collett, Merrill. *At Home with Dying: A Zen Approach.* Boston: Shambhala, 1999. As a full-time resident at the San Francisco Zen Center for four years, and a volunteer caregiver at the Zen Hospice Project, Collett assisted many people during their final days. Collett was graced with this book out of that first-hand experience. He covers the whole gamut: a variety of spiritual as well as practical topics, such as "Why you should help your loved one die at home," spiritual care, meditation, "the Tao of eating and elimination," touch as the "way to connect," and working through grief.

Hutchison, Joyce, and Joyce Rupp. *May I Walk You Home? Courage and Comfort for Caregivers of the Very Ill.* Notre Dame, Indiana: Ave Maria Press, 1999. Joyce Hutchison has served as an oncology and hospice nurse for over 20 years. In this collection of stories, she shares the spirit of those who accompany the dying on their journey of transformation. Joyce Rupp, a "spiritual midwife," an inspirational speaker, and a member of the Servants of Mary (Servite) Community, shares meditations and prayers that accompany and bless each of the 25 stories in this book. It is a collection intended for caregivers, but a much wider range of people could find it meaningful.

McLeod, Beth Witrogen. *Caregiving: The Spiritual Journey of Love, Loss, and Renewal.* New York: John Wiley & Sons, Inc., 1999. McLeod suffered through her own parents' sudden catastrophic illnesses and subsequent deaths only five weeks apart. She has written a thorough book on care-giving, based on her firsthand experience. Beth explores topics such as women and care-giving, spousal care-giving, coping with depression, hitting bottom, end-of-life concerns and spiritual issues, including forgiveness, thanksgiving, and "the urge to serve." She also discusses some practical aspects of care-giving, like the myriad of medical and financial issues that may come up.

Nouwen, Henri J.M. *Our Greatest Gift: A Meditation on Dying and Caring.* New York: HarperSanFrancisco, a Division of HarperCollins Publishers, 1994. Fr. Nouwen, a beloved and timely spiritual writer, is challenged to examine and "befriend" his own death as he returns to his community to help bury a much loved, differently-abled community member. In Part II of the book Nouwen specifically shares three chapters with a focus on caring for the dying.

Smith, Douglas. *Being a Wounded Healer: How to Heal Ourselves While We Are Healing Others.* Madison, WN: Psycho-Spiritual Publications, 1999. Smith has been a hospice worker, a minister, and a therapist. He is on a journey of healing himself from a variety of "wounds," including the death of one of his daughters, a stay in a mental hospital, choosing to leave the priesthood, and a divorce. Finding healing "in the midst of woundedness" has been a significant theme in his life. His reflections are from a universal perspective, including pieces from various religious traditions. He also shares reading and writing exercises for his readers at the end of each chapter.

Smith, Doug (author) and Marilu Pittman (photographer). *The Tao of Dying.* Washington, D.C.: Caring Publishing, 1994. This is a collection of simple reflections from a man who has cared for the dying. Smith shares from a Taoist perspective, honestly and deeply, from the heart. The photographs are beautiful and often moving.

Magazines and Journals

Alternative Medicine. A monthly magazine sharing news and articles about new and ancient healing alternatives. See www.alternativemedicine.com for more information.

Body and Soul. A monthly publication that helps people appreciate the importance of doing what makes them happy in life. One of their mottos is to "enjoy a healthier, more natural, joyful life." They have many articles and ideas on better nutrition, sleep, and general holistic care of the self. See www.bodyandsoulmag.com for more.

Parabola: Myth, Tradition, and the Search for Meaning, Volume 27, Number 2 (Summer 2002). "Dying." To order, call (800) 560-MYTH, or visit www.parabola.org. This issue covers a wide range of topics, including "Why We Wash the Dead: Exploring the Jewish ceremonial washing," "Godfather Death: Storytelling lights the transition," and "The Last Note: How music wakens and heals." It is a beautiful collection of articles, stories, quotes, and well-researched information.

Parabola: Myth, Tradition, and the Search for Meaning, Volume 2, Issue 1 (Winter 1977). "Death." To order, call (800) 560-MYTH, or visit www.parabola.org. This issue includes pieces such as "Learning to Die" by Brother David Steindl-Rast, "The Nature of Death," which shares a sampling of the great traditional teachings about death, and "Faces of Death," by William Doty, a brief discussion of the variety of ways in which people around the world have regarded and coped with the reality of death. Again, this is a wealth of information and perspectives on the topic of death.

Spirituality & Health: The Soul/Body Connection. This is a magazine published four times a year. It is beautifully put together, with articles of a spiritual nature relating to our health and well being. Some sample themes from back issues are: Self-renewal, Be the Light, and The Gentle Arts of Letting Go and Giving Back. It is an attractive publication with colorful pictures interspersed throughout. See www.spiritualityhealth.com for more information.

The Way Through. This journal used to be called *The Daybook: A Contemplative Journal.* It is published by Marv and Nancy Hiles of the Iona Center; the Hiles also host contemplative retreats. Address: P.O. Box 1528, Healdsburg, CA 95448. Phone: (707) 431-7426. Email: marvsam@comcast.net.

Tricycle: The Buddhist Review, No. 25, Vol. VII, No. 1 (Fall 1997). *"The Great Matter of Life and Death,"* Dharma Drum Publications. To order, call ACCESS: (800) 507-BOOK. This issue covers such topics as "How do you want to die?" and "Practices and preparation," and "Life after breath." It includes an interview with Rick Fields on "Living with Cancer," an article on the practice of Tonglen, and many other interesting pieces, including images and artwork that evoke the presence of death in our daily lives around the world. Fax: (212) 645-1493; e-mail: tricycle@well.com.

Music

Charlotte Church, Sony Music Entertainment (UK) Ltd., 1999. Charlotte has some magnificent pieces on this album, including "Guide Me, Oh Thou Great Redeemer" and "If Thou Art Near."

Crossing the Waves, Mara Grey, Celtic Harp, 2002. This is a special collection of ten pieces of harp tunes (some Scottish/English, and one written by her 10-year-old daughter!) which Mara Grey put together at her home on Whidbey Island. Mara has been playing the harp for over 20 years. For more details, see www.natureweaving.com/harper/.

Dream Chants East & West: Soothing Gregorian & Sanskrit Chants for Relaxation & Meditation, Cynthia Snodgrass, vocals; Jim Oliver, keyboards. Cynthia Snodgrass is an Episcopal priest, musicologist, and hospice chaplain. She is the founder of Sacred Sound Institute, "a not-for-profit organization dedicated to education about the spiritual benefits of sacred sound." Sacred chant is described on this CD as being "more than music – it is sung prayer. The power of sacred chant to calm, to soothe, and to bring the listener into the presence of the divine is celebrated in spiritual traditions around the world." On this CD, two sacred traditions, Sanskrit chants from the East and Gregorian chants from the West, are woven together to bring deep, prayerful meditation and spiritual relaxation. Website: www.sacredsoundinstitute.org; e-mail: sacredsound@compuserve.com.

Harp of the Healing Light, Erik Berglund, Oreade Music, 1999. "Erik Berglund's music is designed to inspire, uplift and heal where beauty and harmony are most needed. He plays a Celtic harp.... The harmonies seem to transcend sound to become healing colour and light." (from the CD cover)

Harpestry: A Contemporary Collection, produced by Dawn Atkinson and Diana Stork, PolyGram Records, Inc., 1997. This is a beautiful collection of a variety of pieces for harp played by various harpists.

Japan: Shakuhachi – The Japanese Flute, Kohachiro Miyata, Shakuhachi. Elektra Entertainment, a division of Warner Communications, Inc., 1977. I have learned that the shakuhachi is not unlike the harp, an instrument that can assist us in transitioning to another realm. I share this beautiful CD of shakuhachi music that was given to me by a friend. Please explore further on your own.

Josh Groban, 143 Records, 2001. This is Josh's first CD. I especially recommend the piece "To Where You Are" for those who are grieving.

Music for Efficient Sleep – Sleeping and Awakening, Wind Records. (music from China) According to Chinese medical theories, sleep disorders are mainly due to the breakdown of the relationship of the Yin-Yang Chi. This series of Music for Efficient Sleep is designed to adjust one's emotional condition through music. Subsequently, this adjusts one's Yin Chi and Yang Chi, thus improving sleep quality. Using psycho-acoustic principles and traditional as well as Western classical instruments, this music is both lovely and effective (available in cassettes or CDs).

Quiet Mind: The Musical Journey of a Tibetan Nomad, Nawang Khechog, Sounds True, 1991. "From the Tibetan highlands comes a wordless prayer for peace – and the beauty of meditation, or 'quiet mind.'" Hear Tibetan bamboo flute, didgeridoo, ocarina, Incan panpipes, and silver flute.

Restorative Sleep, The Monroe Institute. For those who need strong and intense recuperation from any body dysfunction: illness, injury, surgery, and the like. It helps produce healing patterns in critical areas and reintroduces normalcy through the system. Hemi-Sync with verbal instruction. Set against the background of sweeping white noise.

Spectrum Suite, Steven Halpern's Inner Peace Music, 1975, 1988. The "Zen-like" quality of this CD instantly relaxes body, mind, and spirit. The luminous sound of the electric piano literally "tunes your human instrument." Each of the seven musical keynotes on this album corresponds to one of your seven chakras or energy centers. You'll experience your heartbeat and breathing slowing down – the perfect CD for meditation.

Tapes

Valuing Death: A Lecture by Ram Dass, at the Pain & Palliative Care Unit Memorial Sloan-Kettering Hospital, ISBN: 1-887474-04-8. Human Foundation Tape Library, 524 San Anselmo Avenue, #203, San Anselmo, CA 94960; (800) 248-1008.

The following are some of the tapes available through Stephen and Ondrea Levine at *Warm Rock Tapes:* P.O. Box 100; Chamisal, NM 87521. They will lead you through guided meditations and provide helpful information as you journey through grief, death, and other life transitions.
Soft Belly: A Contemplation and Meditation
Lovingkindness Meditation/Gratitude Contemplation
The Grief Process: Meditations for Healing
Grief as Healing - 1
A Talk on Forgiveness

Videos and DVDs

A Family Undertaking, **a PBS documentary.** This sensitive and beautiful documentary profiles families who chose to forego a typical American funeral to personally provide for loved ones and their funerals at home. These families are reclaiming a tradition that used to be a natural part of life. They participate in after-death care, designing and building their own caskets, and burying their loved ones on private lands; home funeral guides are available to help with this. To order a copy of this video, call (800) 937-4113.

Appointment with the Wise Old Dog: Dream Images in a Time of Crisis, **by David Blum.** © **1998.** This extraordinary documentary-style piece is a record of David Blum's profound drems and inner work that were a gift to him from his unconscious. Davis was an internationally-renowned musician (orchestra conductor) and author when he was diagnosed with cancer at age 52. He had already developed a strong inner life through an ongoing interactive dream life. After his diagnosis, a series of vivid dreams assisted him in countless ways through the labyrinth of his illness. In this reflective, symbolic, heartfelt piece, David gently leads us through his dream drawings. Not long before he died, he was compelled to reveal his inner journey in order to help others become empowered by our own inner life and gifts. In David's own words, "It's an amazing fact that at a time of dire crisis, people often unexpectedly find themselves supported by a power that makes it possible for them to cope." To order DVD ($29.95 includes shipping and handling), send check to Sarah Blum, PO Box 104, Medina, WA 98039-0104.

Chalice of Repose: A Contemplative Musician's Approach to Death & Dying, **by Therese Schroeder-Sheker. © 1997 Therese Schroeder-Sheker, Paul Kaufman Inc., and The Fetzer Institute. Produced by Sounds True, 1997.** Told through real-life footage, this 44-minute film documents the efforts of the Chalice of Repose Project, the world's only formal educational program in music for the care of the dying. It shows how contemplative musicians offer an "anointing of sound" that can help dramatically alleviate the pain of the dying. Over the past two decades, Shroeder-Sheker's innovative and creative efforts have helped to bring spiritual and physiological comfort to a wide range of patients. She also continues to teach students of music in this vital field. To reach Sounds True, call: (800) 333-9185.

On Our Own Terms – Moyers on Dying, **Interview with Bill Moyers.** Bill Moyers crossed the country from hospitals to homes to hospices in order to put this remarkable four-part, six-hour series together. He captures "some of the most intimate stories ever filmed and the most candid conversations [about death] ever shared with a television audience." The four parts in the series are "Living with Dying," "A Different Kind of Care," "A Death of One's Own," and "A Time to Change." For more information go to www.pbs.org/wnet/onourownterms. To order the films, call (800) 257-5126.

Resurrection, **starring Ellen Burstyn and Sam Shepherd. © 1980 Universal City Studios, Inc.** In this unforgettable story of love and a modern-day miracle worker, a woman has a near-death experience as a result of a car accident. She returns to life with a mysterious ability to heal. She attributes her power to human love rather than divine intervention. The plot thickens as she begins to heal the residents of her childhood town, eventually healing and getting involved with a zealous young farmer.

Shadowlands, **starring Anthony Hopkins and Debra Winger. © 1993 Savoy Pictures, Inc.** In this movie based on a true story, C.S. Lewis, played by Hopkins, is a world-renowned writer and professor. He is a single man whose life is filled with his books and intellectual pursuits, until he meets Joy Gresham. Joy is a passionate, strong-willed American woman who challenges Lewis and slowly begins to open his heart. Their eventual romance opens up Lewis' world in a profound way, but Lewis must also confront the truth that a heart opened to great love must also be open to the possibility of great pain.

To Dance with the White Dog, **starring Hume Cronyn and Jessica Tandy. © 1993 Signboard Hill Productions, Inc.** Sam and Cora are found still dancing cheek-to-cheek at their 50th wedding anniversary. Soon after their anniversary, Cora dies of a heart attack. Struggling with his own health, Sam continues to live by himself under the watchful eye of his children. His spirit begins to fade until, one day, a mystical white dog suddenly appears and takes up residence with him. In time, the dog reawakens Sam to the joy of life and reminds him of the power of his beloved's undying love.

What Dreams May Come, **starring Robin Williams, Cuba Gooding, Jr., Annabella Sciorra. © 1998 PolyGram Films.** After the two children, then Williams, the father in this family, die in automobile accidents, Williams desires to remain close to his earthly wife (Sciorra). With the friendly spirit assigned to help him, he begins to adapt to his new reality that is "heavenly." But when his distraught wife takes her own life, she is condemned to eternal damnation. With help from his heavenly friends, Williams sets out on a perilous and harrowing journey of his afterlife – a quest for everlasting love that will intrigue and amaze you.

Wit, **starring Emma Thompson. © 2001 HBO, a Division of Time Warner Entertainment Company.** This is the story of Vivian Bearing, a rather austere and disciplined English professor, dealing with a serious case of ovarian cancer. While relying on her research-oriented physician and hospital personnel for treatment, Vivian is challenged to reflect on her life and discover what's really important to her. This somewhat heavy and intellectual film is not necessarily intended for someone in the midst of dealing with cancer but might rather be considered a "teaching film" for health care professionals and others who want to learn about the trials of dealing with a serious illness and treatment in some hospitals. (Directed by Mike Nichols and adapted from a Pulitzer Prize-winning drama by Margaret Edson.)

WEBSITES

Cancer Support

www.annieappleseedproject.org Ann Fonfa, a breast cancer survivor, is the founder of the Annie Appleseed Project. She's become a familiar figure at cancer research conferences around the country. She's unafraid to ask the tough questions, and has a great deal on her website regarding the whole gamut of cancer treatment. See her website or read the article about her project, "A Cancer Patient's Best Friend," in *Alternative Medicine,* Nov.–Dec. 2004.

www.cancerlifeline.org : Cancer Lifeline's website.

www.cancercenter.com : Website for Cancer Treatment Centers of America.

www.cancer.org : American Cancer Society's website.

www.harmonyhill.org (see Chapter Eleven)

www.nci.nih.gov : Website for the National Cancer Institute.

Caregiver Support

www.dying.about.com/od/caregivers/index.htm?nl=1 Website provides death and dying resources for caregivers. These resources will help anyone who is caring for a terminally-ill person, as well as healthcare workers who treat dying persons.

End-of-life Support

www.aahpm.org Website of the American Academy of Hospice and Palliative Medicine

www.americanhospice.org Website of the American Hospice Foundation, which has an interactive page for finding a hospice near you.

www.cigna.com/healthinfo/shc99hsp.html Links to hospice "umbrella" organizations in the United States.

www.csum.edu/pethospice The Nikki Hospice Foundation for Pets is the first official, non-profit organization of its kind in the nation. founded in response to a need which is becoming ever more prominent in our society, Its main purpose is "to encourage the provision of hospice care for dying pets, so that pet owners who do not wish to choose euthanasia when their animals are about to depart this life or who wish to postpone it can care for them in the home

245

environment – under veterinary supervision and with adequate pain management and/or symptom control."

www.finalpassages.org (See Chapter 11)

www.hardchoices.com This website is about the booklet, *Hard Choices for Loving People*, and is meant to provide some guidance through education for professionals, patients, and their families regarding end-of-life decisions. It covers topics like CPR, artificial feeding tubes, hospice, living wills, nursing home placement, ventilators, and dialysis. Other related topics like bioethics, death and dying, and the emotional and spiritual issues surrounding the end-of-life are interwoven into this educational website.

www.nhpco.org Website for the National Hospice and Palliative Care Organization.

www.peacefulpassages.org Peaceful Passages is an organization in South Jersey devoted to helping people die in as natural and holistic a way as possible. They help people utilize Complementary Therapies such as massage, healing touch, aroma and music therapies as part of their end-of-life experiences. Through them, you can order a small book called *Peaceful Passages* that shares 60 short, real-life stories about people who have successfully utilized these therapies at the end of their lives.

www.samaritanhospice.org Website for Samaritan Hospice that was founded in 1980 in New Jersey. Samaritan is a non-for-profit organization that contributes to the health and well being of the community. It is a leader in hospice, palliative care, grief support, education, advocacy, and other life-enhancing services.

www.seattleiands.org This is the website for the Seattle Chapter of the International Association for Near-Death Studies. This Chapter meets usually on the first Saturday of each month at the Catholic Community Center in Seattle. Anywhere from eighty to one hundred individuals who have experienced near death experiences gather to share their stories and to support one another in coping their expanded sense of reality. You can read many stories about actual NDEs on this website.

www.virtualhospice.ca/public/splash.asp This is the website for the Canadian Virtual Hospice. It is an interactive network for people dealing with life-threatening illness and loss. You do need to register with them before you go into the website.

www.whitefeatherpublishing.com (See Chapter 11)

www.zenhospiceproject.org This is the website for the Zen Hospice Project. Inspired by a 2,500-year-old tradition, the Project provides a spectrum of innovative programs including volunteer services, residential care, and trainings that seek to cultivate wisdom and compassion through service.

Grief Support

www.bereavementmag.com This is the website and online catalog for *Bereavement: A Magazine for Hope and Healing*. This magazine is intended to be a "support group in print," a friend who arrives in the mailbox six times a year. It was founded in 1987 by Andrea Gambill after years of support group leadership and grief counseling. Having lost her own 17-year-old daughter in 1976, Andrea started one of the first support groups of The Compassionate Friends (see below).

www.dougy.org Located in Portland, Oregon, The Dougy Center was the first center in the U.S. to provide peer support groups for grieving children. They have served 14,000 children, teens, and families since 1982, and the Dougy Center provides support and training to individuals and organizations seeking to assist children who grieve.

www.erichad.com/index.html EriChad is another website that provides resources for bereaved parents.

www.groww.com GROWW was founded by widow Judy Divers. Judy made her transition in 1999, but this organization continues to support grief recovery for all bereaved persons.

www.tearsoup.com This is the website for Grief Watch, a ministry of Metanoia Peace Community, a congregation in Portland, Oregon. It is based at 18th Ave Peace House, site of a variety of ministries focused on hospitality, community, peacemaking, and care of the dying. Its mission is to offer spiritual, emotional and other support to persons who are grieving, and to assist organized efforts which address the systemic injustices within our society which are the source of grief for many.

www.thecompassionatefriends.org The Compassionate Friends is a national organization based in Oakbrook, Illinois. Their mission is to assist families toward the positive resolution of grief following the death of a child of any age. They also provide information to help others be supportive. They are a self-help support organization and have no religious affiliation. They charge no membership dues or fees.

www.thisisawar.com/GriefChild.html This website is dedicated to helping bereaved children recover. It gives a great deal of information on various aspects of grief and loss and has many links you may go to.

www.healingheart.net Healing Hearts for Bereaved Parents is an organization to support parents whose children have died. Parents whose children have died as a result of a miscarriage or stillbirth are also welcome.

www.webhealing.com This is a website to help you understand the different paths to heal from strong emotions. Tom Golden, internationally known psychotherapist, author, and speaker on the topic of healing from loss, shares his insights and books, etc. From his book titles, it seems that he specializes in the masculine aspects of grief.

www.widownet.com This website provides emotional and financial guidance and self-help resources for people who have lost a spouse. The inspiration for it came from a 37-year-old who became a widower after his wife died of cancer in 1992. Topics range from what to do with your loved one's things to how and when you might start dating again.

www.youngwidow.com This website deals with the concerns of any younger person who has lost a spouse. Helps reduce the feelings of isolation and hopelessness. The site includes a chat room and an online library with suggested readings.

Meditation Support

www.carolynmcmanus.com (see Chapter Seven)

www.seattleinsight.org This is the website for Seattle Insight Meditation Society (SIMS), a nonprofit organization devoted to offering the Buddha's teachings on insight and awareness to all who seek them. SIMS was founded by a group of longtime practitioners of the teachings of the Buddha. They intend to create an open and cohesive spiritual community to support the practice of mindfulness in daily life.

Meditations on the Present Moment (CD), by Thich Nhat Hanh, Sounds True and One Spirit. To order, call (800) 333-9185, or go to **www.soundstrue.com.**

Quality of Life Support

www.agingwithdignity.org/5wishes.html This is the Five Wishes Document webpage. This popular document helps you get the care you want, when you need it. It is unique among all other living will and health agent forms because it looks to a person's medical, personal, emotional, and spiritual needs. You are encouraged to look into these five questions now, when you can decide for yourself what you would desire in the future, then discuss them with your family and physician(s). You can order a copy of this document by going to www.agingwithdignity.org/order.html.

www.radicalforgiveness.com This is the website of the Institude of Radical Forgiveness, begun by Colin Tipping. If you are working on any kind of forgiveness issues, this is a wonderful website to explore a new shift in thinking about forgiveness. You may want to consider reading Colin's book, *Radical Forgiveness: Making Room for the Miracle,* or attending a Radical Forgiveness Ceremony being hosted in your area. If you are in the Seattle area, coach Brenda Miller facilitates these ceremonies regularly. Her website is www.brendamiller.org.

www.sacredartofliving.org (see Chapter Eleven)

Acknowledgments

FIRST AND FOREMOST, I wish to thank God/dess and Spirit for the inspiration to compile this material, and then for guiding me through the challenges of pulling it all together.

There are countless beautiful, generous people who have assisted me in this process, but I particularly wish to express my heartfelt gratitude to Laurie Keith, Dr. Kayo King, Dr. Greg Zografos, Rahl Loomis, Donna Baverman, Patricia Zapatka, Jannette Isaacson, Dr. Robert Jangaard, Jaya Sarada, and all the healers who have nurtured, guided, healed, and strengthened me along the way. I also wish to thank...

Edmond Nickson: for his editorial assistance on this manuscript and his clarity, encouragement, humor, good energy, and wisdom.

Cathy Tinker: for her friendship, sustaining prayers, and sharing the book Spiritual Literacy with me that provided the initial vision for this book.

Valerie Lesniak: for holding the open-hearted space for me to spiritually reflect and grow along the way.

Satyavati: for her love and commitment to the Goddess, for her inspirational yoga classes, and for her helpful editorial ideas, not to mention generous spiritual support.

Laura Strong & Jonathan Evelegh: who helped us in our "transition to Whidbey" through their friendship and wise counsel.

Halley Hart: for friendship, encouragement, and "refocusing," when needed.

Reiko Mittet, Wally Fletcher, Mayumi Ochi, Jun Akutsu, John Hannon, and all the networkers and friends in my life who have shared generously with me.

Betty Filley: who so generously shared her knowledge and experience regarding self-publishing, just when I needed it!

Karen Schuetz: for helping me get started with the graphics of this book.

Kimi Jones: for your assistance with the cover, my logo, and all the rest of the graphics, to the "finish line." Thanks for your patience with this involved project!

Anne Marie Evers: for your enthusiasm for my work.

Lee Lawson: for writing the Foreword to the 2nd edition of this book.

Barbara Fandrich: What can I say? My meeting with Barbara was completely serendipitous, and she has helped and cheered me along the last few months of this book's "delivery." You are a beautiful spirit, Barbara, like all those who have helped me along the way, and I so appreciate your professional style and spiritual presence with me.

My daughter Heather: for her tireless encouragement and invaluable help with the computer and my website (I couldn't have done this project without you, Heather!), and all the hugs and laughter and tears along the way, too.

My sisters Janet and Linda: for your faithful love, support, and friendship through the ups and downs, particularly in the aftermath of losing our dad Alan late last year.

My parents, Betty and Al, and Al's recent widow, Alice: for their devoted care of me, through thick and thin.

Gladys Galvin, my great aunt: for reminding me who I am, a child of the Universal God who loves each and every one, regardless of our religious or spiritual affiliation. Thank you, Gladys, for giving me permission to step "out of the box!"

Nan Waldie: for your friendship and collegiality; you "showed up" just when I needed you.

And finally, to all of my hardworking co-workers with hospice who extend their "compassion in action" day after day, and all the beautiful, wonderful, varied people and families I've met through my hospice ministry: Thank you, thank you, thank you for all you have taught me along our fascinating, interconnecting path!

Permissions and Credits

Infinite gratitude for all permissions received to reprint the following materials:

Introduction

"We Are Always Safe," excerpt from *Life! Reflections on Your Journey* by Louise L. Hay. © 1995 by Hay House, Inc., Carlsbad, CA. Reprinted by permission of the author.

"My Pledge," by Diane R. Willett. © 1982 by Diane R. Willett. Reprinted by permission of the author.

Chapter 1. Truth: Letting Go Is Liberating

"When I first came across…," excerpt from "Learn to Die" by Br. David Steindl-Rast in *Parabola*, Vol. 2:1. © 1977 by *Parabola*. Reprinted by permission of *Parabola*.

"I am of the nature to grow old…," by Shakyamuni Buddha, found in *Tricycle: The Buddhist Review*, No. 25, Vol. VII:1 (Fall, 1997).

"Be Alive," by Frederick Buechner, excerpt from *Listening to Your Life: Daily Meditations with Frederick Buechner,* compiled by George Connor. © 1992 by Frederick Buechner. Reprinted by permission of the author.

"Beyond this Breath," by Victory Lee Schouten. © 2005 by Victory Lee Schouten. Reprinted by permission of the author.

"My Religion," by Niah Kinczewski. © 1998. Reprinted by permission of the author's family.

"You should train yourself…," by Shakyamuni Buddha, found in *Tricycle: The Buddhist Review*, No. 25, Vol. VII:1 (Fall, 1997).

"On each branch," by the Seventh Dalai Lama, found in *Tricycle: The Buddhist Review,* No. 25, Vol VII:1 (Fall, 1997).

Chapter 2. Beauty: The Divine Presence Within All Living Things

"By a Plain but Amiable Cat," by Ruth Pitter, from *Ruth Pitter, Collected Poems.* © 1996 by Ruth Pitter. Reprinted by permission of Enitharmon Press.

"By Example…Shall You Lead," by Niah Kinczewski. © 1998. Reprinted by permission of the author's family.

"The Wellspring," by Mark Reiman, from *Through the Perilous Fight: Living a Life of Challenge.* © 2000 by Mark Reiman. Reprinted by permission of the author's family.

"Beatitudes for the New Wilderness," from *Wilderness Spirituality: Finding Your Way in an Unsettled World,* by Rodney Romney. Text © 1999 by Rodney Romney. Reprinted by permission of the author.

"And You Thought They Were Just Blossoms," by Kevin Kawamoto, from *Seattle Post-Intelligencer,* March 28, 2003. Reprinted by permission of *Seattle Post-Intelligencer.*

Chapter 3. Love: The Only Real Power

"Edmond's Out of Body, Near-Death Experience," by Edmond Nickson. Written for this book. © 2005.

"There is a whole universe inside of me," by Helga Erika Svensdotter Luederitz. Written in 2002. Used by permission of the author's family.

"The Golden Rule, Revisited," by Edwin Leap, M.D. Used by permission of the author.

"Love that springs…," by Christine Longaker, from *Facing Death and Finding Hope: A Guide to the Emotional and Spiritual Care of the Dying.* © 1998 by Christine Longaker. Fair use.

"Only Love," by Harley Moor, excerpted from *Visitations from the Afterlife* by Lee Lawson. © 2000 by Lee Lawson. Reprinted by permission of HarperCollins Publishers, Inc.

Chapter 4. Joy: Tuning in to Humor and Gratitude

"His Holiness the Dalai Lama…," excerpt from *Tap Dancing in Zen* by Geri Larkin. © 2000 by Geri Larkin. Reprinted by permission of Ten Speed Press.

"Have you had a good laugh recently?" excerpt from *The Power of Reiki: An Ancient Hands-on Healing Technique,* by Tanmaya Honervogt. © 1998. Fair use.

"Laughter," by William Mann, excerpted from *Visitations from the Afterlife* by Lee Lawson. © 2000 by Lee Lawson. Reprinted by permission of HarperCollins Publishers, Inc.

"The Miracle of Laughter: Where Humor and Spirituality Meet," by Mary Ann O'Roark, excerpted from *Guideposts,* August, 2003. Reprinted with permission from *Guideposts.* Copyright © 2003 by Guideposts, Carmel, New York 10512. All rights reserved.

"A Sandpiper to Bring You Joy," by Mary Sherman Hilbert. © 1979 by Mary Sherman Hilbert. Used by permission of the author.

"Death is nothing at all," by Henry Scott Holland (1847–1918), adapted.

"The Profound Power of Gratitude" section was inspired by *Attitudes of Gratitude: How to Give and Receive Joy Every Day of Your Life,* by M.J. Ryan. © 1999 by Conari Press.

Chapter 5. Trust: Healing into Wholeness

"The Catcher Will Always Be There for You," excerpts from *Our Greatest Gift: A Meditation on Dying and Caring* by Henri J.M. Nouwen. © 1994 by Henri J.M. Nouwen. Fair use.

"Recommendations for the Time When Death Draws Near," excerpts from "What to Do When You Realize You Are Dying," by Nine Lords of Time through Mary Fran Koppa, from *Sedona: Journal of Emergence!* (August, 1999). © 1999 by Love Light Communications, Inc.

"Faith Is…Replacing Worry with Hope," excerpt from *Tough Minded Faith for Tender Hearted People,* by Robert H. Schuller. © 1983 by Robert H. Schuller. Reprinted by permission of the author.

"The Buddhist approach…," paraphrased from *Nothing Special: Living Zen,* by Charlotte Joko Beck. © 1993 by Charlotte Joko Beck.

"The Road of Life," found on the Internet, author unknown. Apparently found in *Holy Sweat* by Tim Hansel.

"Why Pray?" paraphrased from *Healing Words: The Power of Prayer and the Practice of Medicine,* by Larry Dossey. © 1993 by Larry Dossey, M.D.

"Celebrate God…," excerpts from *The Message: The Bible in Contemporary Language,* by Eugene H. Peterson. © 1993, 1994, 1995, 1996, 2000, 2001, 2002. Used by permission of NavPress Publishing Group. All rights reserved.

"The Healing Heart," by Cheryl Fuller, excerpted from *Visitations from the Afterlife* by Lee Lawson. © 2000 by Lee Lawson. Reprinted by permission of HarperCollins Publishers, Inc.

"Understanding Why," by Bernie Siegel, from *Spirituality and Health* (Spring, 2002). © 2002 by Bernie Siegel. Reprinted by permission of the author.

"Don't Ask Why," excerpt from *Legacy of the Heart: The Spiritual Advantages of a Painful Childhood,* by Wayne Muller. © 1992 by Wayne Muller. Reprinted by permission of the author.

"AUGUST 23 – For Robert Shields, 1975-2005," by Craig Oare. © 2005 by Craig Oare. Reprinted by permission of the author.

Chapter 6. Reflect: Life Review and Dealing with Unfinished Business

"My 'Bed of Life,'" author unknown. Found in a clipping from the *Everett Herald,* saved by Jonathan "Harold" Meier; Jonathan died on June 2, 2002, in Everett, WA.

"Some Questions for Life Review," from *Whistling in the Dark: A Doubter's Dictionary,* by Frederick Buechner. © 1993 by Frederick Buechner. Reprinted by permission of the author.

"The long era of judgment…," from *Love Without End: Jesus Speaks,* by Glenda Green. © 1999 by Glenda Green. Reprinted by permission of the author.

"Judgment," author unknown but probably from the days of Lao Tzu in China. Found in *The Messenger: News of the Great Tomorrow,* date unknown.

"Do Not Judge," excerpt from *The Tao of Dying: A Guide to Caring,* by Doug Smith. © 1994 by Douglas C. Smith. Reprinted by permission of the author.

"Ubuntu," excerpt from *No Future Without Forgiveness,* by Desmond Tutu. © 1999 by Desmond Mpilo Tutu. Fair use.

"That's why…," excerpt from *The Message: The Bible in Contemporary Language,* by Eugene H. Peterson. © 1993, 1994, 1995, 1996, 2000, 2001, 2002. Used by permission of NavPress Publishing Group. All rights reserved.

"May peace prevail…," excerpt from The World Peace Prayer Society's *"Global Link"* newsletter, Vol. 38 (Spring, 2003).

"A Course in Miracles" – for more information, see www.acourseinmiracles.com .

"A Forgiveness Meditation," from *Healing into Life and Death* by Stephen Levine. © 1987 by Stephen Levine. Reprinted by permission of the author.

"Every Death Is a Birth," paraphrase from *Experiencing the Soul: Before Birth, During Life, After Death*, ed. Eliot Jay Rosen. © 1998 by For a World We Choose Foundation.

"Theresa," from *Final Gifts: Understanding the Special Awareness, Needs, and Communications of the Dying*, by Maggie Callanan and Patricia Kelley. © 1992 by Margaret E. Callanan and Patricia Kelley. Reprinted by permission of the authors.

"Bless the Road," song by Steve Cooney. © 1999 by Steve Cooney. Reprinted by permission of the author.

Chapter 7. Awareness: Cultivating the Art of Meditation

"The basic fact...," excerpt from H*ow to Handle Trouble: A Guide to Peace of Mind*, by John Carmody. © 1993 by John Carmody. Fair use.

"Breathe and Smile," from *Daily Word* (June 14, 2001). © 2001 by Unity School of Christianity. Reprinted by permission of the publisher.

"The Gentle Art of Blessing," from *The Gentle Art of Blessing*, by Pierre Pradervand. © 2003 by Personhood Press. Reprinted by permission of Personhood Press.

"Planting the Seed," adapted from an article in *Body and Soul* (February, 2002) by Clark Strand. © 2002 by Clark Strand.

"The Way to Do Is to Be," from *Oh, To Be 50 Again! On Being Too Old for a Mid-Life Crisis*, by Eda LeShan. © 1986 by Times Books, a division of Random House, Inc. Fair use.

"A Meditation for Busy People," found in *Daily Word*, date unknown and article not recognized by contact person at Daily Word.

"A Simple Loving Kindness Meditation," adapted from a similar meditation by Stephen Levine.

"Tonglen," paraphrased from "Tonglen: The Practice of Giving and Receiving," by Sogyal Rinpoche in *Tricycle: The Buddhist Review*, No. 25, Vol. VII:1 (Fall, 1997).

"Be Still and Know," from "In an Awareness of God's Presence," in *Daily Word* (November 2, 2002). © 2002 Unity School of Christianity. Reprinted by permission of the publisher.

"Comeditation," paraphrased from "A Sharing of Breaths: Performed for centuries by Tibetan physicians, comeditation is now being used in the West to ease the psychic suffering of the terminally ill," by Olivia H. Miller in *Yoga Journal* (March/April, 1993).

"Meditations to Help Prepare for Dying," from *Peaceful Transition: The Art of Conscious Dying and the Liberation of the Soul*, by Bruce Goldberg. © 1997 by Dr. Bruce Goldberg. Reprinted by permission of the author. www.drbrucegoldberg.com.

Chapter 8. Hope: Reflections on the Afterlife and the Interconnectedness of All

"I am standing upon the seashore," by Henry Van Dyke. Found in *Gone from My Sight: The Dying Experience*, by Barbara Karnes. © 1986 by Barbara Karnes. Public domain.

"Martha," from *Final Gifts: Understanding the Special Awareness, Needs, and Communications of the Dying*, by Maggie Callanan and Patricia Kelley. © 1992 by Margaret E. Callanan and Patricia Kelley. Reprinted by permission of the authors.

"The Journey," by Amanda Sasnett Roebuck. © 1998. Reprinted by permission of the author.

"A Blessing in Disguise: In Memory of My Father and Best Friend, Daniel Alspektor," by RoseAnn Alspektor. © 2005 by RoseAnn Alspektor. Reprinted by permission of the author.

"I was blessed with a mother…," by Josefina Monroy B. © 2006 by Josefina Monroy B.

"Special Signs in Nature," excerpt from *Living into Dying: A Journal of Spiritual and Practical Deathcare for Family and Community*, by Nancy Poer. © 2002 by Nancy Jewel Poer. Reprinted by permission of the author.

"Do not stand at my grave and weep…," by Mary E. Frye, in *Bereavement* magazine (March/April, 1989). © 1932 by Bereavement Publishing, Inc. Reprinted by permission of Bereavement Publishing, Inc.

"Save Your Tears," by Niah Kinczewski. © 1998 by Niah Kinczewski. Used by permission of the author's family.

"Remember Me," by Niah Kinczewski. © 1998. Used by permission of the author's family.

Excerpts from *Wilderness Spirituality: Finding Your Way in an Unsettled World*, by Rodney R. Romney. Text © 1999 by Rodney R. Romney. Publishing © by Element Books, Inc. Reprinted by permission of the author.

"The Dead," from *Questions about Angels*, by Billy Collins. © 1991. Reprinted by permission of the author and University of Pittsburgh Press.

Chapter 9. Spiritual Path: Receiving Strength from Our Faith Traditions

"Many spiritual traditions…," by Anya Foos-Graber in *Experiencing the Soul: Before Birth, During Life, After Death*, ed. Eliot Jay Rosen. © 1998 by For a World We Choose Foundation.

"A Prayer for Courage and Patience," by The Terma Collective, in *Life Prayers from Around the World: 365 Prayers, Blessings, and Affirmations to Celebrate the Human Journey*, edited by Elizabeth Roberts and Elias Amidon. © 1996 by Elizabeth Roberts and Elias Amidon.

"Blessed be the works of your hands…," by Diann Neu, co-director of The Women's Alliance for Theology, Ethics and Ritual (WATER). www.hers.com/water. Public domain.

Excerpts from "The Lord's Prayer," translated by Ron Roth with Peter Occhiogrosso, in *The Healing Path of Prayer*. © 1997 by Ron Roth and Peter Occhiogrosso. Fair use.

"Healing Prayer," by Rabbi Rami M. Shapiro, originally in Tangents, now out of print. Used by permission of the author.

"Words of Infinite Light," excerpts from *Gratitude to Nature*, by Masami Saionji. © 2003 by Masami Saionji. Reprinted by permission of the author.

"I Corinthians 13," excerpt from *The Message: The Bible in Contemporary Language*, by Eugene H. Peterson. © 1993, 1994, 1995, 1996, 2000, 2001, 2002. Used by permission of NavPress Publishing Group. All rights reserved.

"Beatitudes of Peace Pilgrim," excerpts from *Steps Toward Inner Peace,* by Peace Pilgrim. Never copyrighted. Public domain.

"Blessing of Light," Traditional Irish blessing found on the Internet and also in *Earth Prayers from Around the World: 376 Prayers, Poems, and Invocations for Honoring the Earth,* edited by Elizabeth Roberts and Ellias Amidon. © 1991 by Elizabeth Roberts and Elias Amidon. Public domain.

"Ute Prayer," found on the Internet and in *Earth Prayers from Around the World: 376 Prayers, Poems, and Invocations for Honoring the Earth,* edited by Elizabeth Roberts and Elias Amidon. © 1991 by Elizabeth Roberts and Elias Amidon. Public domain.

Chapter 10. Grace: The Transforming Power of Grief

"Random Thoughts," by Cecelia T. Perciballi-Clayton, in *Bereavement* magazine (January/February, 2001). © 2001 by Bereavement Publishing, Inc. Reprinted by permission of Bereavement Publishing, Inc.

"Non-Attachment," by Niah Kinczewski. Used by permission of the author's family.

"Grief Can Open Up the Compassionate Heart," excerpts from the work of Amber Watson. Used by permission of the late author's partner/executrix, Leah Kosh.

"No matter how brave…," excerpt from *Up the Golden Stair: An Approach to a Deeper Understanding of Life through Personal Sorrow,* by Elizabeth Yates. © 1990 by Elizabeth Yates McGrael. Used by permission of the author and Upper Room Books.

"Cry When You Are Sad," by Jonathan Piccirillo, from *Chicken Soup for the Preteen Soul,* compiled by J. Canfield, M.V. Hansen, P. Hansen and I. Dunlap. © 2000 by Jonathan Piccirillo. Reprinted by permission of the author.

"Letting Go," by Kathleen M. Garner, from *Thanatos* (Winter, 1994). © 1994 by Florida Funeral Directors Association. Reprinted by permission of the Florida Funeral Directors Association.

"Affirmations and the Final Destination," by Rev. Anne Marie Evers, from *The New Times* (August, 2002). © 2002 by Anne Marie Evers. Reprinted by permission of the author.

"Even if death…," by Dilgo Khyentse Rinpoche, from *Tricycle: The Buddhist Review,* No. 25, Vol VII:1 (Fall, 1997).

Chapter 11. Resources for Healing and Further Inquiry

"There is a Law…," from *The Healing of the Planet Earth: Personal Power and Planetary Transformation,* by Alan Cohen. © 1987 by Alan Cohen.